The Twilight of Politics

THE ITALIAN LIST

MARIO TRONTI

The Twilight of Politics

Translated with an Introduction
by Matteo Mandarini

LONDON NEW YORK CALCUTTA

This book has been translated thanks to a translation grant awarded by the Italian Ministry of Foreign Affairs and International Cooperation.

Questo libro è stato tradotto grazie a un contributo alla traduzione assegnato dal Ministero degli Affari Esteri e della Cooperazione Internazionale italiano.

Seagull Books, 2024

First published in Italian as *La politica al tramonto*

First published in English translation by Seagull Books, 2024

Paperback ISBN 978 1 80309 374 1

Hardcover ISBN 978 1 80309 373 4

British Library Cataloguing-in-Publication Data
A catalogue record for this book is available from the British Library

Typeset by Seagull Books, Calcutta, India
Printed and bound by WordsWorth India, New Delhi, India

CONTENTS

Translator's Introduction

It is by now routine to introduce Mario Tronti with a discussion of *Workers and Capital*, a near-legendary book first published in 1966, and one of the very few postwar Marxist texts to have provided a radical reinterpretation of the very bases of this rich tradition. Perhaps only Althusser's 'structuralist' reading can be said to have surpassed Tronti's text in terms of theoretical influence. Anyone who knows Tronti through that work will be surprised at the one presented here, published 32 years later—in a context marked not by a rising tide of working-class and emancipatory struggles, but in what we might call the time of the Great Restoration, after the conclusion of the 70-year rivalry between great ideological systems embedded in opposed socioeconomic power blocs—and appearing in English at a time when the dialectic of enlightenment calls for an apocalyptic sensibility as the only true realist standpoint.

The question of continuity and rupture in Tronti's decades-long theoretical development is, as in the work of all great theorists, an important one, but one I can only approach here in a rather impressionistic form. Neither continuity nor rupture alone explain a trajectory that is thoroughly dialectical, but without the pacifying reading of the tripartite structure of the Hegelian dialectic of *Aufheben*: *to cancel, to preserve and to raise up*. The dialectic at work is rather that of the fragment, of Benjamin's 'dialectical image', crystallizing contradiction, providing an untimely image that contains—without neutering—the conflict and tension of an epoch. Tronti is most certainly an epochal thinker, albeit one who forces us to rethink what an epoch and its twilight might mean.

Of Tronti's books, only two are available in English at the moment. After 55 years, there is finally a (poor) translation of Tronti's *Workers and Capital* (1966, 1971), and now this book, originally published in 1998.[1] In addition, aside from the extracts from the former published in *Telos* in the 1970s, more recently we have seen the publication of two collections of Tronti's writings: *Leaping Forward: Mario Tronti and the History of Political Workerism* (2012),[2] drawing again on the 1966 text but showing the sharp discontinuities and radical departures within that very text (itself composed at various different political moments in which it sought to intervene); and, thanks to the excellent work of Andrew Anastasi, *The Weapon of Organization: Mario Tronti's Political Revolution in Marxism* (2020), a collection of articles, letters and talks from 1959–67 which provides a substantial and precise overview—thanks also to a very useful introduction by the editor—of Tronti's theoretical and political development over this crucial period of Italian political history.[3]

The book translated here is, in many ways, a radical departure from those, in which the foremost figures were (nearly) all from the Marxist tradition: above all Marx and Lenin, but also Brecht. Yet, often hidden from sight within that early work (and almost invisible in the English translation of it) were a number of other thinkers and writers from the great bourgeois modernist tradition, which is to say, of that moment of greatest self-doubt—before the fall—of bourgeois consciousness, in which *form* itself became undermined, transgressed against, shattered and reconstructed, which reappear—as silent interlocuters—in *The Twilight of Politics*. This haute bourgeois period was one where the

1 For a critical review of this translation, see Matteo Mandarini, review of *Workers and Capital*, by Mario Tronti (David Broder trans.), *International Review of Social History* 65(3) (2020): 547–50.

2 Michele Filippini (ed.), *Leaping Forward: Mario Tronti and the History of Political Workerism* (Maastricht: Jan van Eyck Academie, 2012).

3 Mario Tronti, *The Weapon of Organization: Mario Tronti's Political Revolution in Marxism* (Andrew Anastasi ed. and trans.) (Brooklyn, NY: Common Notions, 2020).

supreme bourgeois consciousnesses recognized that its self-confidence was now thoroughly misplaced and threatened on all sides and that the very forms of bourgeois thought, style and representation would need to be shattered and recomposed—a bourgeois constructivism that some bourgeois conservative revolutionaries recognized would need to be at least as radical as Soviet Constructivism. So, hidden away—though not so invisible for eyes able to see, as one of those great bourgeois thinkers might have put it—in *Workers and Capital* were Friedrich Nietzsche, Max Weber, Thomas Mann, Ernst Jünger, Robert Musil, Carl Schmitt, Paul Klee, Arnold Schoenberg, Martin Heidegger, Joseph Schumpeter and others—members of that great bourgeois class which, recognizing the degeneration of its own conditions and telos, attacked the forms upon which it had itself depended, with a view to constructing a new sensorium, a new 'Great Politics', and a multiplicity of new orders, new forms. These figures, crucial throughout Tronti's theoretical development, come increasingly to the fore in his work. But they are subjected to the radical class analysis advanced in *Workers and Capital*. For Tronti, thought within capitalism, if it is not to present itself as the placid surface of ideology, is riven by class conflict—but both sides of that conflict, of necessity, exist in each class, for a class always stands in contrast to another, a conflict that thereby constitutes it. Unity is only an ideological effect of domination; all unity ultimately falls into an un-composable two at war with its other.[4] No resolution was possible, no restoration could be conceived, conflict was all.

4 Alberto Toscano, in reading a draft of this introduction, rightly noted that perhaps Tronti did not go far enough and that there is a danger in considering each of these classes as homogeneous, in not understanding each class as itself riven by differences. Perhaps one should reflect—to draw on Mao—on the necessity of thinking of contradictions *among* the people and not only 'between ourselves and the enemy' (Mao Zedong, 'On the Correct Handling of Contradictions Among the People' [27 February 1957] in *Selected Works of Mao Tse-tung*, VOL. 5 [Beijing: Foreign Languages Press, 1977] [available online: https://bit.ly/3yDSTXS; last accessed 21 May 2024]).

Aside from these nineteenth- and twentieth-century sources, there are other critical ones that go back to the dawn of the early modern era—to Machiavelli and Thomas More—that exemplify another aspect, increasingly central to Tronti's thought, what Franco Milanesi calls 'the political use of history'.[5] By this, of course, Tronti does not intend the rewriting of history to serve a political purpose—such as was described by Leon Trotsky as 'Stalin's school of falsification' or as we witness in the narratives of the greatness of a plucky little island nation able to extend its 'influence' across the globe, forgetting the murderousness of its pluck. What is intended is history as a means of interrogating and unpicking the present: 'History does not offer only homologation and identity, but it is an extraordinary field of comparisons, analogies, differences'[6]—allowing us to use such comparisons, analogies and differences to prise open the apparent unity of historical periods. Machiavelli, who in his *Discourses on Livy* approached the Roman historian's work in this way, proceeds by outlining the causes of decadence and corruption in politics. This is a theme at the heart of *Twilight*, to which Tronti returns again and again—as he does to that of the 'age of the masses' and of 'Great Politics',[7] where the greatness stems not simply from a quantitative expansion of the masses, but also from a 'great thought' that takes hold of the masses and alone confers greatness on a 'cause or action'. The 'Great Politics' that Tronti repeatedly invokes is the one that reached its high point when it was embodied in two great counterposed blocs: the collective capitalist and the workers' movement. If this return is nostalgic, it is so only in a way analogous to the sensibility of great bourgeois

5 Franco Milanesi, *Nel Novecento: Storia, teoria, politica nel pensiero di Mario Tronti* (Milan: Mimesis 2014), p. 107.

6 Milanesi, *Nel Novecento*, p. 107.

7 Friedrich Nietzsche, *Beyond Good and Evil: Prelude to a Philosophy of the Future* (Rolf Peter-Horstmann and Judith Norman eds, Judith Norman trans.) (Cambridge: Cambridge University Press, 2002), p. 132.

thinkers of the negative that he celebrates, 'who by virtue of their delicate nature, morbid eroticism, dubious heredity, over-refined aesthetic sense and sickly nobility of spirit, were estranged from their immediate world of bourgeois health and vitality.'[8] So if it is a question of nostalgia, it is a nostalgia that is anything but a comforting escape, for it instead blasts open the present by comparing its poverty to the 'age of the masses'. The comparison reveals that it was not the quantitative expansion of the masses that was pivotal—since the growth of the masses is greater today than it ever was—but their politicization:

> The dichotomous view of society, of the world and of humanity either is or is not political. It either acts and thinks politically, and hence is present; or it does not act and does not think politically, and then is absent. It is not a case of visibility but of existence. Those who generously maintain that the division into classes is not visible but continues to exist console themselves and their friends with a faith in glorious tomorrows. It's true, the working class is not dead; on the contrary, it is probable that at the world-scale it is destined to expand quantitatively. But the workers' movement is dead. And the class struggle did not exist because there was a working class; the class struggle existed because there was the workers' movement. [. . .] There is no organized force that expresses here this duality, no theory unites this world, no collective consciousness of struggle allows for a voice of antagonism to be heard. There is no politics. Hence, there is no real contradiction.[9]

8 Peter Gordon Mann, 'The Good European in the Great War: Thomas Mann's Reflections of an Unpolitical Man and the Politics of the Self, Nation and Europe', *Journal of European Studies* 47(1) (2017): 39–40.

9 See pp. 79–80 below.

Another reason why nostalgia is an inaccurate description for Tronti's relationship to the past is that it typically leads to resignation and contentment. Tronti instead turns to the past to forge weapons. In *Twilight*, the weapon serves as a warning to the 'progressive' Left, which at the time was on the crest of the Third Way wave across North America and Europe. Tronti's political retelling of history is one that diagnoses, as does Machiavelli, the decay and corruption of the present, thereby turning on its head Fukuyama's celebration of the 'End of History'—and it does so by pitting politics *against* history. Whereas the advocates of the Third Way took up the mantle of free markets and globalization as the inescapable direction of history, Tronti pits history as the realm of 'necessity' against that of politics as the domain, if not of freedom, of 'possibility'. Politics is always an event, an action, a decision that intervenes within the necessity of history; a decision that acts like a clinamen, causing the apparently smooth and linear paths of atoms to barge into one another and derail necessity. It operates always within the contingent. There is—by definition—no necessity that politics will take place, let alone succeed; it is a rare event that depends upon the concentration and quality of collective subjects.

History–technology–economy–capitalism form an indissoluble whole, against which Tronti pits politics–party–masses–socialism. The twentieth century is, for him, the contraposition of these rival forces. That's not to say that capitalism has no politics (any more than socialism has no economics), but that it subordinates the political to the economic—turning it effectively into the administration of the existent. Socialism attempted to subordinate the economic to the political, and with the taking of state power, for a time it succeeded—for good and ill, as Tronti will readily admit. Not only does capitalism not *not* have a politics, it is impossible without modern politics, which alone can provide the ability to administer great processes and great masses. It is not by chance that absolutism was the form necessary to the expulsion of peasants from the land necessary to turn them into wage workers, 'free' of land and other forms of sustenance; or that commercial society demanded a politics of state non-intervention or liberalism;[10] or that democracy became the political form necessary to productive capital and the necessary capital–labour compromise of Fordism. Indeed, the historical period that Marx discusses as that of 'primitive accumulation'—the land clearances that created the class of wage labourers—coincides with the process of 'primitive accumulation of the categories of the political'. The point is not that capitalism does not have a politics—such a claim would be absurd—but that it subordinates this form to another, to what Heidegger would call 'technology', which we might more commonly speak of as 'the economy', and which Tronti here simply calls history.[11]

---

10 'The same bourgeois consciousness which celebrates the division of labour in the workshop, the lifelong annexation of the worker to a partial operation, and his complete subjection to capital, as an organization of labour that increases its productive power, denounces with equal vigour every conscious attempt to control and regulate the process of production socially, as an inroad upon such sacred things as the rights of property, freedom and the self-determining "genius" of the individual capitalist. It is very characteristic that the enthusiastic apologists of the factory system have nothing more damning to urge against a general organization of labour in society than that it would turn the whole of society into a factory.' Karl Marx, *Capital: Volume I* (Ben Fowkes trans., Ernest Mandel introd.) (Harmondsworth: Penguin, 1990), p. 477.

11 It is worth pointing to an early example of the politics–history opposition, appearing in the 'Postscript' to the 1971 edition of *Workers and Capital*: 'This is a process of the massification of the working class, whereby the workers grow as a class; a process of internal homogenization of industrial labour-power, where politics always precedes history—because, for us, it is true to say that politics is workers' struggles that leap qualitatively ever-higher, and history is capital that renews, on this basis, its technico-productive structures, its organization of labour, its instruments for the control and manipulation of society, and substitutes, following the objective indication of its class adversary, the parts of its mechanism of power that from time to time become obsolete' (Mario Tronti, *Workers and Capital* [David Broder trans.]

It is important, nevertheless, to also highlight some 'unfashionable' or problematic aspects of Tronti's thinking. Most obviously the Eurocentrism. This aspect of his thinking should be accounted for and understood—whether or not it is to be 'excused' I leave to the reader to decide. I shall merely try to present how I think Tronti might respond to the critique. This 'Eurocentric' thread runs deep and is not based in any claim to superiority of European culture, or at least not in any straightforward sense. Take, for instance, the claim:

> *Socialism*—what this word signalled can be achieved, if it can *still* be achieved, only in one continent. The Left should look courageously at the European world. If there is to be any further political civilization for the world, it cannot but still come from here. Hence, only politics can save us.[12]

At face value, this might appear as a claim for European culture to take up the reigns and assume the 'white man's burden'. But this uncomfortable passage, and there are others, might best be understood as one that claims not that the centrality of Europe stems from any intrinsic greatness, but from it being the site where modern politics—'Great Politics', as Tronti discusses it in this book and elsewhere—is realized as the *active intervention of the masses into history*, bending, for the first time, necessity to the will of the many. For it is in Europe, he argues, that for the first time the masses became an organized force, such that for the only time before or since, they caused history to quake—not only nationally or regionally, but also globally—at the level of the two opposed camps of the workers' movement and of the collective capitalist.

It should be noted that this has echoes of the anti-'Third Worldism' of Tronti's mid-60s writings, when he accused those who revived Lenin's

---

[London: Verso, 2019], p. 323; translation modified). I would like to thank Andrew Anastasi for pointing me in the direction of this passage.

12 See p. 119 below.

dictum that the revolution would happen where the imperialist link in the chain was weakest (in Lenin's time, of course, Russia) of justifying 'opportunism' or what we might prefer to call an attitude of political passivity, betting all on the anti-colonial struggles, allowing everyone else the comfortable position of bystanders awaiting the struggles of others. Tronti did not downplay such struggles, but argued that these were secondary contradictions, in that a victory for movements of national liberation—or resolution of such contradictions—would do nothing for the central capitalist contradiction of capital and labour. Hence Tronti argued that 'the chain must be broken not where capital is weakest, but rather where the working class is strongest',[13] and hence in the advanced capitalist countries with organized workers' movements. One might well argue that such 'echoes' are today problematic, especially once one recognizes that the 'margin' is much more thoroughly integrated with the 'core'—the hyper-exploitation taking place in the 'periphery' is not marginal but central to accumulation strategies of the corporate behemoths of today. And, so, this does more than raise the question as to whether Europe can still be seen to be the centre of a potential 'political civilization'. Might one not rather argue that, just as the rules will, for now, 'be written by the central banks alone, on behalf of national capitals, organized according to great spaces, USA, Europe, [the] Pacific', that it is only at the level of each of these blocks that 'a politics can save us'? Might one not argue that each of these areas calls for the development of a '*political* culture of conflict',[14] of large-scale organized collective forces in struggle with the structures of governance? This would be to argue that capitalism, in globalizing economically and technologically, has had to bear with it also the structures of politics, a degenerate and perverse politics subordinated to capital's processes of accumulation,

13 Tronti, *Workers and Capital*, p. *xxix*.

14 Mario Tronti, 'Ancora su utopia, proseguendo una discussione', *Infiniti mondi* (2020) (available online: https://bityl.co/OXPf; last accessed 18 May 2024), p. 12.

but that is nevertheless focused on the great masses—even if only to constrain and contain them. It would, in any case, be difficult to claim that great powers like China did not also see—in living memory!—a 'Great Politics', in which large masses come onto the historical stage and, for a time, make history tremble before it.

These reservations aside, at the heart of this book is Tronti's attempt to hold together a view of the longue durée of political history with a critique of the 'dictatorship of the present',[15] to help us escape being 'chained to the bars of an eternal present [. . .] which deprives us both of the freedom to look back and to see ahead'.[16] Tronti provides an example of such a political use of history in a recent piece, from which I have already drawn:

> In recent weeks, we have been subjected to the unbearable triumphalist rhetorical celebratory chatter for the 30-year anniversary of the fall of the Berlin wall. It's true that the winners write history. But is it possible that one is unable to set out a well-argued, well-documented counternarrative, in this case too, regarding the promises that have not been kept and the dramatic consequences that have followed?
>
> Of 1989, and of 1991, a far more epochal date, we are shown the face of liberation and the internal one of restoration is hidden from us. And what is told is a rigged history. The entire 'anti-twentieth century', since the eighties, has been an age of Restoration. With a capital *R*. Similar to the historic one that followed the French Revolution and the Napoleonic age.

15 Tronti, 'Ancora su utopia', p. 13.

16 Mario Tronti, 'Desperate Hopes', *Autonomies* (2020) (available online: https://bityl.co/OXPj; last accessed 18 May 2024).

> Either we see these two together—moment of liberation and practice of restoration—or one fails to understand what happened.
>
> The visible wall has fallen, which prevented the move from East to West, but above all, I repeat, with the collapse of the Soviet Union in '91, an invisible wall has risen that impedes the passage from present to future; from, to say it with Bloch, the 'here and now' to the 'not yet'.[17]

Such a political use of history develops a counternarrative to the dominant one that blinds us to the possibility of reclaiming a past that Tronti claims as his own, not so much by way of the operation of nostalgia, nor as a mere 'correction', but through an approach that is at once epistemological and political, in that it 'comprehends and conserves a certain [partisan] past'. That past is marked by the conflicts that compose it. Thus, against a culture of social cohesion, he calls for a culture of conflict to infuse our understanding and our action. Here, perhaps, is Tronti's central lesson: that more than contradiction (which demands a solution), a political culture of conflict, embedded in a partisan viewpoint, is the only window we have onto past, present, and future. Without this, we are blind. Without this, we are left in an eternal present that reinforces the existing structures of power or—worse—that advances the cause of an age of Restoration unable to stave off but hastening the End of days.

Tronti died at the age of 92 on 7 August 2023, closing his 'age of the patriarchs', a phrase that he repurposed on occasion of Pietro Ingrao's 90th birthday, taken from Carl Schmitt's reply to Ernst Jünger's letter on the occasion of the German jurist's 90th birthday. Schmitt and Jünger, two thinkers from the period of the global state of exception of great politics, would have been on the other side of the barricades—'There is no great politics without a great adversary'—had Tronti not missed the

17 Tronti, 'Ancora su utopia', pp. 13–14.

historical moment of the state of exception, when political action could be truly transformative. His 'misfortune' in having missed that moment is perhaps our good fortune, since it meant that this politician lent to the world of philosophy (as he was wont to say), provided us over a long career with the theoretical tools to orientate, guide and confront the enemy, and diagnose the epochal impasse of the present. 'It is only "clear-eyed pessimism", unflinching recognition of our predicament, that opens up a hopeful space beyond it.'[18] For now, as he tells us in the postface to this English edition, 'nothing more can be done, all has to be given up to the stupid "spirit of the times". But the last word is never spoken.'

18 Oliver Eagleton, 'Therborn's World Casting', *New Left Review* 144 (November–December 2023).

A Note on the Translation

The word *tramonto* can be translated in numerous ways: 'sunset', 'twilight', 'dusk'—and the relation to a setting sun is typically what would spring to mind. It can, however, also mean 'decline'. Oswald Spengler's *Untergang des Abendlandes*, for instance, is translated into English as *The Decline of the West*, and in Italian as *Il tramonto del Occidente*. 'Good style', in English, typically calls for variety, although this conflicts with the philosophical demand for consistency in the use of concepts. The extent to which *tramonto* is a concept rather than a metaphor here (although this opposition is hardly watertight) is open to question. Hence, whenever the term appears and wherever it might be in question whether we are using the same term, I shall insert the original in square brackets.

Tronti is known as a very refined stylist, although in a manner that challenges what in Italian typically characterizes refinement: long sentences, broken up into a complex variety of subclauses, often ornate if not florid. Tronti's style, contrastingly, is fragmentary, syncopated, not pretty but clinical, incisive, violent as a scalpel is as it pierces flesh. I have, as much as possible, tried to retain this aspect. One of the drawbacks of doing so is that I have had to make some choices that are problematic. For instance, sentences are sometimes mere grammatical fragments. More problematically perhaps, Italian remains somewhat gendered, with the male pronoun dominant. In English, one might correct this by moving between two genders (although this sometimes means losing some precision as to the referent of a sentence), or supplement (he or she), or come up with rather ugly solutions (s/he). I have opted for 'he', as in the original, and accept that this is problematic though stylistically more in keeping with Tronti's work. For despite his championing of the Italian feminist 'philosophy of difference', this has not found its way into his writing.

Central to Tronti's entire theoretical practice is the assertion that truth is always determined from a point of view, perspective, standpoint. This is connected not only to his specific reading of the Marxist tradition, with roots in Lenin and Lukács, but also to his Nietzscheanism and Weberianism. In the original, Tronti speaks constantly of the 'part' [*parte*] or the 'partial' [*parziale*]—this is not a reference to the limitedness or 'one-sidedness' to be opposed to a truth to be found only in the totality. Quite the opposite. Only the 'part' can grasp the whole, and it does so in political practice. These terms are linked rather to the claiming of partisanship or belonging to a part, to one side. This clearly has the same root as *partito* or 'party', as in a 'political party'. I have had sometimes to use rather cumbersome expressions such as 'partisan standpoint' for *parzialità*, which literally means 'partiality' but more precisely claims to 'belong to one side' [*essere di parte*]. To say 'keeping to one part' or to be 'a party to' has different resonances, such as those of bias, limitation or formal representation (see the subsequent sentence) that is not necessarily present in the Italian. I have therefore noted the Italian in square brackets where the root to part/partisanship is not present, e.g. in cases where I have opted for 'side' as a better translation.

Lastly, Tronti often quotes without reference, or even without citation marks. I have often tried to trace the reference and reinsert the citation marks for ease of reference. All footnotes with the attribution [Trans.] at the end are by the translator.

Matteo Mandarini

The Twilight of Politics

A Brief Antiphon

This book is born from within. This is not usual for a book of political philosophy. But here, thought experiences a particular state of exception. Today, it is not politics but the crisis of politics that must be thought about. We can say that, in many ways, this is unprecedented. And, as such, it must be confronted with an unprecedented argumentative force. This is necessary in the face of the opacity—the grey of representation—with which the collapse of political action expresses itself today. The tenor of the text—the obsessive return of certain motifs, the theme's repetition with variations at once intended and obligatory—stems from this. The repetitions may be disturbing—because they jar with the common sense of intellectuals. But the broken style of the investigation follows the impossible harmony of the framework. To read contemporary events in the language of the classics is a contradiction that has always accompanied me as a writer. It is too late to change.

I want to communicate a state of theoretical desperation. I think I have succeeded, in excess. But that's fine. The maxim is always the same: at the point of the greatest danger, there is also that which saves.[1] Thought must probe the bottom of the history of the workers' movement's soul; whatever it costs in terms of the necessarily crude form assumed by the use of concepts and the capitulation of words. The criterion of honesty

1 The reference is to Hölderlin's 'Patmos': 'But where there is danger the saving powers also grow.' Friedrich Hölderlin, *Selected Verse* (Michael Hamburger ed. and trans.) (London: Anvil Editions, 1986), p. 193. [Trans.]

emerges once you reach the point that you must know—or at least seek—how things really went. To set out again from there, not so as to hope, but perhaps to begin again to act. At this delicate pivotal point, pertaining to an existential fact, it is easy to grasp the oscillation between *Kulturpessimismus* and will to power. For the culture of crisis, this is an intimately cultivated love; for the organization of force, it is a temptation imposed from without.

Each of us bears history within oneself. It is not one's own history. We are utterly indifferent to biography. It is a case of great history, that of the men and women who unite and divide themselves in society, and in the consciousness of it, which—to this point—has been politics. We introject and analyse in various ways its different passages and stages and places and times. More than other epochs, the 1900s drives us to do so. We can say of this [the twentieth] century that it produced history at such a height and with such intensity that, by its end, it is exhausted and empty. There is a battle over its periodization. This book does not evade it—choices are made, questionable, subjective, functional to a logic internal to the subject and only along this path seek to glean partial truths. I believe there to be a masculine difference in setting out from oneself. It needs investigating. A mysterious cave where concrete life and historical time, ideas and shadows, eternal events and immediate contingencies confront and become muddled with one another. A knot that becomes more complicated as experience accumulates. Then thought intervenes to decide for itself.

So, this decision that is entirely one of political thinking and almost not at all political, must be judged. There is here a 'what is to be said?', not a 'what is to be done?'. A backwards swerve imposed by this phase. It should be clear that I am aware of this. 'Distance' is a mystical condition of the modern political. One must try to throw flashes of light onto the night of contemporary politics. The aim is not to clarify, to 'illuminate', but to understand, to 'comprehend'. This is a political time without self-awareness: a tombstone placed on the past, and for a future only the one granted by the present. We cannot.

Looking at it from the end of the twentieth century, the political times I have travelled through appear to be a failure. It was not the demands that were too high; the instruments were inadequate, the ideas poor, the subjects weak, the protagonists mediocre. And history, at a certain point, ceased; mere news was all that remained. No more epoch; just days and more days. The miserabilism of the adversary closed the circle. There is no great politics without a great adversary.

Today, there is fear of the political criterion. But one should not suppress the friend/enemy; it should be civilized. Civilization/culture in conflict. Political struggle without war; the nobility of the human spirit. The message is there. In the bottle of this allusive symphony of psalms.

Mario Tronti
7 October 1998

Theme with Variations

POLITICS HISTORY TWENTIETH CENTURY

'[B]ecause I believe that this would be the true way to go to Paradise: learn the way of the Inferno so as to escape it.'

Niccolò Machiavelli to
Francesco Guicciardini, 17 May 1521

'Since there is no longer any truth after Nietzsche, from Nietzsche to Weber, a new criterion arises, that of honesty.'

Jacob Taubes, *The Political Theology of Paul*

Politics against History

The political and the modern are born together. At the foundation—the root of modernity—lies politics. There is a specifically modern sense of doing/thinking politics. This fact is one aspect of the problem. For us, politics is not eternal human history. It is one's epoch comprehended with the intelligence of action. Let us suspend the distinction between *das Politische* and *die Politik*. Sapid meanings hide behind and are represented in this distinction. Not masculine and feminine, but neutral and feminine. Here politics will be conceived in the singular. As it was at the origin of modernity. Then afterwards: from the prince's *virtú–fortuna* to the universal rights of man;[1] and so, from the time that goes

1 *Virtù* and *fortuna* are two critical concepts to Machiavelli's thought. A useful explanation of them can be found in the notes to Peter Bondanella's translation of

from the triumph of politics in Europe to the twilight of politics in the West. Taken as a whole, this arc of time is our contemporary history. We are old inhabitants on a great ancient world. The antiquity of the modern: in this way shall we speak of politics.

We should recount, narrate, thinkingly. There is no such form. There is no *roman philosophique*. And neither should we provide one. The entirety of modern history can be found in the modern. And vice versa. Two forms of destiny in a single life. They have often walked in step; sometimes they have stood in contrast. The latter is the case of the twentieth century: the place where politics attempted 'to storm heaven' and history imposed one of its 'tiger leaps'[2] into the past. There is a divarication in power between politics and history. The power of history is naturally endowed with force, materially 'formed' by processes over the longue durée. Reason, always on its side and, more still, a reason that develops but does not progress: the mysterious evolution of things, in a way that is neither linear nor circular but rather is a spiral. In this, the ancient has got its revenge over the modern. Löwith described the conceptions of history. We have been able to judge them. The divine design of the history of salvation has failed. And its failure—God's defeat—is not dated from Auschwitz but from long before, from forever, the eternal

the text: 'This power was recognized by both classical antiquity and medieval and Renaissance writers as the arbitrary force in human affairs that makes it extremely difficult to predict the outcome of any event. [. . .] *Virtù* is related to the Latin *virtus* and *vir*, is a decidedly masculine quality, denoting ingenuity, skill, and ability. It can rarely be rendered accurately by references to our present-day association of the word with moral "virtue".' Niccolò Machiavelli, *The Prince* (Peter Bondanella trans.) (Oxford: Oxford University Press, 2005), pp. 92–93. See also 'Virtù' in the excellent *Dictionary of Untranslatables: A Philosophical Lexicon*, edited by Barbara Cassin (Princeton: Princeton University Press, 2014), pp. 1202–7. [Trans.]

2 The reference is to thesis fourteen of 'On the Concept of History', in Walter Benjamin, *Selected Writings, Volume 4: 1938–1940* (Howard Eiland and Howard W. Jennings eds) (Cambridge, MA: Belknap Press, 2003), p. 395. [Trans.]

history of the modern era—just to limit ourselves to what existentially concerns us. The great Christian Middle Ages were the cradle of this mad design of a final celestial city, attempting everything and anything, from Augustine to Innocent III, and not succeeding in anything, if not to accentuate, to the limit-point of life, the tragic history of human freedom. There was no final surrender to the modern, due to the resistance of the *katechon* of the Church, an anti-historical modern power and historical anti-modern power; a *complexion oppositorum* in eternal struggle and in contingent accord with the times of the [twentieth] century.[3] But it was politics that, in modernity, was the legitimate heir to the Christian philosophy of history; all of politics—realism as well as messianism, tactics and eschatology, utopianism and pragmatism. Otherwise, why would the categories of the political have to be—as they were—secularized theological concepts? Politics against history, compelled to seek, for itself, force against the power of the other. Only when it found it was it occasionally able to win.

Politics does not have a design of its own, it needs to give itself one as required, delivering it to a temporal subject. It never contains the rationale of things, knowing that the same things return while being unable to accept this condition. Hence politics is compelled to demand progress within development, but it is precisely this that disempowers it, leaving it disarmed in the face of the great return of the epoch—with its insuperable obstacles—and, thereby, politics remains caught within the immediacy of the phase in which it exists. In this case, Weber's iron

3 Reference here is to Carl Schmitt: the notion of *Katechon* (the 'restrainer' or 'withholding power') is a critical one for Schmitt in his *The Nomos of the Earth: In the International Law of the Jus Publicum Europaeum* (G. L. Ulmen trans.) (New York: Telos Press, 2006), pp. 59ff. See also Massimo Cacciari, *The Withholding Power: An Essay on Political Theology* (Edi Pucci trans., Howard Caygill introd.,) (London: Bloomsbury, 2018). For *complexio oppositorum*, see Schmitt's *Roman Catholicism and Political Form* (G. L. Ulmen trans.) (Westport: Greenwood Press, 1996). [Trans.]

cage of history imprisons politics. For politics is contingency, is occasion, is the short term, here and now, falsely, ideologically, named decision; whereas history is permanence, regularity, repeatability, it is the longue durée, it is necessity, fate, destiny. The entire modern era, the epoch of the subject, has enormously accentuated the force of objective processes, of impersonal mechanisms, of system-logics, of the material laws of movement. Political economy is the great metaphor of the modern: with the economy as noun and politics reduced to an adjective. The anatomy of civil society, as bourgeois society. The unrepeatable greatness of Marx lies in his having worked/lived for the science of this universe of ideas and relations. The greatness of his limits lay in not leaping over the horizon of the critique of political economy. The course of his life was wrought by the symbolic form of the existence of the revolutionary intellectual, this tragic figure of modernity.

A conscious political occasionalism lies on the other side of an achieved political realism. Marx's political thinking lies atop the barricades of the imagined Parisian workers, the eighteenth Brumaire of the little Napoleon, the Blochian concrete utopia of the communards, the organization of the First International—and there one finds the seeds of the *Grundrisse*; while it is not there in *Capital*, where it should have been, and is instead crushed there between the indecision of a theory of development and a theory of breakdown. *Das Kapital* should not have had the subtitle 'critique of political economy', but 'critique of economy and of politics'. Marx sought the point of crisis of the system mechanisms in the economic contradiction and was unable to find the contradictory grouping of forces able to challenge these mechanisms from within and without. It gave way to a century of reforms, but the anti-capitalist revolution when it erupted was 'against *Capital*'—in Gramsci's brilliant quip. Nothing of this is new. But the new, bitter truth, unwelcome to many, is this: a vacuum has appeared in the failed search into the places and forces of political conflict, discussed here in the apparently obscure terms of the contrast between politics and history. The vacuum of politics has been filled by an ethical emergency: emergency in the dual sense of the rising up of a dimension of the dominant reality that is, in its own way, critical; but also in the sense of the contingent action to escape from a phase, accepting the necessity of the epoch. This is the only opening that bourgeois consciousness has left for a programme of opposition to the permanence of the status quo: ethical revolt—an impotent cry of refusal against world injustices, without even one of the decisive injustices being so much as grazed by it. But one must measure ones' actions against the time of history, not against human injustice. If possible, one must do so on equal terms: not damning the times but struggling with them. Searching for more than critical points of contradiction, for the instruments able to challenge history's ordering of itself on its own grounds, on the basis of its own—apparently eternal—laws; because it is as such that they appear to those who experience historical processes politically. Modern politics is born of this dramatic demand. For this reason, it is born armed. And it is born 'against'. Politics bears upon itself the signs of its heretical conduct towards tradition: rupture, sin and guilt, scandal. It requires much greater 'fervour' [*impeto*] than 'respect' because it is necessary to 'conquer either by force or by deceit'.[4] The cold decision to expel morals from the territory of politics stems from this. Modern politics chooses to locate itself beyond good and evil. All political theory concerning the greatness of the modern, from the early 1500s to the middle of the 1600s, thinks of the world and of human things against the history immediately surrounding it. Machiavelli against the history of Italy; Bodin and the *politiques* against the history of France; Suarez and the Jesuits against the history of Spain; Althusius against the history of the European continent; Hobbes against the history of the world-island of England. And here, with the first English revolution,

4 Machiavelli, *Prince*, p. 29. [Trans.]

the synthesis of the European civil wars of the time—with the New Model Army, the first political party in the West—ends the process of primitive accumulation of the categories of the political in modernity. History is defeated. Politics wins. Capitalism can be born.

What followed is a tale of the tables turning. Considered strategically, as a whole, what followed involved many other things. But already the second English revolution, the 'Glorious' one, and then the beautiful one—as Arendt would have it—of the Americans, were models of the political use of defeat by long history. The birth of political economy was the first decisive defeat for politics; a defeat of its primacy, its autonomy, in terms of its status as self-sufficient thought/action. Economics has, since its classical period, rightly postulated itself as a science. It has been. It is. A First science, which within modernity has taken the place of First philosophy. In it, the substance of social being is grasped empirically and measured quantitatively. *Homo oeconomics* is man in general. Economic science is modern metaphysics, inasmuch as it is meta-history which is engaged on a daily basis with the foundation of modern history, with the only unfathomable Absolute left after the death of God. The neoclassical economists understood more and better than all others: Marshall, Walras, partly Pareto, and the 'pure' economists, Menger, Böhm-Bawerk, precursors and prophets of econometrics. The most abstract calculus with the most probable empirical consequence, with the greatest approximation to concrete conditions of production and the market. They united economics, anthropology, psychology and mathematics: an intellectual operation that proved a winning one over the long course of history. The Second International proved its mediocrity by suspecting nothing of all of this. From that time, economics no longer needed to posit itself as 'political economy', because politics was reduced to 'economic politics'. The highpoint of this is the twentieth century—Lord Keynes!—who used politics, subjugating it, so as to save economic society from the quasi-breakdown of the Great Crash. Economics has known how to use politics; politics has not known how to use economics: the tragedies of the century, for our side, can all be found encased within this formula. This case must be reopened but without, out of kindness, letting flee the evil spirits that inhabit it. The God of history cannot be defeated by the Lord of this world: the demon of politics—but it can be fought and, in the struggle, recognized and, finally, it can even be loved. To fight who you know cannot be defeated; opposing this world lucidly, knowing that there will not be another. Once again, not an ethics but a politics for the future—if there is to be a future for politics.

Capitalism is not dead. And yet its illness—in Marx's accurate prognosis—is terminal. From a certain point onwards, all the parabolas have begun to take a downward turn. Then again, the entirety of the Modern has been the opposite of the Annunciation. The Gospel has lived within modernity, *in partibus infidelium* [in the land of the unbelievers]. This was known from the beginning. It is no coincidence that, at the start of the modern era, one finds the Reformation as well. Luther understands Paul's difficulties in speaking to modern people. But it is from this time that Christianity begins to adapt itself to the new world. It was the Calvinist ethic that interpreted the spirit of conquest of the capitalist entrepreneur, but it was Roman Catholicism that gave political form to the subaltern people of God. The two reforms—that of Wittenberg and that of Trent—from that time till today set the Protestant ethic against Catholic politics. The Church of Rome has been a great subject of modern politics, interpreting politics in purest autonomy from *religio* itself—yes, bound by faith, but in the worldly form of the Kingdom. Let us leave to one side 'secular' modern consciousness, which has understood none of this, but it is unpleasant to have to tell the internal critics and modernizers of the Church: only in this context has the annunciation of Advent maintained itself. There was no reason why the Christian message should survive the irruption of modernity—which spoke entirely against this happening. Only the Word of the Father, having become worldly political action, was able to save the Son from a second death without resurrection. An impossible undertaking, realized. True, historical *historia salutis* [history of salvation]. A response worthy of the challenge that the rebirth of human reason posed to the eternal movements of the human heart. Let us not forget: if on the one side they were enlightened, because they were privileged intellectual elites, on the other side it was the murky, ever-oppressed world of the simple folk who asked to be heard, to speak, to act. There, between the Renaissance and the Reformation, struck the victor, as burgeoning bourgeois society became identified with modern history. When the modern era became one with capitalism, politics—I say again—either became subordinated to the economy, resulting in today's *homo democraticus* as the form of *homo oeconomicus-politicus*, or existed only as a violent eruption of organized minorities. There were 'ugly' revolutions before and after this identification of capitalist economy with modern history won out; both before and after kings' heads rolled. There were Cromwell and Robespierre, *Behemoth* and *la Terreur*, Levellers and Jacobins, first religious civil wars, and later, revolutionary civil wars. The twentieth century provided further evidence. When the Belle Époque came to an end, capitalism appeared as that which bore 'war in its breast like a hurricane',[5] compelling democratic socialists to become communists, capitalist development in Russia was forced to mutate into the October Revolution, the no-longer-bourgeois form of the modern state became the dictatorship of the proletariat. And when President Hoover's 'prosperity is just around the corner' became Wall Street's Great Crash, capitalism was saved not just by Roosevelt's Keynesian policies but also by Hitler's military politics. One can choose different periodizations of

---

5 The historian Giovanni Procacci ascribes this phrase to Jean Jaurès (leader of the French Socialist Party before the First World War) via Palmiro Togliatti (general secretary of the Italian Communist Party during the years of exile under Fascism, and in Italy until his death in 1964). See Silvio Pons, 'L'unione sovietica nella politica estera di Togliatti', *Studi storici* 33(2–3) (1992): 444. [Trans.]

the twentieth century, but from the 1910s to the 60s, 1914 to 1956, capitalist society and modern history experienced a critical moment, one of difference, contradiction and conflict. The entire epoch of the world civil wars, and its conclusion, was necessary to recover an organic relationship of reciprocity and common development. The more violent that age of war, the more reliable this age of peace. The state of exception, within globalization, becomes a local fact. Political sovereignty has become objectified again in economico-financial mechanisms. The state lives on because it survives in the Nation. But there is no longer government. In the world economy, the space of politics exists only in the form of municipal administration.

Modern history has always reduced politics to a sovereign decision over the exception. Normality, legality and peace have always led politics to one of its cyclical crises. Great politics has no history; there is no continuity, no development and certainly no progress. It intervenes, occasionally, through fractures, interruptions, upendings. Whether from above or below—for that is not the discriminatory criterion. Politically, the function of personality or the function of the masses carry the same weight in modern history. They are interruptions, not necessarily violent ones, in the course of events, plunging into the river's current. Intimately, existentially bound to the modern human condition. Modern politics specifically has had to tear out the roots binding it to the earth where politics in general was born. Hence modern politics has no origin. It is not born. At a certain point, it exists. That's all. This is enough to turn every immanent providentialism, every divine design, all calls for a future, all illusions of a better world into a broken toy in the hands of a naughty child. There is this mysterious persistence of the word—politics—that has induced many, all, into error. It is not the only obscure aspect. There is in politics a trait of irrationality, of unreason, it is irreducible to its meaning, which cannot be understood and yet needs to be. From Augustine to Weber, the demonic temptation that affects the soul of politics has been revealed. The Christian critique of ancient politics and, more generally, the degree of kinship of modern politics with political Christianity is a great theme that needs confronting separately, unravelling the skein by pulling on another thread and tying it anew to a knotty mass of other internal problems. In the same way that Christian politics breaks with the terrestrial city, so too modern politics breaks with the polis. It is no longer the inhabiting of the polis—as the etymology of the word states—which is what defines modern politics. In the same way that the polis is a mythical tale of the Greeks, so too the citizen is an ideological narration of the moderns. The *citoyen* exists in written Constitutions; the *Verfassung* of the state does not provide for it. *De Cive* speaks of power and refers to the *Leviathan*. One begins again from *The Prince*, seeking to win back command. After which comes the consent of the citizens. That is the subject, this is the object of politics. This is the transposal of the tree onto new earth. An operation that will also require new heavens. Marx's heaven of politics is the ideology of the rights of man. This is one of Marx's flashes of brilliance. He had not wanted to see *bourgeois* politics, the *bourgeois* rather than the *citoyen*, as a political figure. He had not wanted to see within capital, as its internal contradiction, the specifically capitalist form of the political. He had not, for reasons of class hatred. For him politics was still that of the Greeks—that of the ancient gods and heroes; it could not be delivered to the moderns—to merchants and bourgeois bosses. There is a nobility to politics, for Marx, as in all authentic revolutionaries. This is a variation of the nobility of spirit. The spirit of politics blew where it wished in modern times. And the great 1900s, which is to say its first half, was at its level. Then, 'O, what a fall was there . . . !'[6] in this second half of the century through which we've been cursed to live.

---

6 William Shakespeare, *Julius Caesar* 3.2.192. References are to act, scene and line. [Trans.]

The Great Twentieth Century

The slogan 'the end of history' is not just stupid. The fact that it was coined by a Japanese American should not prejudice us into instinctively rejecting it. In reality, maybe it is history that has started again, the history that has always been, where the real is the rational and the rational real; that is, where domination has achieved consent, power has become legitimized in institutions, where thesis and antithesis such as freedom and oppression have become synthesized dialectically. This is the democracy of the moderns. The West, Europe, realized modernity. Politics has fought, within this process of realization of the modern, against the return of the ever-the-same in history. Gods, heroes and 'titans' in the figures of singular individuals, of Jacobin elites, of groups of Bolshevik leaders, of the masses organized in trade unions and parties, where 'titanic' masses fight unwittingly against history—indeed, believing the opposite, that they were the bearers of history. It is untrue to say that the modern has not—and cannot—produce myths. The rising sun, the 'tomorrows that sing', the 'dream of a thing'[7]—at bottom, all of them *did*

7 The rising sun is a communist symbol that in Italian is sometimes referred to—as it is here—as *il sole dell'avvenire*, literally: the sun of the to-come, of the future. The 'tomorrows that sing' (*Lendemains qui chantant*) is the title of an autobiography by the French communist journalist and politician Gabriel Perí, who was shot by the occupying Germans in 1941. The 'dream of a thing' is the title that Pier Paolo Pasolini gave to his first novel, *Il sogno di una cosa*, composed in 1949–50 but not published until 1962. He draws the expression from the Italian translation of a phrase from a famous early letter of Karl Marx to Arnold Ruge, which Pasolini places—in a partially modified form—as epigraph to the novel. In Marx, it reads as follows: 'Hence our motto must be: reform of consciousness not through dogmas, but by analysing the mystical consciousness that is unintelligible to itself, whether it manifests itself in a religious or a political form. It will then become evident that the world has long *dreamed of possessing a thing* of which it has only to be conscious in order to possess in reality' (Marx to Arnold Ruge [September 1843] in Karl Marx and Friedrich Engels, *Collected Works*, VOL. 3 [London: Lawrence & Wishart, 1975], p. 144). The

presuppose the end of history, of human history as it had unfolded till that point. Marx called it the prehistory of humanity. In truth, it was the only history that we know, which should be brought to a close so as to pass over to an era where there would no longer be history. A horizon of final salvation has always defined the space-time of politics in the modern age. Great politics has always demanded a context of religious faith. There was a need for political theology so that modern politics could prophesize and organize the desperate attempt to knock history out of joint. Indeed, the struggle has been between the war of politics and the resistance of history. The struggle turned, time after time, on the substance, determined by the accelerated or retarded transitions of the epoch. Politics did not challenge the modern, it completed it. It was an impossible endeavour because the completion was at the beginning. The two symbolic events that lie at the foundation of modernity, the primitive accumulation of capital and the industrial revolution, leave epochal marks of inconceivable violence. The greatness of capitalism is that it built social progress upon these events so terrible for humanity. The misery of capitalism is that upon this social progress it planted the most perfect form of dominion over humanity: freely accepted dominion. Was it possible, from that beginning, to not arrive at that end-point? It was not. But one must praise politics for having heroically sought to divert the course of that swollen river. We became divided between those who wished to raise the embankments to stem the furious torrent of water and those who sought to excavate the riverbed, shift its bends and erect dams to contain the water's force. To domesticate the savage beast, allowing it to remain free; or to subjugate and cage it? Reformists and revolutionaries—to look back at them from the present, they appear to be a single thing, drawn from one family. There once was the workers'

---

phrase I have placed in italics reads in the English translation as: 'dreamt of possessing something'. [Trans.]

movement. Bernstein and Lenin are closer to each other at the end of the 1900s than when they stood in opposition at the end of the 1800s. It was the century of Labour (uppercase), Accornero has argued.[8] It was also the century of Politics (upper case).

A great subject. That of the relationship between worker politics and modern bourgeois history: one of the highest, most intense, extensive and profound contrasts/conflicts that an era has ever produced. Contrast and conflict: in the former case, almost a fact of nature, a physical law of opposition between two elements; in the second, a social fact, the choice of organized struggle between two subjects. After the modern political revolutions, immediately after, came the modern social class struggles. The most sensitively aware historians found in the former the signs, the seeds of the latter. We can, in any case, safely claim that the class struggle is the fruit of the mature stage of modernity. Not only is it vain to seek it prior to the existence of capitalism with the ideological instruments of a materialist philosophy of history. It is also pointless to seek it in early capitalism, at a time when the processes of the structural transformation of commodities and money into capital, of human labour into wage labour-power and of society, and the world as a whole, into 'experiment and industry' were underway. The worker subject is born only after the birth of capitalism, in the classical transition from manufacture to factory production. Only thereafter will the development of capitalism depend upon working-class struggle. It is true that the industrial proletariat should be seen within the long history of subaltern classes. But not as the direct filiation of them, which might be scientifically demonstrably derived from a poor economistic sociology. Slaves, serfs, early industrial workers have nothing in common but their chains. But the material with which those chains was forged was different. The golden chains of

8 The reference is to long-time friend and collaborator Aris Accornero, *Era il secolo del lavoro* [It was the century of labour] (Bologna: Il Mulino, 1997). [Trans.]

today's post-worker employees, or of second-generation self-employed workers,[9] are not the same as the iron and mud of the past. And here too, it is as if we said, and some indeed say it, that today on this earth we are all indirectly productive wage workers, in services, in knowledge, in communications. But the relationship of continuity of factory workers with the struggles of subaltern classes, and of us with factory workers as a potentially dominant class, is now based on other grounds. It is here that politics comes back into play. And it travels another route. A symbolic route of belonging, not to the world but to a part of the world, a partial standpoint that cannot be gathered up in a totality. It is in tension with the epoch, with a passion for the defeated of history but for those defeated who fought—hatred for the natural rulers, those born for it, for looking down, sitting on the thrones of wealth and power. The workers' movement and modern capitalist history, together they do not bear the markings of a normal episode in this eternal struggle; they exhibit the irruption of a state of exception, symbolizing the 'political form' assumed, for the first time and perhaps for the last time, by the contrast/conflict between the low and the high of society. The heights of this struggle have led modern politics to a point of no return. There is no type of political normality that can be posited after this type of state of exception. Order assumes another—non-political—shape: the economic-financial cosmopolitanism that we call globalization. This is not itself a novelty. For it was precisely this that was inscribed within the beginnings of the modern that, now, after the age of politics, has been consummated. The world market was already implicit in the market of the nation-state; the world-system of production was already implicit in the process of factory production—in the same way as the poverty of

9 See Sergio Bologna and Andrea Fumagalli (eds), *Il lavoro autonomo di seconda generazione. Scenari del postfordismo in Italia* (Milan: Feltrinelli, 1997), and, in English, Sergio Bologna, *The Rise of the European Self-Employed Workforce* (Milan: Mimesis, 2018). [Trans.]

continents was implicit in that of the wealth of nations; the crisis of industrialism in industrial machinism; the virtuality of financial exchange in the arcane of commodity-money; the end of labour in labour-saving; the death of the modern person in the alienation of the worker. Nothing is truly new under the sun of capitalism.

Where then is novelty? The paradox: it is a past novelty. One that remains. Worn out, but intact. Lost and present. 'Untimely'. It is the irruption of the workers' movement into modern history. Warning: this must be kept well in mind for the rest of the discussion. The workers' movement is here, at once, class and class consciousness, struggle and organization, theory and practice, the world of ideas and the ensuing actions. This is completely unprecedented. An absolutely modern event that modern history had ignored, that it then had to endure and ultimately overcame. The workers' movement, with Marx and without Marx, encountered modern politics—expressed it, inflected it, organized it. Not only. It also led politics to its final results, pushing it towards an exponential growth until the apocalyptic point of its precipitous fall. The workers' movement was the last great subject of modern politics. The 'great crash' of its ensemble of power provoked its 'breakdown'. The *Zusammenbruchstheorie*[10] did not serve capitalism as an economic mechanism, but it did in terms of political order. Problem: if capitalism was born with modern politics, and it rooted its development alongside it and with it escaped from its crisis, can capitalism survive the end of modern politics? What if we read the '89 of the 1900s, two centuries from the '89 of the 1700s, as the end of the political parabola of modern

10 *Zusammenbruch*—or breakdown—is a Marxist notion (the extent to which it is Marx's remains in dispute) naming the point at which the contradictions inherent to capitalist development would fundamentally undermine it. Perhaps the most famous discussion can be found in Henryk Grossmann's *The Law of Accumulation and Breakdown of the Capitalist System*, now in *Henryk Grossman Works*, VOL. 3 (Jairus Banaji and Rick Kuhn eds and trans.) (Leiden: Brill, 2022). [Trans.]

capitalism? Does the closure of the age of politics open onto a general crisis of capitalism or onto the parturition of another capitalism? Or, as is more likely, first the one and then the other? Only senseless questions—lacking good sense—can now attack common sense. What is required is a mad season of mature thinking, not even revolutionary but merely realistic-prophetic. The workers' movement did not lose a battle, it lost the war. More than that, it lost the age of war. It was a battle over the longue durée, culminating in our century's world civil war. The historical condition of the crisis of foundations that ensues must be carefully scrutinized. Without the workers' movement, within this form of peace, politics is no more.

What ensured the survival of politics over the course of the hundred-year peace (1815–1914) that Polanyi uncovered for us? It was thanks to the class struggle, which stepped in and placed itself at the heart of the 1800s after the age of reforms and bourgeois revolutions that had opened with the second English revolution and culminated in the Napoleonic wars. It is class struggle that, for the first time, transforms war into politics. Throughout the nineteenth century, it played the same civilizing role that the *jus publicum Europaeum* did in the preceding two centuries. But the early bourgeois right acknowledged war and regulated it, whereas the early proletarian struggles took its place and negated it. Operating at these lofty heights, we must once against give the social class struggle this noble significance in the history of the human species. Solidarity, cooperation, mutual assistance, in work and in struggle; self-organization, the spontaneous uprising from the ground of an autonomous, antagonistic conception of the world and of life that alone defines the rising of socialism; it is the long, slow historical passage of a Lessingian education of humanity.[11] Extraordinarily, here politics did not fight against history

11 A reference to Gotthold Ephraim Lessing's *The Education of the Human Race* (1777–1780). See Lessing, *Philosophical and Theological Writings* (H. B. Nisbet ed.) (Cambridge: Cambridge University Press, 2012), pp. 217–40. [Trans.]

but incorporated it, integrated it, bent it to its will, made it serve its needs. Politics has this capacity to produce exceptional events, which have something miraculous about them when compared with the usual course of things. And modern politics has, in this respect, been scandalous to bourgeois normality. The forms and ideas immediately assumed, at the dawn of class consciousness, by the consciousness of the individual alienated industrial worker, those of collective appreciation of a common and potentially liberating human condition, in the factory and in life—this too is capitalism and modern history; but from the opposite perspective: unpredictable and—for those times—uncontrollable. The figure of the worker who consciously becomes social mass is itself an example of the history, the political history of the modern subject. The labour that is productive of capital, the 'great misfortune of being a productive worker',[12] has transformed the person, who in the labour process is subordinated and dehumanized, into a superior form of human being, the subject of a process of free re-appropriation of self. The 'I' that becomes 'we', the 'we' that becomes 'part', the part that declares that, in emancipating itself, the proletariat emancipated the whole of humanity. That which is whispered in one's ear must be bellowed from the rooftops: this is the liberty of the moderns.[13] Not the private law of the citizen to become bourgeois. Not the modern state in place of the ancient *polis*. Or, as we say today in a facile and vulgar age, of the market in place of politics. Not the mass humanity of democracy that is sold the illusion—money as against image—of being a modern individual. A

12 Tronti does not provide a reference for this quote, but similar expressions appear regularly in Marx. For example: 'To be a productive worker is therefore not a piece of luck, but a misfortune' (Marx, *Capital*: *Volume I*, p. 644). [Trans.]

13 On the opposition between the 'liberty of the moderns' and 'liberty of the ancients', see Benjamin Constant, 'The Liberty of the Ancients Compared with that of the Moderns' in *Political Writings* (Biancamaria Fontana trans. and ed.) (Cambridge: Cambridge University Press, 1988), pp. 308–28. [Trans.]

process of generalized human liberation opened and then was interrupted. Everything went into reverse from that point. The temptation of an apocalyptic reading of events competes here with the will to think them. We need the latter to win out. Otherwise, we would have to agree with Sergio Quinzio: 'History descends from the gods to the heroes, then to the high priests, to the nobles, to the bourgeoisie, and finally the proletariat. There are no more steps.'[14]

The workers' movement did not fight against modernity, it fought within the contradictions of modernity. This point is essential. It was thus also in the one-hundred-year peace of the 1800s, as well as in the world civil wars of the 1900s. If one fails to grasp this, one risks confusing the workers' opposition, *absolument moderne*, with things alien to it—such as Catholic traditionalism, economic or political romanticism, or the conservative revolution. The workers' movement is a child of the early modern and father to the late modern. It is located at the heart of modernity, in a crucial passage of this history, between the violence of the beginnings and the horrors of the results. Initially, it cultivated the vocation to redeem those events from evil. It was then increasingly involved and participated in the pure and raw necessity of what was possibly an even greater evil. In the middle was Marx's generous emphasis on capitalism's 'progress'. And the struggles and the organization of proletarian wageworkers to humanize the conflict with the bosses. The programme to convert war into politics is struck and overthrown by the thunderclap of 1914. The truce is over. The world of yesterday dies.[15]

---

14 Sergio Quinzio (1927–1996) was an Italian Catholic philosopher and theologian with whom Tronti struck up a profound intellectual conversation as Tronti's attention turned to the long history of the categories of the political in the modern period, which Schmitt had so memorably described as being 'secularized theological concepts'. Carl Schmitt, *Political Theology* (G. Schwab trans.) (Chicago: University of Chicago Press, 2005), p. 36. [Trans.]

15 The implicit reference is to Stefan Zweig's *Die Welt von Gestern: Erinnerungen eines Europäers* (1942), an autobiographical account of early-twentieth-century

One sets out again from the arrival point, from the defeat of the Napoleonic armies on the battlefield. The concert of European powers gives way to the first form of world conflict. In a century, modern history had produced world capitalism. The world war becomes its natural political form. The only difference between war and politics—we know this from von Clausewitz—lies in their respective means. Politics—says modern history—is either war, or it is not. Modern politics has, with a dose of realism, taken note. The generous proletarian illusion of the international class struggle as a substitute for the war between nations falls in 1914 with the war credits voted for by German social democracy. The figure of the internationalist worker forced to become a soldier of his nation is the tragic figure of our epoch. That superior human person, the possibility of the Overman that the struggles of labour had announced, is brutally upended and defeated. The 1900s get underway. Modern history becomes, once again, the violent history of peoples and states, of individuals and classes, of races, of religions. The tragic penetrates everywhere, from the ramifications of feeling it insinuates itself into the folds of human thought. Being towards death becomes the theme of philosophy. Political theology speaks of friend/enemy. The impolitical discovers *Romantik* anti-modernity. The Parallel Campaign intrigues the man without qualities.[16] For some time now, all forms have been shattered. Words are lost in nonsense. Figures break within the soul. Sound approaches silence. Someone, precisely in this century, taught us that an energy accumulates in the air of a great epoch; it

---

Vienna, the collapse of Austria-Hungary and the author's flight into exile as the Nazis rose to power. Available in English as: *The World of Yesterday* (Anthea Bell trans.) (Lincoln, NE: University of Nebraska Press, 2013). [Trans.]

16 The Parallel Campaign refers to the national campaign (one similar to that planned in Germany) to celebrate the seventieth jubilee of Emperor Franz Joseph in 1918—a central theme of Robert Musil's unfinished masterpiece *Der Mann ohne Eigenschaften*; available in English as: *The Man Without Qualities* (Sophie Wilkins trans.) (London: Picador, 2015). [Trans.]

remains as if suspended in an inexpressible time, is apprehended, intuited, only via signs by mad visionary spirits, until the collision between opposed currents stemming from lower and higher parts of society, where the clash of geopolitical motives issuing from the powers of the earth and of the seas, where the contrast of ideological apparatuses that flow from the becoming-mass of material interests provoke a temporal explosion. A great epoch recognizes itself in great conflicts. Greatness must be paid for: with the breaking of norms, with the establishment of states of exception, with the irruption of the tragic into the political; not emergencies but crises, not transitions but leaps that compel history to renounce natural evolution to the point of making it act and think beyond itself.

The Small Twentieth Century

So far, the great history of the twentieth century. Here, politics had to raise itself to the height of the epoch. The true age of great politics runs from 1914 to 1945. Then it throws out light and shadow; it carries subjects and ideologies, it consolidates forms, behaviours, languages, stiffens cultures, and thereby undergoes countless trials of survival for at least another two decades. In the long afterglow of that history, in the 60s, we were all happily mistaken. It was an optical illusion. *Theoria* understood almost everything, but *praxis* subverted absolutely nothing at all. There is a reason for this. From the workers' struggles to the protest movements, it was as if the red proscenium curtain descended and brought the performance of the epoch to an end. To us, to many, it seemed as if an era was opening up. It was a happy delusion, because it helped us—through a process of estrangement—to definitively escape from the representation of the old world. From this was born that mode of thinking differently about those same things that return. We could indeed see red on the horizon, but it was not the glow of dawn, it was the twilight of the setting sun. At the end of the 60s, the decline [*crespuscolo*] of the West was complete. After, came the small twentieth century. History again undergoes the great fear of politics, and lowers the level, seeking normality, pushing away the chalice of the cross. To defeat its enemy, great politics, history has but one means: scaling down politics itself, downsizing its ends, its instruments, subjects, deleting horizons, neutralizing conflicts. History belongs to the winners, politics to the defeated. The nearly realized dream of history is depoliticization. The small twentieth century is our era of restoration: the legitimation of values in place of the legitimation of the monarchy. Those who observe with the myopic eyes of rights fail to see that everything in the substance of the balance of social forces has returned to the way it was before the age of great politics. Today, there is little in the way of 'being able to dare'; much in 'being able to see'. 1989 is an event of the small twentieth century, of the end of the twentieth century. By that time, history had for some time wiped away the greatness of its beginnings. There was no collapse, neither of walls, nor of powers, nor of systems, even less of ideologies. Merely the slow extinction of a soulless body. The slow burning out of a sputtering candle. An unprecedently mediocre scene. We can only grasp part of it. We cannot see the dark side of the planet. Politics, which presided over the birth of socialism, is entirely absent at the moment of its death. In the so-called new beginnings, and above all in the protagonists who announce it, the end of modern politics has already taken place. There is a metaphor with figures: the endeavour beginning with Lenin ended with Gorbachev. Two worlds, two different centuries: on the one side politics, on the other a strange activity the nature of which is unclear. It's true. Those systems could not be reformed. But only because they needed to be subjected to a continuation of the revolutionary process. In that way, perhaps, one might have opened anew the chapter of revolution in the West. We say: perhaps. Because the more probable hypothesis is that: with politics having become extinct in the postwar small politics of the twentieth century, no idea or practice of revolution was any longer possible. Socialism, the real one, the realizable one, never was, it could not be a politically autarchic endeavour. The communist attempt to build socialism in one country will remain a tragic political utopia of modern history. Once the fog of edifying interpretations of these human events has cleared, it will be understood that the violence of certain processes lay in the material conditions of the processes themselves, rather than in the wickedness of the personalities that expressed them. The demonic was in the history of the times, which were geopolitically determined. It lay in the destructive energy that modernity accumulated in the course of its magnificent and progressive destiny.[17] This is the history that remains unfinished. The spectacle is merely suspended. We find ourselves chatting in the interval.

We must set out a fundamental argument here, in opposition to this revisionism, to this ideology of the second half of the twentieth century that turned the 1930s into an absolute in which all cows are black. While Nazi totalitarianism applied its ideas, communist authoritarianism contradicted its own theories. The critical point lies in the relationship of politics to modern history in these two cases. In the case of Germany, the contrast to the modern was based upon the reading of a cultural tradition, bent towards the interests of a Lebensraum, of living space, whose wellspring lay in the dark history of the epoch. In the case of Russia, the contradiction to the modern was only practical, forced upon it by circumstance, by its experimental character, not willed but endured, which was the consequence of a necessary political attempt that was historically impossible. The conservative revolution and the workers' revolution were two true protagonists of the first half of the

17 Reference is to Giacomo Leopardi's poem 'Lenta ginestra', or 'Broom, or the Flower of the Wilderness': '*the magnificent, progressive / destiny /* of humankind'. Giacomo Leopardi, *Canti* (Jonathan Galassi trans.) (New York: Farrar, Strauss and Giroux, 2010), p. 291. [Trans.]

century, two great subjects of the great twentieth century. The one is irreducible to German totalitarianism, the other irreducible to Soviet socialism. Just as the Reformation and Counter-Reformation were in reality Protestant Reformation and Catholic Reformation, because, in the early-sixteenth-century context of the birth of modern politics, the idea and practice of religious reformation had reached maturity; so in the first half of the twentieth century, in the epoch of world wars, the idea of revolution had reached maturity, no longer merely as politico-institutional transformation but also as total subversion, both political and cultural. Clearly, we are seeking different categories to understand what happened, forced as we are into these conceptual leaps by the insufferable opinions of intellectuals, who view the solution to all issues in terms of a facile evolution. We set out from the hypothesis that the essential aspect of the century is yet to be understood; in contrast to the victorious thesis that what happened is obvious. Rather, history poses questions to the politics of the defeated party. If in Russia there was indeed a 'revolution against *Capital*',[18] how could this not mark all that followed from that attempt? The contradiction can be found in Lenin. The political directions that flow from *State and Revolution* overturn the economic analysis of *The Development of Capitalism in Russia*. And the contradiction can be found in Stalin. The practical establishment of socialism overturns the theoretical directions of revolutionary Leninism. All of Stalin's 'Asiatic' violence goes in the direction of politically accelerating the processes of social modernization of the resistant and restraining archaic relationships. To transform the revolution against *Capital* into a revolutionary process was not an activity for beautiful souls. And then. How can one fail to observe that the attempt to build socialism in

18 This is the title of a famous article by Gramsci 'La rivoluzione contro *Il Capitale*', *Avanti* (24 November 1917); translated in Antonio Gramsci, *Pre-Prison Writings* (Richard Bellamy ed., Virginia Cox trans.) (Cambridge: Cambridge University Press, 1994), pp. 39–42. [Trans.]

one country takes place in the age of the world civil wars? Every time one tries to understand, one is accused of justifying. But *die Weltgeschichte ist der Weltgericht* is not a good place to pick up the thread of our argument.[19] One may write a phenomenology of the political spirit of the twentieth century without rooting it in a philosophy of modern history. And indeed, there is no port of arrival. There is no absolute knowledge to achieve. There is a relative truth to win, to tear from things, being rigorously honest with oneself.

The failure of socialism in Russia can be dated very early on. It coincides with the failure of the revolution in the West. Lenin was aware of this when he launched the ingenious idea of the NEP.[20] He thereby sought to extend over the long term the sudden break of October. Capitalism could not be immediately overthrown; it would have to be pressed into the service of primitive accumulation of the economic conditions for socialism. This is the task of a political power that guides, directs, controls, holds the reins of the movement that is not all, because all is the final aim that justifies the means. The Keynes that inspired the New Deal would have existed without Marx, but not without Lenin. The political hand that leads capitalism out of crisis follows the movements

19 'The history of the world is the Last Judgement'. A line in Friedrich Schiller's 1786 poem 'Resignation: A Fantasy', it is used by Hegel in *The Philosophy of Right*, § 340. [Trans.]

20 Lenin initiated the New Economic Policy (1921–28) in order to rebuild an economy destroyed by war and civil war. The NEP envisioned a degree of private ownership, competition and market exchanges in certain sectors of the economy alongside state ownership of large-scale industry. In 1922, as the civil war in Russia drew to an end, he presented the NEP as a 'retreat', but in the course of an extended metaphor of a mountain climber intent on reaching the utmost summit, he explains that at times the climber may be 'forced to turn back, descend, seek another path, longer, perhaps, but one that will enable him to reach the summit'. Vladimir I. Lenin, 'Notes of a Publicist' in *Collected Works*, VOL. 33 (Moscow: Progress Publishers 1980), p. 204. [Trans.]

of the hand that wanted to lead it to development. The stroke of genius lies here in Lenin as man-of-government: when one speaks of strategic vision in the field, great politics over the short term, *voilà un homme*! who knows what that means. There is a point here which was not truly considered at the time, but which perhaps we can perceive better now that the century has passed. That high reformism in one enormous country, which was largely backward, needed the continuity of a revolutionary context that, if not world-wide, certainly needed to be Europe-wide. Could Marxist socialism win in the country where it had been voluntaristically imposed, just at the time it was defeated where it had been born? This by no means banal thesis of historical revisionism interprets German Nazism as the response to the establishment of socialism in Russia. A violent response, just as violent was the response of the European powers to the Bolshevik success of 1917. There are lapses of memory that we should endeavour to remedy: it is the liberalisms of the West that unleashed the civil war in Russia. Ultimately, capitalism—when politics puts its very survival in doubt—always replies with war. And it is easy to grasp how far the civil war conditioned the form of party adopted by the communists in power. Hence the thesis is, partially true, but truer still is the contrary one: the terrible 1930s in Soviet Russia are also a response—reprehensible morally, ill-advised politically—to the on-field victory of German totalitarianism, its neighbour. Germany and Russia, at that time, exhibited a sort of stellar political hostility. This problem of the history of culture remains outstanding. It is also an intimate motif of recognition within the condition of the twentieth-century European soul. Leave to anyone who wants it the Italian national-popular[21] and, worse still, American civilization! Everything was already written in the signs, weighty spiritual signs of a rift within modern consciousness faced with

21 For an extended critique of the 'national-popular' in Italian political culture, see Alberto Asor Rosa, *The Writer and the People* (Matteo Mandarini trans.) (London: Seagull Books, 2021). [Trans.]

the bourgeois splendours of the god of progress. Our *Heimat* lay in the period straddling the nineteenth and twentieth centuries, in Germany and Russia before their unexpected rise to monstrous leviathans. There is no other word for it. There was our Heimat. And in that 'there was' lies the entire tragedy of the political that began there and that today has ended in nothing. It lacks even the shape for a tale.

What remains is the aspect of political reasoning. The great reformist path of the NEP falls due to the failure of the revolutionary path in Europe. Because, traditionally, reformism and revolution are two paths to arrive at the same objective. So it was, as we have seen, post-Marx, who gave rise—like his teacher Hegel—to a right and a left current. They maintained a common critical dogma: capitalism would be overcome by socialism. The division was over the means. In truth, there was a difference of 'sensibility'. The revisionists did not say: the end is nothing. They said: it is pointless to proclaim it, it must be organized in the movement. The orthodox did not refuse gradualism. They said: this is the work of tactics, which must prepare the conditions for a strategic leap. In both cases, there was a primacy of politics. Only the degree of intensity assigned to it differed. For this reason, the greatest difference expressed itself on the terrain of organization. In the workers' movement, reform and revolution have been inseparably complementary. The workers' movement was this set of practices sustained by theory. When the theories began to cave in, the practices were no longer able to hold, neither together nor independently. It is a disingenuous illusion to make oneself heir of only one of these traditions. Today no reformism is possible, whether socialist or, worse, social democratic, that does not contain a critique of capitalism and envisages its overcoming. The practical reformist whose mind no longer retains any revolutionary thoughts performs a merely provisional function of rationalization, normalization and neutralization of mechanisms that are both the winning ones and that belong to the enemy. On the other hand, there is no revolution possible, whether communist or, even less, of workers, without a long slow march, profound and gradual, within those economic and institutional mechanisms to disassemble them from within. The revolutionary in word only, incapable of reformist patience, merely keeps the votive lamp lit before the icon of a sanctified antagonism. It is not true that wrapping matters in the coils of this unusual discourse means running up against the facts. There is an almost infallible recipe to enable us to approach the truth of things today. Take the common sense of mass intellectuality. Turn it into its opposite. You will be close to gleaning the—relative—truth.

The evidence in favour of the hermeneutical usefulness of this procedure lie not only far back in the century but lies closer too, in our own experience. After 1956, in the early 1960s—a period of de-Stalinization, a relaxing of the Cold War and international détente—it was perhaps still possible to reform the socialist system. Why did it not happen? Because of internal resistance, certainly: due to the weakness of the subjective forces leading renewal, to the viscosity of the dominant structures of power, to the closure of any free circulation of public opinion and the consequent, consolidated and almost institutionalized absence of theoretical consciousness of the processes underway. But there is another 'fact' that one chooses not to see. Socialist reformism was once again left isolated in the international context of the class struggle. Only concerted pressure from the West that, in one way or other again could have advanced—in new terms—the great challenge of the revolution in Europe, might have been able to invest and overthrow the powerful internal resistances to that system. With the explosion of neocapitalism, new conditions had been created for workers' struggles and unexpected movements of contestation. In a few rare places, these latter elements unified quite spontaneously. What was lacking was the lucid idea of joining this reunified form for the self-organization of conflict in the West with an organized movement of internal reform of Soviet socialism. These are not the most sophisticated and novel set of reflections on this complex interweaving of problems. We wait for further investigations by Rita di Leo to shed light on many obscure points that have here been merely touched upon.[22] The fact remains that, sure, history is not made with maybes, but the maybes that did not take place occasionally illuminate the obscurities of history. The lost chances for advancement not only do not return, but often also trigger burdensome reversals. Subjectively, social democratic and communist parties were absent, together. That was the time of *Ostpolitik*, not of governments but of struggles. The real break with the recent history of the USSR required an audacious inner split, a split from one's own recent history in the West; one that might inaugurate a strategic turn that, from within the 1960s, might have reopened a season of great politics in a modern anti-capitalist opposition. Democratic reformers in Russia could have won only if European democracy had regained a revolutionary vocation. Dreams, visions a là *Symphonie Phantastique*.[23] The reality is greyer. But it is precisely the grey colour of the course of history that is better understood by seeing than analysing. Weber was wrong to say: those who wants to see should go to the cinema. This is the century of the cinema, after all. Rather, Wenders is correct when he says: the world is in colour, but black and white is more realistic.

Something else is true. One must, with sober vision, discern behind the ideological spectacle of this so called global and virtual postmodern of the final years of the twentieth, the reality that is merely a little, ancient world. In the end, the 1800s returned to defeat our century. At the helm again are all the old social relations, now secure, because the age of

22 Rita di Leo was an economist of socialist economies who after the dissolution of the Soviet Union became professor of international relations at the Sapienza University of Rome, where she remains professor emeritus. She is a long-time collaborator of Tronti's, going back at least as far as the time of the establishment of the founding journal of political workerism, *Classe Operaia*, in 1963. [Trans.]

23 1830 symphony by the French Romantic composer Hector Berlioz made up of episodes, some hallucinatory, in the life of an artist. [Trans.]

politics—the only one that could have troubled the modern idea of domination founded upon the economic—is over. Two vast winning processes. The market, the paradigm of a totalizing modernity—commodity-money-capital—does not win because of its world scale but for its individual dimension. The historically capitalist relation of reproduction—money-commodity-money—is now *in interiore homine*. The individual is the princely category of the modern. When a process wins here, it wins everywhere. Like the other terrible process: the alienation of labour passes from the particular industrial worker to the generic, neutral man. Having reached and overthrown the boundary of the mass worker it turned to the universal figure of the citizen. From the Taylorized factory to bourgeois civil society. Alienated labour, by enslaving itself, enslaved all of humanity. As we have already in part seen. The *citoyen* is no longer the bourgeois in the heavens of politics. The heavens of politics have crumbled upon us along with all the Greek gods. The bourgeois no longer needs the *polis*, just as capital no longer needs the state. They, certainly, have emancipated themselves. Now they are free. And it had to be so. Because it was written in the character of the beginnings. Let us state honestly: this is an age of Restoration. But without Romanticism. On the contrary, it is in essence neoclassical. A shamelessly futuristic neoclassicism. It has been called: conservative modernization. It's like that, more or less. Restoration via innovation, this is what the consequences of peace have deposited after the age of the world civil wars. In the end, politics has had to sign an unconditional surrender. One talks again of ancient politics or of Eternal Politics so as to exorcize and demonize modern politics. It can all be found narrated in the petty quotidian existence of the 'last men'. This fateful encounter, this progressive superimposition of *homo oeconomicus* and *homo democraticus* has brought the game to a close once and for all. It is no longer possible to use the contradictions of the modern. But without use of contradictions, we are left with an impossible politics.

Nostalgic Inhabitants of the Century

Impossible modern politics. It came to fruition with the heroic attempt of the workers' movement to become the state. Which meant: the apocalyptic decision of the subaltern classes to become the dominant class. Only modern politics could force open this untraversable passage. The categories of the political, secularized theological concepts transvaluated, shaped the modern process of revolution. Over the long history of the modern, there are few subjects of such processes. Not the nation-states of the absolute monarchies, not the ensuing liberal colonial empires, not even the confederation of democratic states, which were exercises in the domination by economic interests that were, yes, political but without spirit—pure force, war without human greatness. Perhaps the *complexio oppositorum* of the political form glimpsed in Roman Catholicism is equal to it—but only after having renounced the Church, with the Kingdom but not the Institution, with the people of God but not the Papal hierarchy, at once *eschaton* and *katechon*. The workers' movement, heir to the struggles of the subaltern classes, gave itself a philosophy of history: historical materialism, the prehistory of humanity as the history of class struggle in all societies to ever have existed. It is pointless to prove its scientific validity. It is not a case of science, whatever it claims, but of ideology. It was a witting false consciousness; a symbolic construction aiming at partisan mobilization. The objective: to organize part of society against the other, producing, through this novelty, a partisan mobilization. But with respect to its other aspect, the workers' movement did not give itself a philosophy of politics as the irresistible expression of power, of organized force for a condition of permanent conflict from the base of society to the heights of power. The communists saw this better than others, but they did not see it all clearly. When one speaks of the absence of a Marxist theory of the state, it is of this that one must speak. Moreover, missing was a Marxist critique of politics at the same lofty heights as the Marxist critique of political economy. And so, the liberty of the moderns was bequeathed to the liberal tradition, popular sovereignty to the democratic tradition, and one was left—not even with an idea, but—with a practice of absolute power drawn from the early modern state; a bad, primitive synthesis of Prince and Leviathan. No contingent historical condition in the construction of socialism could justify this. It is a complex discussion, which we should confront using different instruments. The error lay perhaps in the premises: the idea-project that fundamentally united the communists of the West and the East, of introducing the masses into the state. It is the failed communist attempts from Russia to China to Italy that compel us to rethink modern politics critically. But the objective of bringing the masses into the state was accomplished in the guise of contemporary Western democracies, setting out from that form of realized democracy that—as has been argued—was Soviet socialism. This was the strategic research thesis advanced by Rita di Leo. Her studies have for some time broken with traditional analytical frames and started new studies into socialism. For this reason, official opinion keeps them at a safe distance. Masses and power: seen from Canetti's Mitteleuropa—Russia and America emerge as world experiences more intimately linked than Tocqueville's prophecy foresaw. It was the workers' movement that was to become state, thereby changing, revolutionizing by this very fact the modern idea of power. A side [*parte*] that would win, with struggles and from government, that active consent to the exercise of its authority on the field and conserve it over time. Force endowed with spirit that intervenes in the social relation to disassemble and reconstruct it. Active consent, because the decisions are shared and developed collectively; conscious political decisions. In the limit-idea of the extinction of the state, in the communism of every cook can govern,[24] one saw a frontier beyond politics, after a

24 Reference is to Lenin's 1918 pamphlet 'Can the Bolsheviks Retain State Power', where he argues that although the Bolsheviks realized that 'an unskilled labourer or a cook cannot immediately get on with the job of state administration', he called for

hyper-political passage. Why this two-step did not work is not at all clear, even though today people exhibit such certainty in everything. The only thing that is clear is the result: precisely because the going beyond, the overcoming of modern politics did not take place, then de facto what remained—and at that point all that remained—was this nihilism of the end.

But why all of this at the end of the twentieth century? What really happened? The roots of the workers' defeat are at the present time buried beneath successive layers of false interpretations. This discussion is the beginning of an archaeological dig to bring them to the surface. Its commencement presupposes a brave abandonment of ethical commitment for the sake of truth, and the uncomfortable adoption of a criterion of honesty. It's true, this had already occurred in the opposition of *Kultur* and *Zivilization*, between Nietzsche and Weber. But then the workers' revolution represented the problem. And the conservative revolution followed in its tracks. It seemed then—in the second and third decades of the twentieth century—that a new need for truth was born. It imposed its law, a terrible absolute. Innocent victims, ideas, persons could only sacrifice themselves on the altar of what had to be. That was the great 1900s. Our generation is perhaps the last fortunate one. Because in spirit, even before coming into existence, we were combatants of this long total war. We were still able to immerse ourselves in its living memory, not the one in books but in that of men and women, the people/class first and then culture/civilization, these two admirable pairings that the

an immediate break with the prejudiced view that only the rich, or officials chosen from rich families, are capable of *administering* the state, of performing the ordinary, everyday work of administration. 'We demand that *training* in the work of state administration be conducted by class-conscious workers and soldiers and that this training be begun at once, i.e. that a *beginning* be made at once in training all the working people, all the poor, for this work.' Lenin, *Collected Works*, VOL. 26 (London: Lawrence & Wishart 1964), p. 113. [Trans.]

twentieth century celebrated and then destroyed. Witting inhabitants of the century, we would like today to look at it from the summits but are obliged to look at it from the nadir of the end. One must not only know what side [*parte*] one is on, but also on what side [*parte*] one would have been on. In the epoch of truth, there was no room for doubt. Within the First World War, I would have been a Russian peasant soldier who followed Lenin's revolutionary instructions to not fire on German worker soldiers but, instead, to turn my gun on the Tsarist generals. I would have occupied the factories in the *biennio rosso*.[25] On 21 January 1921, in Leghorn, I would have moved from the Goldoni theatre to San Marco.[26] 'Naturally', I would have become an underground antifascist militant. I would have gone to Spain with the communist-organized International Brigades, ideally without firing on the anarchists. During the Resistance against the Germans, I would have been a partisan in the mountains—perhaps this would be the only time I would have felt like an Italian in the entire wretched history of the motherland. I would have endorsed the Salerno Turn,[27] agreed on by Stalin and Togliatti, conscious of the duplicity necessary to establish the best conditions for a revolutionary process in Italy. I confess: this is nostalgia for epochs I was unable to live through. This, for us, is *Die Welt von gestern*. Not the

25 The 'two red years' were 1919–20, when the intense class conflicts took hold in Italy as it had in a number of other European states. Most famous were the 'factory councils' established in Turin and Milan. See, for instance, Antonio Gramsci, 'Soviets in Italy' (1920), *New Left Review* 1(51) (1968): 28–58. [Trans.]

26 The reference is to the Leghorn Split that took place at the XII Congress of the Italian Socialist Party at the Goldoni theatre, when the communist (or 'maximalist'), comprising Antonio Gramsci, Amadeo Bordiga and Amedeo Terracini, among others, broke away to establish the Italian Communist Party in the San Marco Theatre in Venice. [Trans.]

27 The *Svolta di Salerno* (the Salerno turn), was when Palmiro Togliatti, the historic leader of the Italian Communist Party, returned to Italy and agreed to enter a unity government in April 1944. [Trans.]

imperial kingdom of Kakania,[28] nor the Parisian *belle époque*. But the *Weltbürgerkrieg* [world civil war]. Born in the heart of it, we breathed the air, drank the milk, absorbed the energy of the epoch that remained around and in the form of a tragic memory for many years. For that great epoch to be forgotten, a generation of little men had to emerge. They did so. To be against that history, that certainly would have been 'great politics'. Opposing its tragic results, cultivating it in its dramatic illusions. Great history always carries dark impulses in its collective unconscious. The task of great politics is to raise them to consciousness to free the field of human action. To clarify, not to illuminate but to intervene and transform. Here was the anti-enlightenment and, if you like, anti-rationalist vocation of Marxism. It was lost, not in favour of a good use of critico-negative reason, but in favour of the bad use of beautiful and positive feelings.

Conventional wisdom gets the order of factors completely upside down. Whatever is said today is not pertinent to the theme, even less to its variations. Revolution was wrong to make itself the midwife of history. It is capable only of begetting monsters. The monsters of the twentieth century belonged to the history of the time, only later to the politics of men. Politics' fault lay rather in not knowing this in time or thoroughly enough. Revolutionary politics should have restrained and, at the same time, liberated: restrain forces, liberate subjects. An enormous task was left unformed, was not grasped in thought. *Virtù* and *fortuna* found themselves happily together at the start of the century; the end of the century finds them desperately alone, separate and hostile. And so, from

28 *Kaiserlich* und *königlich* (imperial and royal) was the nomenclature for the institutions of Austria-Hungary that Robert Musil ridiculed with the name of 'Kakania' in *The Man Without Qualities*. For a useful discussion, see Stefan Jonsson, *Subject Without Nation: Robert Musil and the History of Modern Identity* (Durham, NC: Duke University Press 2000), p. 221. [Trans.]

where should one start again? The fortune of living memory. Knowing that it is against all banal political *virtù*. The rule of which is to forget. One can listen to historical memory in the narration of the protagonists. It can be read about in books and reconstructed from documents. To live it means finding oneself in a prolongation of a time that is changed compared to before, but not so much as to make way for that weak and distorted image that is a 'new beginning'. The century cannot be cut in half like an apple. The age of war, which in the twentieth century coincides with that of politics—one might tremble before this statement, but it is true—ends not in 1945, but in the 1960s. One might vaguely agree with the idea of the 'short century'. After all, Hobsbawm is the only recent historian towards which one might feel some fondness. With respect to the others, be they called Nolte or Furet, you realize immediately that you are confronting enemies. One can speak of 1914–89 only on the pessimistic condition of seeing in that '89 of the century the precipitate of the slow decadence of the 1980s and 70s. The century is no shorter if one speaks of 1914–68. The twentieth century had already begun earlier, in that extraordinary passage of the history of spirit that, from the last two decades of the nineteenth century to the first ten years of this, never failed to provide symbolically tragic signs of that which was to come. The figurative arts, literature, music, the sciences—they all tell us the same thing, all are at war with their own forms. Only philosophy will come later, that owl of Minerva that requires things to have passed. The destiny of the 1900s is already there in the passage from Nietzsche to Weber. Genial, mysterious and not particularly significant stellar symbologies. The same decade that Marx dies in London, Kafka is born in Prague, Nietzsche is snuffed out in madness—the century can officially begin. Once things are seen no longer to originate from there, it's clear that the twentieth century has ceased or that a minor twentieth century has begun. And yet there was no caesura, no leap, even less could one speak of breakdowns. There was an imperceptible subsidence in the historical terrain; an unidentified drift in the continents of politics; an exhaustion of the modern in the products of its origin—and, at a certain point, we found ourselves here, in a world unrecognizable that, without knowing it, is always the same: formless because unconcerned with the search for alternative forms; in a condition of stagnation without desperation—this cultural coma of the West that is impossible to interrupt once the dramatic glare of its setting sun is extinguished.

From when can we date this victorious deconstruction? The scandalous answer is to name 1968 as the watershed moment between the great and the small twentieth century. To some extent this is an arbitrary periodization. But here too one should overturn the commonplace intellectual opinion that expends on the symbolism of the 1960s the enlightened bourgeois apologia of a new beginning of anti-politics. A thorough sociological hermeneutics should endeavour to shed light on the conceptual distinction between 'contestation' and 'conflict'. Class struggles and anti-authoritarian struggles were not the same thing—and should not have been. But failing to maintain continuity between them snapped the long chord of their history in favour of a short-term uprising. Organized forms and non-institutionalized experiences, parties and movements share the blame for failing to understand one another. A historic set of events ended without another beginning. Ironically, the origin of the crisis of politics lies there, in the very desire to put authoritarian power in crisis. The relations between history and politics are murky, confused, ambiguous, unresolved and—ultimately—unpredictable. At the point of the greatest danger, there also is what saves. At the point of the greatest opportunity, what we can lose can be found.

The slogan 'students and workers unite and fight', the virtuous bridge between 1968–69, between youthful spring and the workers' 'hot autumn', between the children of the flowers and the rugged pagan race,[29] was an Italian miracle. It was a demonstration of how the Italian case incorporated the best of the European political situation. Elsewhere, starting with the USA through to the French May events, 1968 was anti-worker and anti-political. And since the workers and politics were the only two opposition forces within capitalism, once the field was cleared of these, the road was open for a new victorious image of the old world. Imagination took power. The real neocapitalism is not the Fordist, developmentalist and Keynesian one of the early 1960s, but the one that is post all of this. The capitalism of the 1980s and 90s, following the work of the Trilateral Commission and the revenge of the economic right in the guise of Thatcher and Reagan; then—with a different set of political alliances—it lands in the Europe of the Maastricht Treaty. This period brings together all manner of things—from Japanese Toyotism to the Southeast Asian Tigers, to Yeltsin's Russia to post-Deng China, and so on and so on. Of course, the extraordinary generation of the 1960s did not ask for this heterogenesis of ends, but, while undeserved, it was the result. Never had such a renewal of the ruling class occurred as after that wave of protest. After the passing of the 1960s and slowly through the subsequent years, never before had there taken place such an extreme process of uniform knitting together of a caste as a body at the top of societies and political systems. It was extreme because it occurred across all fields, from industries to markets, to the professions, from academies to the workplace, up to the new frontiers of communications technologies and virtual realities. And it was uniform—this is perhaps the most

29 Tronti describes the new, 'mass workers' of the late 1960s as 'a rugged pagan race, without ideals, without faith, without morality' (*una rude razza pagana, senza ideali, senza fede, senza morale*) in a famous expression from 'Estremismo e riformismo' in *Contropiano* 1 (968): 46. The *Autunno Caldo* (Hot Autumn) is the name given to the period of intense industrial conflict, primarily in northern Italy, which ran from the autumn of 1969 to the start of 1970. [Trans.]

striking and important element—because what followed was an unstoppable uniting and homologation of ruling classes that up to that point had lined up in opposing camps, and in civil struggles that had assumed democratic guise. This set the stage for that process whereby left political groupings in Europe, having broken all links with the preceding history of the workers' movement as well as losing all notion of the categories of modern politics, would become increasingly interchangeable with those of the right with which they formally alternated. The minor history of the twentieth century begins in 1968. In place of conflict, compromise; in place of belonging, contamination; in place of ideologies, interests; in place of cultures, issues; in place of parties, groups; in place of the noble contest of relations of class forces, the stupid anarchic violence of acts of terrorism. In place of politics, ethics at best. Nothing but a leap back to a time before modern politics.

Since that time there has been only one genuine revolution, the feminist one.[30] The only case of a movement that has delivered new thinking. And has shifted relations, changed laws, overturned common sense and destroyed 'good sense'. Because it came from afar. The need for liberation from a millennial oppression by the other side of the heavens. These two characteristics always qualify and expose a political phenomenon able to compete as an equal with the noumenon of history. The first is the irruption of a direct opposition, agonic, 'polemic' in the literal sense of the term, the one that divides in two with no possible synthesis, the opening of an *either/or* that unleashes a struggle of *Freund–*

30 Tronti speaks of the 'feminine' rather than 'feminist', but it rings rather oddly in English, and it seems quite clear that throughout this passage the reference is to feminism. He is thinking specifically of what is sometimes called the Italian feminist thinking of difference, more specifically that thinking developed around the 'feminine philosophical community *Diotima*' (www.diotimafilosofe.it). Founded by Luisa Muraro, Adriana Cavarero, Wanda Tommasi and Chiara Zamboni in the 1980s, it also has strong links with the thought of Luce Irigaray. [Trans.]

Feind. The second is the long duration of the problem, deep rooted in the history of time, epochal and relatively eternal. The workers' movement was defeated in part because it allowed itself to be enclosed within a too-narrow stretch of time. It was unable to turn against modern history the weight of human needs unaddressed over a long historical period. It had not wanted or, perhaps, it was unable to take a deep breath and immerse itself in all the past revolts of the world's oppressed and, from there, not await but press on to prepare for and organize the event of the retribution to come. Moreover, lost was the lofty tension of opposition, 'lofty' as in elevated, because no longer overseen and cultivated within the vulgar forms of violence. Instead, it becomes a part of the culture of *et-et*, of the 'on the one hand and on the other hand', and taken as far as the reactionary idea of systemic complexity that had its real origin in the dialectical finale of *Aufhebung* [sublation], the overcoming that retains within itself not what is always there but what it considers it has overcome, the suppression of the negative so as to return to a bolstered positive. The Real-Rational movement of the entirety of modern history. The greatness of Hegel is that he told us this history as it was. Marx did well—on this basis—to grasp the laws of movement of capitalism. But to go beyond this, rather than setting out from Hegel, perhaps it would have been better to set out from Kierkegaard. This discussion should appear precisely here, in the context of a conversation about the feminist revolution. No, it should not substitute for the workers' movement. This is not its place in the world. It must not be and it is not. But it does have those characteristics of direct standing in opposition and of a long history. Enough at least for it to be the irruption of an element of the negative that is potentially un-subsumable by what was once known, in an eloquent expression, as the constituted order. Here we find a paradox of the twentieth century, one of the many. This is a century that has been, first tragically then comically, paradoxical. The contradiction man/woman, masculine/feminine, had its preferred ground alongside and autonomous from the other great contradictions of the epoch, traversing the first half of the twentieth century: workers and capital, fascism and democracy, capitalism and socialism. It's problem—fear not—was worthy of the age of world civil wars. But that great contradiction exploded while the other contradictions had gone extinct both practically and theoretically. The problem missed its epoch. This needs to be understood and its consequences interpreted. The women's revolution falls within the small twentieth century. This fact cut off its wings as it flew to the solitary summit of its problem. It is the case of the critique of the ideal of man, modern man, bourgeois and citizen, which from women's standpoints are found to be the same thing: exclusive citizens of the city, with wealth and power on their side, the gods, friends of the modern polis. It is the case of the crisis of the practice of the 'last man' and of the desperate subjective tension to go—running, leaping, 'dancing'—towards the Overman. Feminists were right to set out from the tragic heroine Antigone, passing via the Christian mystic Marguerite Porete,[31] and arriving at the worker Simone Weil. Symbolic stations of a long history of alternative life, or rather, existence. A feminist revolution could only have won in the age of great politics. Today, after the end of this age, it can only be—and is—a cultural revolution. Precious but poor. Precious for the condition of the individual, poor in relation to the future of the world.

It creates a thinking that is distinct from all others, that of difference: a concept of philosophy galvanized by the condition of woman. In this sense, in its substance as thought, difference is a category of modern politics. In its practice, it is modern politics realized. It cannot do without conflict; it cannot do without force; it is without legs if it does not stand

31 On Marguerite Porete, see Joanne Maguire Robinson, *Nobility and Annihilation in Marguerite Porete's 'Mirror of Simple Souls'* (Albany, NY: State University of New York, 2001). [Trans.]

on the legs of realism and utopia; it cannot but create willed false consciousness; it cannot but inflect the strategic framework of liberation with an emancipatory tactic. This is the paradox. This political eruption of the female in history occurred once politics was also beyond its crisis, on the way to its breakdown. The women's movement found itself heir to 1960s processes of civilization, modernization and secularization. Not very much given the apocalyptic charge of its sudden emergence from history's deep pulsations, those of the modern individual and of modern social and civil relations. Only great politics could have advanced this other sense of life, which originated—at the end of modernity—from the female of humanity. The women's revolution has yet to be defeated, as the others of the century have been, but it must know that it must play out its difficult destiny and its joyous freedom within this miserable age of restoration.

Paix impossible, guerre improbable[32]

The century dies and the millennium is extinguished without messianic portents of salvation. The play's chorus happily approves. The happy ending is just around the corner. All will end in jubilee. Is there anything more tragic than Johann Sebastian Bach's *Weihnachts-Oratorium* [Christmas Oratorio], BWV 248? Is there anything more painful than the birth of a Son of God fated to die, or rather, to be killed? If the consequences of peace lead to the end of politics, this is now the problem we need to reflect on. A situation that is indeed new. Modern history has coexisted, in conflict, with modern politics. What history will there be now without politics? It is never said: this situation of anti-political peace is also born of victory in a war. The age of world civil wars does

32 'Impossible peace, improbable war': this was the title of the first chapter of Raymond Aron's book on the opening of the Cold War, *Le Grande Schisme* (Paris: Gallimard, 1948). [Trans.]

not end in '45. What ends then is the second phase of the twentieth-century permanent war, when a third phase opens. The Hiroshima Bomb, rather than Churchill's 'Iron Curtain Speech' in Fulton, is the act that signals the start of the Third World War. Inter alia, Roosevelt was gone, Truman had taken his place. The USSR is told that the peace can be organized together, while knowing that at that time the world is under the ominous hegemony of the United States. All of Stalin's manoeuvres in Eastern Europe so as to create an anti-Western cushion, as well as the beginning of the long march of the Chinese revolution, are necessary countermeasures. A politico-military confrontation[33] begins. The world is arranged into two camps, perhaps as never before, or perhaps not since the break signalled by the Reformation and the ensuing religious wars. And indeed, the bipolar geopolitical order is charged with opposed ideological motivations. While the USA proposes the brilliantly conceived Marshall Plan, the USSR transforms the Third International into the Cominform. Typically differing ripostes of two opposed systems. The entire contrast of capitalism and socialism can be interpreted as the conflict between economy and politics. Even the victory of the one over the other can be read that way. The workers' movement represented this, ultimately Weberian modern vocation of politics. The thesis of the workers' movement as the last great subject of modern politics is confirmed *in articulo mortis*, at the point of death: since the end of the history of the workers' movement, there has been no place for politics. Who could deny that there is a line that runs from Machiavelli to Lenin? Even the capital-relation was born and grew up with politics. But in the twentieth century an extraordinary event took place. The working class that became State through the revolution led by the party, subtracted politics from capital; in turn, capital—not only for this reason but also because of it—underwent the quasi-breakdown of the Great Crash. To

33 In English in the original. [Trans.]

escape it, it needed to draw from socialism—provisionally but strategically—the reversal of relationship of economy to politics. Had not Keynes taken 'a short view at Russia'?[34] The Second World War—the continuity of world politics by other means—completed the work. After which both capitalism and socialism emerged strengthened in their natural historic vocations: the one economic, the other political. Let us try to look at the Cold War through this historically determined pairing of friend/enemy. One sees an entirely different landscape from the one typically observed. The power politics of the USSR was not something that could have remained undone. It was something more than a defence against objective capitalist economic power. It had been inscribed by force into the original characteristics of the construction of socialism in one country. It never had the opportunity to enjoy a period of peace. There had been a permanent revolution. A long and continuous state of exception running from the civil war in the years straddling 1920 through to the Cold War of the 1950s. The communist attempt to establish socialism was the following: political government not of normality but of a historic exceptionalism. And in the state of exception, sovereign is he who decides. Who decides when another front opens in a war immediately after the peace imposed upon the Nazi war? With rules one administers a home, with laws one governs a city and with relations of force one determines spheres of influence. In 1947, peace was already over and war had begun. And the form it assumed in the third-world conflict is extremely interesting. Raymond Aron defined it better than others.

A lucid rereading of the period would be a fruitful exercise, were it not for these hysterical and anything-but-disenchanted times, in which jealous possessors of good intentions do little more than exhibit astonishment in the face of the appearance of evil in history. The concept of

34 See John Maynard Keynes, *A Short View at Russia* (London: Hogarth Press, 1925). [Trans.]

Cold War is an original historical concept: an armed war, not a fought war. War without war, not because of the ethical wishes of peoples but by virtue of an entity that is anything but abstract: the weapon that has won the subjective right to a majuscule: the Bomb. A paradigm of modernity: the greater the destructive power of a weapon, the closer to zero is the possibility of it being used. The nihilism of technology. The positive reason of science, having reached the point of producing the conditions for the apocalypse, comes to rest on the brink of the abyss; it does not advance, it does not reverse, it remains suspended in the middle of a phase. This suspension of decision was named the balance of terror. Peace was not defended by a treaty, by a conference, by diplomacy or by a compromise. Peace was not a child of pacifism. War was defeated by war. For the first time, it found a limit within itself. Perpetual peace, at least as far as concerned the twentieth century's 'world war' character, was assured the day in which atomic parity between the rival powers was reached. Thus, socialism saved the peace. Only force beats force. Politics has taken this regulative idea of human history as setting the tone for its activity. It has in this way contributed to the progress of humanity. The Cold War continued, without war, the age of the world civil wars. A masterpiece of the cunning of history. These were still the noble years of life choices. Humanity should be grateful to those Western scientists, nuclear physicists—including Italian ones—who picked a side, one opposite to that assigned to them. They thereby contributed to establishing that armed equilibrium that prevented the use of arms. They accepted the division of the world into opposed blocks, but in the unprecedented setting of a conflict of powers without direct armed encounter. This is an incredible fact: war was confirmed as something too serious to be left to generals. It was politics that then made war. That is great politics: organizing conflict without unleashing war. Small politics is: annulling, constraining, masking conflict for the love of peace. Small politics, in the end, renders politics redundant, superfluous. Without conflict, no politics. Without modern politics, there is no more politics. The end of modern politics coincides with the end of the workers' movement organized on the world stage. The politics of two opposed world systems, led modern politics to its ultimate consequence, compelled it to completion. After this, the return to a single world system for all is not the pacifying transition to a post-political age but a regressive leap to a pre-political epoch.

There is no doubt. Here lies a danger. As soon as one retires into the *arrière boutique* of political self-consciousness and rediscovers the tattered clothes of ones' old ideological group identity, the thread of a romantic view of the past weaves together purposeless scattered sentiments and great causes trampled under the feet of tiny men. And yet. The time today is the totalizing one of the universally valid decision, as if it were improbably the only real one, or at least the only one permitted. Whereas once, in the world of yesterday divided in two, there was the polemical time of alternative decisions, partial investigations into dual truths. Masses of the people and single intellectuals—and it was precisely the intensity of the time that enabled the people and intellectuals to be the same thing—chose, they would be aligned, their courage came from knowing what side to line up with. The price to be paid was high: in the form of doors closed, intolerance, self-limitation, self-constraint, renunciation. But there was value in being divided across politico-ideological frontiers while keeping the military trenches closed off from direct conflict; in an international class struggle without a world war, this is—I say ironically—the New Model Army of the twentieth century, retaining, potentially, the political strength to overcome the violence of war. Modern politics had reached the apex of its power. The battle of ideas, the *engagement*[35] of culture, the politicality of art, the faith of militants, the prestige of the leading groups, party discipline—all of these elements together

35 In French in the original. [Trans.]

marked the dramatic aura of the epoch with a unique affirmative character. Can one still claim this? In the 1950s, [Norberto] Bobbio was wrong, Togliatti was right. It was the age of political decision-making. Cultural choices followed, along with stewardship, as they always do. As if the culture of today does not follow, obediently, the paths of the *pensée unique*, moreover without saying so, perhaps even unwittingly. Bobbio is right in the 1990s. The liberal utopia is the quotidian practice of Markets, of Banks, the Bourse, the ideology of industrialists and professors, and, lastly, the Gospel of politicians without politics, who today are the true *intendance*.[36] The reason for this decline in meaningfulness, for this loss of recognition, this triumph of appearance and this breakdown in quality of Weber's two professional vocations of the twentieth century, of the politician and the intellectual, await explanation. Perhaps it will be necessary to work on a partisan [*di parte*] anthropology from below, that judges the masters of the earth and justifies all the others. And the others are not only the poor, the simple folk, the outcasts, the excluded, but also, among these and from these, above all those who have been tempted to become the dominators; those who have sought, with the means at their disposal, to overthrow the eternal conditions of the world; those who have sought to do so from a collective anxiety for justice or revenge, which is the same thing. They tell us that every human being is born with the potential for interiority. And let us leave aside the divine call or election. The one we know, and know it well, is the social call or election. Privilege divides and mandates. The potential of the one is cultivated, that of the other suppressed. Today more so than yesterday, within the new division of the world, and the new division of society, both are increasingly well masked, falsified, concealed, unexpressed.

Great history is more egalitarian than small and mediocre history. The common man needs to be dwarfed by events to recognize in himself

36 In French in the original. [Trans.]

the quality of individuality. That 'in himself' is as if awakened and challenged, its strength put to the test. This is a condition that modern history has discovered, understood and valorized. The conflict within it was permanent, only the degree of intensity, diffusion and violence has changed. Modern society sees not only war as a continuation of politics by other means; it also sees the economy as the continuation of war by other means. But while in politics and war either the one or other wins according to which form of the organization of intelligence and force is superior, in the case of the economy it is always the same one who wins: the possessor of capital and power. It is true that the market is the *Zivilization* of war but within civilization, and modernization, and in the case of globalization, the winners and losers are predestined; this is in contrast to *Kultur* and revolution. In the free market, workers have never won politically, other than when they have been allowed to gold-plate their chains. Classical social democracy understood this, from its Marxist position and, consequently, prepared the tools of organization. And political socialism—the socialism of the state, the socialism of the communists—understood this more radically still, with one foot already in the accelerated age of wars. While in the great twentieth century politics retained primacy over the economy, the outcome of the clash remained uncertain. Messianic hopes in the transformation of antiquated social relations sustained the hearts of the masses and the intellect of persons. Politics was what it had to be to change things: a collective passion, something more than the 'I think', 'I am',[37] this metaphysical

37 The allusion is to René Descartes' Archimedean point of the *cogito*: 'I am thinking, therefore, I exist' which he arrives at as the firm foundation of truth from which knowledge could be built ('Discourse on the Method' in *The Philosophical Writings of Descartes*, VOL. 1 [John Cottingham, Robert Stoothoff and Dugald Murdoch trans] [Cambridge: Cambridge University Press, 1985], p. 127). For a fascinating reading of Descartes as figure of the ascending seventeenth-century bourgeois class, see Antonio Negri, *Political Descartes: Reason, Ideology and the Bourgeois Project* (Matteo Mandarini and Alberto Toscano trans and introd.) (London: Verso, 2007). [Trans.]

foundation of the modern individual. The politics that in the twentieth century of wars became revolutionary, attempted this—soon to be vanquished—storming of heaven. Substance that—according to Hegel—became subject along with the modern, as subject was grasped and transformed into a collective self-conscious subject, a class with class consciousness that, in freeing its own side [*parte*] liberated the totality of humanity. It was not a declaration of principles: all men and women are free and equal, so too the servants, the slaves and the subjugated. This is the emancipatory, universalistic ideological paradigm of the bourgeois revolutions. For us, the opposite is true. Once the oppressed, the exploited, the subjugated are liberated, all will be equal. Only by freeing that part will humanity be free. Magnificent, apocalyptical vision of universal history from the standpoint of a political partiality—these were the markings of proletarian revolution. Communism in the twentieth century was this collective agitation of things, which emerged, exploded and was rooted in an organized political will. It is not the name that was left stuck to an experience that in the wretchedness of its end had nothing to do with the greatness of its beginnings. Without a thorough spring clean of some ideas and some words, this century will die incomplete, misunderstood, and finally, precipitate from the summit of its tragic area of life.

Force against Violence

In the decadence of the century, in the depths of its origin, lies the fall of the idea of communism. If the workers' movement can be said to have been the last subject of modern politics, the communist form of organization, as party and as state, was the final expression of the workers' movement. There is a story of the relationship between communism and the categories of modern politics that should be retraced and judged, not only in terms of the results but also through the premises, the shifts, the turns, the affinities and incompatibilities, the unkept promises and the *dura lex sed lex* [the law is harsh, but it is the law] of the mechanisms of movement of the social world, which are—as ever—subjugated by the eternal alliance of power and wealth. It is too early to speak of the communism of the twentieth century, not because we are too near to—what they call—the horrors of the end, but because a gaze able to see still needs to mature within us. The path of that Ekhartian nobility of spirit must advance and grow by virtue of the 'separation' capable of opening us to the catharsis of tragedy. That of which we may speak is the minor episode that goes under the name of the collapse of the socialist system. A farcical end, parodic, a comedy without leading actors, neither princes nor peoples, neither leaders nor masses: first, the reformers or grave-diggers, all are pale ghosts in the night of politics; the others are remote-control audiences led towards the artificial paradises of the West via the dissolution of a society. 1989 is not, will not be, an epochal historical date, despite the spectacle put in place by the pied pipers of the counterrevolution. Nothing begins in 1989, because nothing ended there. It took three years, from 1989 to1991, to bureaucratically certify the death that had occurred many years before. The socialist systems survived the end of socialism. Taking up again that thesis that for me too leaves a bitter taste: the communist attempt to construct a socialist society had failed by the 1960s, ironically, at the same time as the explosion of contestation in the West. Forms of organization and forms of movement that were then in opposition, will fall together. And on this basis the entire process of modernization ran its course. It was brought about in part by the innovative drive of the new capitalism, but politically it took a conservative direction. No practice of reform goes forward if it is not accompanied, nourished, substantiated by a thinking of revolution. The reformists will never understand. For this reason, they shall never win. We have learnt that this is true for reforms under capitalism and socialism. The 20th Party Congress[38] had neorevolutionary qualities—that really was a great and dramatic event. But that was still the age of politics, subjects were still classes, parties were the instruments, force took the form of the State, the masses were active protagonists of history. We were right, as young communist intellectuals, to be on the side of the Hungarian insurgents; but—here lies the insoluble problem of the revolution in the West: State socialism was not wrong to shut it down with the tanks. It was war. In Hungary and at Suez, the accounts of the two blocks were settled internally. The world Cold War discharged its repressed energies on the periphery of the empires. And even post-Stalin, those same internal critics of Stalinism were compelled to admit: the war continues. What can be accepted in '56, can no longer be accepted in '68. Prague is the beginning of the end of socialism. Perhaps only from then and there might the system have been reformed. Prague was a city symbolic of Mitteleuropa. At the end of the 1960s, these uprisings appeared to link the two divided sides of Europe—the West and the East. The process was firmly in the hands of the communist party, which had been renewed in men and ideas. There were a few democratic naiveties. But had they been deployed wisely, by perceptive leading groups, it would not have brought ruination but would have helped. And, above all, the Cold War was practically over. When a war is not fought, there is no formal peace treaty to end it. This too is a novelty. Détente is not yet, it never has been, peace. It was neither peace nor war. In this suspended state of exception, without return to normality, socialism, in all solidity, survived itself, survived the occurrence of its own failure as a system.

---

38 The 20th Congress of the Communist Party of the Soviet Union took place between 14 and 25 February 1956. This is where Khrushchev delivered the famous 'Secret Speech' condemning Stalin's 'cult of the personality' and accusing him of distorting the principles of Marxism–Leninism. [Trans.]

There is here a hard truth we must speak of, hard like the name of the steel to be found in a man's name.[39] Socialism did not survive the age of world civil wars. It burst forth within it, born by virtue of it, it lived within it and won for it. Socialism did not provoke, unlike capitalism it did not bear war in its nature. It rather underwent it, suffered it, and at the same time it used it, needed it as a moment of total mobilization of the people against the external enemy. It was no great novelty. It was behaviour typical of every authoritarian system. The novelty, rather, was in this marriage of 'Great Russian' nationalism and mass democracy. It is no coincidence that the highest point of internal cohesion of this immense nation made up of many peoples was during the anti-Nazi Great Patriotic War. In the immediately subsequent years, the true heir of the Austro-Hungarian Imperial-Royal political system, a confederation of peoples under the inflexible care of the little Father, was the USSR. And that was not Stalin; it was the party. Moreover, a substantial part of Western intellectuals discovered socialism through this fascinating figure and fell in love with it, despite rapid disillusionment and precipitous betrayals. The Cold War had imposed a *prorogatio* to the conferring of authority, which—if possible—was even more totalizing than in the past.[40] What put it in crisis, was the end of such *prorogatio*. The politics of détente was capitalist great politics. Perhaps the last example of it. This is because afterwards, through to today, there is no more need for it, since any credible enemy is lacking. Then, that state of confrontation without war and without peace was lethal for the socialist systems. Socialism, extracted from the political struggle, was forced to compete on the economic terrain, which is where it lost. When there is no longer politics against the economy, capitalism always wins—with and against

39 Iosif Djugashvili is better known as Stalin, a word derived from the Russian for 'steel'. Hence Stalin or 'man of steel'. [Trans.]

40 In Roman law, a *prorogatio* extended a commander's rule (*imperium*) indefinitely beyond a limited-term magistracy. [Trans.]

everyone. Shifting the ground of confrontation from the political to the economic was the winning card of anti-socialism. The struggle over technology lies here. The categories of the political in the twentieth century found this unique ground of application. They did not withdraw from it, they occupied and subjugated it. After The Bomb, the production of evermore sophisticated weapons of offence and defence was the privileged terrain of politics. Here too socialism found itself in difficulty. As it did in the other—apparently innocuous—place of peaceful application of technology, in the so-called space race. There the symbolic was interwoven with the scientific and the ideological in a comic mixture where, in the end, the idea of human progress worked—as always in the modern era—as a mask for economic development. Man's ridiculous steps on the moon did nothing to reduce, even by a single centimetre, the distance in wealth and power that divides and opposes human social relations within each country or between different worlds. We can safely say that futuristic flights from the world, even technico-scientific ones, confirm and consolidate human injustices. In this century, science has been the handmaid of politics. It did not serve the Prince; it has been a function of systemic mechanisms. To the point of taking the place of traditional ideological apparatuses. After the wars, socialism was literally disarmed: the economy, science, technology, ideology, these twentieth-century arms of politics, were no longer in its hands. It is not peoples' desire for freedom that won. Neither was it the military-industrial complex of capitalism that did so. What won was an economic-scientific-technical-ideological assemblage, without great politics, independent of it, a deadly compound of innovation without transformation, which was the reverse of the conservative revolution, a sort of revolutionary conservation of things. The two theatrical images left for posterity are surprising and depressing: on the one side and the other, the rickety protagonists of the event, and the audience that is still there, applauding.

The historical paradox that socialism decays and dies after the wars must be explained over and again. It will never become part of intellectual common sense. Although well-targeted minority investigations will be able to define and demonstrate it. The proletarian revolution of the twentieth century finds itself within the first Great War; the construction of Socialism in One Country lies in the interwar period; the last possible reform of socialism, de-Stalinization, is situated within the Third Great War. These are three decisive episodes. The rest of the twentieth century is minor history. One might say that revolution and war are Siamese twins; two bodies with a something in common. But this Young Hegelian idea of freedom and fate, despite appearances, does not belong to us. We are children of the culture of crisis; our intellectual father is negative thought; even when we speak of political theology, we hurriedly add negative political theology. When our discourse comes dangerously close to the approach of the philosophy of history, it is as if the grip of the words withdraw, forewarned and disenchanted. Politics is historically determined. This is true above all for modern politics. Marx's scientific oeuvre finds itself in the hundred-year peace. Marx is born once the European civil wars are over, in the heart of the Restoration. The episodes of revolt, 1848 and 1871 Paris, where he finds presages—from a perspective typical of revolutionary thought—of proletarian character, are already responses to unbearable historical conditions. The classical current in which he situates the presence of the workers' movement is the struggle over the working day. This is an organized presence within production, which accompanies, precedes and drives the passage from manufacture to industry. Here the workers' movement—and we repeat this important point—performs the specific task of civilizing the modern social class relation. The passage from Chartism to the first two Internationals is a case in point. The entire nineteenth century can be read in terms of the underlying organized civil expansion of the forms of social solidarity, against the isolated, individualized, egocentric figure of the boss. Already at that time, the workers' movement encountered modern politics in its function as civilizer of the forms of war characteristic of the *jus publicum europaeum*. Already in the 1800s, the substance of modern politics takes the form of the worker subject. It is the 1900s that changes the framework of the one and the other, forcing the one and the other to assume a different form. The peaceful development of capitalism failed in both Russia and in the West. The process of monopolistic concentration, the financializaton of the capital relation, the brutality of colonialism and hence the imperialism of capitalism are a great anti-modern mutation. It should be read as such, exploding the orthodoxy of economic categories. A regression of civilization, even if over the longer term they again become its driver. This is a typically capitalist dialectic: only via enormous immediate imbalances can expanded equilibria eventually be reproduced. This is the foundation of the organic relationship between capitalism and war. For this reason, the era of world civil wars was necessary. Workers and politics found themselves speaking in the language of the epoch, wittingly, as it should be with great subjects. The workers' movement was forced to become Leninist and communist, so to become State through the revolution. Modern politics was compelled to continue the war with other means, and after two hot world wars, it learnt to do so with the Cold War.

This constraint over the mid-term affected the short term. The subaltern classes, who by nature and history have a vocation for peace, have—during their revolts—replied with force to violence; in one case, replying with the force of revolution to the violence of war. The working class recognized itself not in that human destiny, but in this. Indeed, we can say it invested into it the added value of its social specificity. Modern politics taught it the preventative use of force. Modern history taught it that force and violence are two concepts that are not only different but also opposed. Force is a relation of forces; a collective dimension of conflict; conscious masses in movement: struggle and organization; organization and struggle; growth of calculated pressure on the contradictions of the hostile camp; knowledge of them to strike in the right place at the right time. Force calls upon understanding. Conflict is knowledge. The blow force strikes must always be a civilized act. *Macht* and *Kultur*. Force needs to be able to see. It is violence that is blind. It strikes where it can. And it aims to destroy. It is individual, even when it has the mass in its sights. It does not know, it does not want to know, it confuses and wants to confuse. The weak choose violence. She who has force has no need of violence. The act of violence is always a manifestation of barbarism. Even when it is modernity's imposition upon ancient relations. Modern history has learnt to be violent in new ways. *Gewalt* and *Zivilization*. Force is the negative of resistance; violence is the positive of aggression. Symbolically, the two decisions define two distinct spheres: the declaration of a strike and the terrorist act. These are ideal-typical forms of action characteristic of the modern age. The strike is the collective decision par excellence: an action that interrupts an activity, it is a saying no, no to the continuation of work, nonviolent struggle, conflict without war, rational calculation of the balance of forces to shift positions, ones' own and that of others. The workers' movement is represented by this form of social action, where the individual worker becomes conscious and employs force along with comrades against a hostile party. There are many other types of struggle, but with these same qualities. The forms of struggle reveal the aims of the movement. Terrorism is initiated by individuals and groups of individuals against groups: it is a positive, demonstrative action, striking one to teach hundreds; it is a political fundamentalism, a crude elemental being-towards-death, where the individual who fights is annulled even before the individual who is fought against. There can be no noble aim for a decision of this type. And violence ends up subtracting force from the part for which it thinks it is fighting. The height of human maturity within society is expressed in the peaceful use of force. There is a sort of infantile regression in violence against persons. This last slice of the century has revealed the little terrorism of the armed political, religious, ethnic groups. The great twentieth century produced the great terrorism of systems: totalitarian or authoritarian or democratic. Mass extermination, blind violence, positive and demonstrative exhibition of deadly actions—it was that of the Lagers and the Gulag, but it was also those of the carpet bombing of civilian populations and, the decisive one, atomic terrorism. In the search for a final solution, no system and no ideology is innocent. The twentieth century dies upon this cross: force as violence, politics as war, being as death. Let us ask ourselves: why, when one says twentieth century, does one think of this and not of the age of rights?

Workers and Politics

The workers' movement in the twentieth century was swept away by the destiny of politics. The encounter of the workers with politics took place with Marx. But as an encounter, it was unfinished. Attraction/repulson, love/hate. Marx did not grasp the specifically modern character of politics. He correctly critiqued ideology and stopped. He anticipated the future of capitalism with great foresight; he did not divine the future of politics. The age of war as provisional concrete ordering of the world of tomorrow escaped him. It is doubtful that in his work there is a *Zusammenbruchstheorie* of the economic system. There is no question that the possibility of a breakdown of politics is absent from his thinking. That is exactly what took place a century after his death. Was it the case, then, that modern politics could not function? Could it only end in catastrophe under the weight of its insoluble contradictions? The tragedy of the political in the twentieth century was not that of having entered the age of world civil wars, but of not having come out of it; of not having exited with a 'great politics' alternative to war. Capitalism was probably unable to do so. The idea and practice of war between men was too organic to it. But why did socialism not do so? That's the unsettling question. Here lies the failure of the workers' movement. Not with having cancelled here and there some parliamentary democracy or other. Or in having silenced the odd poet of the soul. The place, the time, is that of the historic failure of the working class—which awaits being thought through as a whole. The working class: it has been unable to emancipate itself from its subaltern origins to become ruling class, dominant in a new way, hegemonic. It became trade union, it became party, it became government, it did not become State, which is to say, Order, Kingdom, *Verfassung* [constitution]—each of these word-concepts has its own historico-theoretical meaning. In the East, the assumed form of domination is that inherited from modern history rather than from modern politics, which is to say, politics reduced to State understood in the historical sense of the monopoly of violence. The communist form of the workers' movement was the first to grasp the political turn of the twentieth century. While classical social democracy remained attached to the nineteenth-century forms of organization and political action, the Bolsheviks grasped this shift in the rhythms of historical time, the enormously increased intensity of the political moment, they felt the accumulated energy of the epoch's atmosphere that exploded and it really was a vanguard, among other vanguards, that opened and read in other tongues the book of the century. To grasp the occasion of revolution: this is only possible for those who are a step ahead of their epoch and know how to await it on the threshold. Letting it—the occasion—pass, without grasping it: anyone can do this; it's enough to remain concealed within ones' time without seeing the signs of its crisis. Then, everyone saw the criterion of the political, the law of hostility within war, on the fronts, between nations. Lenin, almost alone saw friend/enemy in the alternative between revolution and war. Better to submit to an inglorious treaty than to continue the useless massacre. Against war as European history, politics as Russian revolution. Twentieth-century communism is born here. Two watchwords reverberated more forcefully than the thundering cannons: Land, Peace! And the spectre haunting Europe assumed a marked human face, that of soldiers, workers and peasants. The politics of October lands a hammer blow on history as war. It doesn't definitively win. It will be vanquished. We have already seen how the years following the revolution were conditioned by the war. And yet. The communists are the only ones who attempted to realize socialism. In a single country, in a hostile world, in conditions that were for the most-part pre-capitalist. The other forms of the workers' movement never took on the challenge. Today, only those who have deleted socialism as maximal programme are entitled to call themselves socialist. The communists failed in the attempt to build socialism. And if they failed, everything leads us to believe, and indeed all do believe, that socialism was impracticable. It is no small acknowledgement. One must set out from here to measure the new relation of forces with capitalism. Besides, if the workers were unable to defeat capital, capital appears today practically invincible. That is the present state of things. We are all—the European left—post-communist. In the sense that we come after that experiment which was attempted and failed. One could try to take stock, materially, of how—after that attempt—the workers of the West and the disinherited of the world were stronger, how potentially freer and how much better the conditions of existence they found themselves in were. Of how much capitalism was forced to change following the great fear of the workers. Question: can one really be sure that there would have been a *welfare state*,[41] despite the struggle to achieve it, without the threat of proletarian dictatorship? Would there have been a reforming capitalism, be it Rooseveltian in the

41 In English in the original. [Trans.]

United States or Labourist in Britain, without the presence of the Soviet Union at the heart of the twentieth century? Today, the certainties can be solely discovered in the heads of our great archivers. Incapable of enclosing a process with the tragic sense of the end, they suppress it, deny it, condemn it, they ward off the cross, three times before dawn they swear to have never known it. There is another path, untrodden and alone: to declare oneself heirs of the defeat of the revolution and, at the same time, heirs to the revolution.

Only communism has been capable of the great mediation between workers and politics. Mediation is necessary. Because the workers are not, have never been, the general class. Here lies their strength and the difficulty, for them to win with that force alone. Partial interest, not particular. Of a part, not of a body or of a social rank. A part, however, that represents a central contradiction for a long phase of modern history: that of human labour within the capital relation. All the other contradictions enumerated today are ripples on the sea of tranquillity when compared to this one. The workers' movement solved the historic contradiction in politics. At varying degrees of intensity. The communist form of organization was the highest degree of intensity through which the workers expressed politics. The relationship between the working class and modern politics—which from Chartism to classical social-democracy gave a glimpse of the possible encounter of vocation and profession—squeezes the communist workers' movement into a form, that of the party, which had to translate the partiality of the factory into social generality; and it had to do so before capital, on its own initiative and with its own tools, did so against the workers. This is ultimately what happened, through successive gradual integrations, as the rest of the workers' movement waited for more favourable conditions. Once again: the Russian Revolution failed in the West. The great opportunity was that of the early 20s. Here lies the inspired foresight of the Leghorn Split. It was not the birth but the weakness of the first European communist parties that explains their defeat then, and the ensuing ones later. When communist parties, in a few countries, were strong enough—after the Second World War—it was already too late. And it was wise then not to attempt it. The communist form of organization carried to completion the parabola of modern politics. The workers' movement was, in nature and history, anti-Jacobin, anti-anarchist and anti-populist. The communists realized, in theory though certainly not always in practice, this historical nature. Modern politics, in turn, risked succumbing to dangerous temptations in relating Jacobinism, anarchism and populism. The communist form of political party, while not dependent upon a single model, attempted to and did provide an original solution: that of the relationship of vanguard/masses, of hegemonic collective intellectual and diffuse subaltern culture and, to deploy more Gramscian terms, of Prince and people. This very attempt was born but was unable to grow. It could have succeeded only if the construction of socialism had done so. Without that construction, and with the fall of this one, the form of organization went extinct. We can put it as follows: the party did not acknowledge the autonomy of the State in socialism; and it did not acknowledge class autonomy within capitalism. But modern politics was precisely this game of autonomies, of the social from the political, of the political from the social, of the economic from all of these, of the institutional from the juridical, of this from that—differences that were to be governed, 'fox' and 'lion', through the instrument-form of the party, the great subject of mediation, or subject of the great mediation between masses and State. This communist project was a realistic-utopian one. Realism and utopia: the qualities that founded the modern criterion of the political. In 1989, Niccolò Machiavelli dies. And along with him, Thomas Moore.

The question that remains not only unresolved but also untouched, still pending is: why did the communist movement, which emerged powerfully from the age of wars, crumble with the peace? The political consequences of the first two world wars saw the consolidation of the communist camp. The end of the Cold War, without winners or vanquished, maintained or at least left a certain balance of forces. The answer is as terrible as the question. Thought cannot fear itself. It advances over a mine-strewn earth. Its ability lies in not setting down its foot in the wrong place. It must reach the extreme edge of the problem. And from there it must seek a possible solution. The sense of boundaries, spoken of today, is a sign of the tendency to moderatism in intellectual opinion—from which no original idea can appear, not even under torture. No, better to bear upon one's shoulders the labour of the concept. So then. Here is the answer: socialism was unable to be anything but War Communism. And the official identification of the communist movement with such a socialism proved fatal. Afterwards, there was no place for any other form, or figure; for any other horizon, or vision, such as one that might see a new beginning in the decline of the West. Because the communist movement, the final representation of the workers' movement, encountered modern politics at the time of politics' end. The twentieth century is the time of the end of politics. Modern politics was born to overcome war, it was instead overthrown by it. The armed globalization of conflict between nations subjugated the categories of the political, it bent them and reduced them to itself. In the Cold War, with the great weapon that remained silent of necessity, politics attempted one last time to avenge itself. But détente did not mean *Weltpolitik*. It meant *Weltökonomie*. It became clear that the world wars served the definitive globalization of the economy. Capitalism won on this terrain definitively. And here the communist movement, the one anti-capitalist movement on the world stage, in terms of its origin more than its results, collapsed.

Better to set out on the basis of this tragic fact than that of the passing of an illusion.[42] The most tolerable of all the arguments about 1989 of those that are impossible to listen to, said: the construction of socialism failed, but the reasons that moved it are intact and stand before us in the contemporary world. A variation: the communist movement usurped a name, but communism remains in the heart of humanity, the ideal, unfulfilled horizon. More or less the sentiments of Norberto Bobbio and Cesare Luporini. Up to a few years ago, we liked the well-meaning statement by Bloch: communism is what humanity has always understood by 'moral'. Reassuring arguments by thinking believers of which all trace has been lost. Perhaps the reasons for the socialist revolution remain present, but they no longer lean towards that idea, towards that myth, that objective: there are different names for different sensibilities. How those reasons express themselves, if they do, is a mystery. There is no scientific analysis capable of revealing it. Perhaps there is a religious feeling that sets out from the world periphery and can be converted into a revolutionary political theology for the West. But it's better to let it go. In the hearts of the 'last men', one cannot see much, given the darkness: sepulchres lie empty after the Resurrected one has fled. Communism is no longer even the simple thing so hard to do, of which Brecht speaks.[43] So-called complexity has done away with its elementary natural constitution and turned it into an acrobatic task for athletes of the spirit. The future does not belong to it. Only a 'tiger leap' into the past of the twentieth century will educate us as to what it was. We will then understand that, in the course of the century, communism meant 'being communist'. A modality, a form, an experience, a choice of human existence. This

---

42 *Le Passé d'un illusion* is a book by François Furet, in which he takes aim at the communist movement and ideology. [Trans.]

43 Reference to the song 'In Praise of Communism' that appears in his play *The Mother* in Bertolt Brecht, *Collected Plays: Three* (London: Methuen, 1997). The phrase reads: 'It is that simple thing / Which is so hard to do' (p. 116). [Trans.]

free horizon of life showed itself to be vaster than obligatory realizations of history. Perhaps the error lay in taking on too much and bearing alone the weight of the construction of socialism. Communism was originally a movement of the negative. It is a 'no' of history to itself, as it had been to that point. Hence, it is a dimension of pure, true politics. Not the abstract idea, but the political name counts. It is born, and the communists become historical subjects in the apocalyptic scene onto which the twentieth century opens. They signify the realization/overthrow of modern history: war is realization, revolution is overthrow. The decision for the name of communists and the event of the political leap of history that followed, overwhelmed at a stroke gradualist reformism, the death of Marxism, democratic civilization, capitalist modernization: all practices and ideas that were old already, that the start of the century had done away with and that this end of the century represents as though they were unprecedented future opportunities. All of them came, all of them come from an age that had muddled positivism, historicism, neo-idealism, scientism in a rhetorical nineteenth-century synthesis of faith in the ineluctability of human progress. The twentieth century, which was born sweeping away all this history, dies by presenting it to us as the present. The communist decision for revolution was a deviation from its own time. It is located, ingeniously, within the twentieth-century revolution of forms. When in all language as well as art, science, in all of knowledge, and then in consciousness and beyond its shadowy limits, came the liberatory leap from the old forms; there was revolution in the forms of politics as well, that is, in the eternal social language of humanity. Hence with the name of communist, the workers' movement did not limit itself to the encounter with modern politics, but in the context of exception it transformed and revolutionized it. The Prince became Party; Utopia becomes State: the course of history is overthrown by politics. The ancient soul and the new forms—according to the young Lukács' splendid image—meet in the accursed figure of the victorious proletariat.

The communism of the twentieth century is not only this. But it was this for such a long time, so deeply and intensely, that the age of decadence and death too becomes, as in the second half of the century, a minor history. This type of intellectual operation is always useful in trying to rigorously locate great epoch-making events in a period of years: join the two wires, that of the beginning and that of the end, to see whether a current passes between them. *Urzeit*, *Endzeit*: and nothing more. The 'between', the time between is important but not decisive. In-between there is a settling down, an adaptation and correction, which might be deviation or involution. The socialism of the communists: the glow of the beginnings, the greyness of the end. In 1989, we were all nonchalantly within the process. The process was quantitatively enormous; qualitatively it was of a very lowly level. The worst of the reactions was that of fear in being overwhelmed by the collapse. One tried to make believe that it was the case of a mere change of names, whereas it was a world that ended. We realized later, one bit at a time as we picked away at the thread of the little, vapid, useless and damaging things that followed.[44] In the death of socialism, what counted and will count for the future is, more than the event itself, this abyssal disproportion between the significance of what happened and the wretchedness of the individuals who managed or represented it. Nothing is more hopeless than a final decision without decisive thought and without tragic action. Something devastating must have happened in the two preceding decades to bring about a situation of this type. The Lefts of the West are not

44 Reference here is to the stormy debate that took place in the Italian Communist Party after the collapse of the Berlin Wall, over the need, or otherwise, of changing the party's name, and to the multiple splits and renamings that took place in the aftermath of the decision to drop reference to communism by the majority faction of the former PCI. [Trans.]

authorized to absolve themselves, or rather, to celebrate themselves for having passively witnessed the progress of socialism's fatal disease. First, because they certainly were not protagonists of an exhilarating path of their own. Second, because against their wills, the Lefts should have known that the two destinies, the workers' movement and the construction of socialism, had crossed paths once and forever, and that the justified break from their forms was something different than a break from the substance of the attempt. For what had really happened after the age of wars is that history took the century in hand again and expelled politics. In words that are less grandiose but more vexing, we can say that capitalism took back the exercise of its hegemony in its entirety, with its own strategic weapons of economic force, financial power and technological violence. Cultures, ideology, mass common sense, private good sense, mass media opinion, followed. To have thought that the breakdown of socialism was in the end more fitting than the reform of socialism was the suicide of the workers' movement in the West.

Unfortunately, we need reluctantly to learn to repeat what we already know. It is an illusion to believe that a thought is understood as soon as it is stated. There is not only the opacity of this reality, which enables everything but also the apprehension of events. There is, here, the habit born of the society of the image, of discourse without thought. And so. The construction of socialism failed in a single country, and so did its application to a field of nations militarized for war, because the revolution in the West failed. It was defeated after the first war, and it failed to get underway again after the second; it snoozed during the third, while still leaving open a path towards other revolutionary prospects within capitalism. The European left should look at itself when it thinks of the debacle of socialism in the twentieth century. Here too the Italian case, has a specific character. The Italian communists were neither true socialists nor politically correct social democrats. The consensus they had was rooted in the noun 'communist', the adjective 'Italian' aimed to give an original form to the project contained in that name. The popular slogan of Gramsci-Togliatti-Longo-Berlinguer, marked symbolically over an arc of 60 years the continuity of a search for a democratic path to revolution in Italy, for the West, after and alongside and against the Soviet construction of socialism. Its Western form tended to configure itself as a civilizing of revolution, as its modernization, infusing it with culture and complexity, moderating it, a modern subjective re-translation of the by-now-archaic and forced break of 1917. Not the 'gradualism' of reforms, but the revolutionary 'process'; which is to say, the revolutionary process through reforming gradualism as well. One can carry out numerous anodyne readings of Gramsci's works and of Togliatti's endeavours, but this was the sense and the signal they gave for the period that was to follow the age of war: that the movement of the revolution, in each passage, should assume the task of finding consensus, and culturally grounding those passages via a popular and intellectual mobilization from which it was to draw its strength and organize its institutions; and to do so in order to overcome resistances, exercise hegemony and express decision. A great project of collective praxis conducted from above. The limit was perhaps that of not having sufficiently elaborated it theoretically with the instruments of twentieth-century thought. We are all responsible for what we did not do. Can the framing of this process once again become current? *No*. That was one epoch. This is another. Now there is the opposite. The practice of modern politics and the idea of the process of revolution could only stand together. Separately, neither the one nor the other can exist. Between the time of the beginning and the time of the end, the spark of historical energy does not light. *Iskra*[45] is spent. The prairies can only burn today through self-combustion.

45 The reference is to the newspaper, *Iskra* (The spark), edited by Lenin, among others, the aim of which was to set off the spark of revolution in Russia. The first issue came out in December 1900. [Trans.]

Once Again, and in Conclusion, on the Autonomy of the Political

Before us, close enough to touch, there is another *Kehre*, a turn. The phase of the autonomy of the political comes to an end.[46] It was a long path, contested, contradictory, misunderstood, incomplete. From the early 1970s to the late 1990s, a period that does not amount to an epoch. The debate around it suffered from this. And practical action suffered from it even more. It is commonplace for everyone to speak ill of the autonomy of the political—and that everyone practices it more or less well. The science of politics knows not what it is. Political philosophy placed the problem *in capitivitate*. Politicians felt the need to rebuff it with moralistic disdain. But the autonomy of the political is nothing but modern politics. It is the name modern politics assumes in the twentieth century. The autonomy of the political presupposes the state of exception in modern history; this was the situation of the three twentieth-century wars. In fact, the criterion of the political is discovered and applied there. Our adoption of the autonomy of the political has suffered Machiavelli's 'misfortune'. Its theoretical adoption coincided with its practical inapplicability. After the 1960s, there was no more state of exception. The normality that today is claimed as an objective is the contemporary historical condition of the last three decades. In this period, absurd, pointless, isolated acts of violence have taken place, all within the Kantian cemetery of perpetual peace. The entirety of the preceding discussion—as we have seen—is melancholically marked by

---

46 See Mario Tronti, 'Autonomy of the Political' (1972) (Andrew Anastasi, Sara Farris and Peter Thomas trans), *Viewpoint Magazine* (26 February 2020) (available online: https://bit.ly/4bGk6aF; last accessed 18 May 2024). For an interpretation of this essay situating within the context of Tronti's thought, see Andrew Anastasi and Matteo Mandarini, 'A Betrayal Retrieved: Mario Tronti's Critique of the Political', *Viewpoint* Magazine (25 February 2020) (available online: https://bit.ly/3yrLBGU; last accessed 18 May 2024). [Trans.]

an 'angry longing' (*zornige Sehnsucht*, as Hölderlin writes from Tübingen) for what the communist workers' movement, and not others, might have done and did not do: impose-conduct a state of exception without war, after the wars, with politics, thereby continuing the great twentieth century and bringing the epoch to completion. This destiny was written in the communism of the revolution. Within the first great war and against it. The culpability of the communists is to not have fulfilled their destiny. For this reason, I say: communists must be condemned for some of the things they did, but also for things they did not do. Moreover, there remains a strong doubt that they did those things because they did not do the others. Not only would the opening of a path to revolution in the West have helped the process of the reform of socialism; but also the reform of socialism and critique of capitalism, soldered together through new experiences of government and the state, and with subjective movements of the masses would have closed the era of wars, reopening the political age of social upheavals. World capitalism would not have stood by and watched. But capitalism fears strength and can suffer under it. To survive as an economic system, it adapts itself to any political system. It should have been forced into this epoch of the second half of the twentieth century. Capitalist societies recognize the autonomy of the political. They seek to use politics, but politics can seek to use them. Only the friend-enemy of politics and economy, both between socialism and capitalism, within capitalism, could have reopened a conversation and an epochal passage. A very difficult game. Perhaps it is one which we may have lost. But at least a prospect might have remained open. The calamity today is that the defeat of the workers' movement presents itself without possibility of rescue. To govern without politics is impossible. So one does not govern. One administers the home. Aristotle would have called it natural chrematistics. The great politics of the day by day is the highest art [*arte somma*]. It seeks the intellectual grasp of the long view, and the practical ability to play it out over the short term. It seeks the decision of strength, and the strength of decision. The art of honest dissimulation united with the ethics of conviction. Modern political men and women are by nature bicephalous. Unity of intents and duality of behaviour together, in dis-harmony within the same person. The politician of universal principles is, if possible, ethically worse than the politician of everyday praxis. The ethics that, in the sense of Weber's professional politician, are the only ones worth considering. Politics is closer to mysticism than mathematics. Although between mysticism and mathematics, between soul and precision there is—as Music taught us—a secret correspondence. As there is in the twentieth century, where beginning with Mach one ends up with Diotima.[47] Without this path, there is no journey of spirit. Here is a daunting reef that over there is out of reach. A solitary time will be necessary to be able to touch it with thought. From the public sphere, one can no longer see the intimate nature of things. And yet for a time it could be seen. The greatness of politics in the first half of the twentieth century and beyond was its implication of life. Existence and freedom—situation and freedom, as the young Luporini keenly saw[48]—is a theme that dug deep into the feeling of the times. One should isolate and revisit it. Intense experiences, both feminine and masculine, have, in differing and contrasting ways,

47 Ulrich, the protagonist of Robert Musil's *The Man Without Qualities*, is charged with establishing a general secretariat for 'precision and soul' (pp. 636–55), i.e. that refuses the opposition between the world of intellect and that of feeling, aiming to unite the world of science, of mathematics, with that of soul—of love, art, and culture. Diotima, Ulrich's cousin, represents the romantic anti-rationalism that sets soul against the modern world. For a useful discussion, see David S. Luft, *Robert Musil and the Crisis of European Culture 1880–1942* (Berkeley, CA: University of California Press 1980), especially pp. 239ff; and Robert Musil, 'Commentary on a Metaphysics' in *Precision and Soul* (Burton Pike and David. S. Luft eds and trans) (Chicago, IL: University of Chicago Press 1990), pp. 54–58. [Trans.]

48 The reference is to Cesare Luporini, *Situazione e libertà nell'esistenza umana* (Rome: Editori riuniti, 1994[1945]). [Trans.]

already done so. It is necessary to do so again from the standpoint of political thought. Because never as in this century has politics expressed the greatness of human existence. It is true, it has also expressed the worst hideousness of the human heart. But happy is the tragic epoch in which the quality of being woman and of being man can contend with the quality of a history-making epoch. Here too one encounters the true test of knowledge of which part of the world deserves to die and which part of man has the strength to survive. The wretchedness of these years is to take as decided, without a struggle, the result of this contest. One part of the world has won that does not deserve to live simply because, in the end, it found itself fighting with another part that was already dead. A scenic fiction, a theatrical trick that, however, in the epoch of appearances, ends up valorizing a system of life historically best able to destroy values: the absolutism of capitalism, the barbarizing of civilization. Here we find that the part of humanity that survives the social selection of the species is that feral mass nature: the ancient-bourgeois as *homo oeconomicus* and modern-subaltern as *homo democraticus*.

So too ends the season of research as tactics. The idea that politics is thought in the same way as it is carried out: in conflict, with adept moves and the force of ideas; advancing, attacking and circling the adversaries' positions; taking the adversaries' thoughts as prisoners and freeing and engaging one's own; imagination and knowledge; sight of the entire frontline and care over the battle here and now. The opposite of academic thought and of political non-thought. As such, these characteristics of research are here to stay. What does not remain is the basic motivation. In this sense, there is a phase change. There the pace, the rhythm, the tone, the sign, the historic location, the very form of choice, the theoretical decision were all tactically organized to supply munitions to strategic practical action. A superior mode of doing culture from Marx to the end of the revolution of the twentieth century and, thereafter, in a more contradictory fashion. Belonging—a noble word. Not belonging to someone but keeping to one's side [*parte*]; being on that side [*parte*] with others; recognizing oneself as of that side [*parte*] against another. Not to think for oneself but for that side [*parte*]. Often forgotten is that before it was the organized representation of a political party it was a social class. The words commitment, *engagement*,[49] do not state the essential: they exhibit the thing from outside. The 'treason of the intellectuals' was the concerned cry of a reactionary.[50] And the successively repented accusers of the 'god that failed' are characters who either understood shortly before or shortly after.[51] When in doubt, I would advise you not take them as teachers. Finally, the curse fallen on the idea of the 'organic intellectual' must be borne patiently, as we await this liberal-democratic night of the good witches to pass. In the meantime, let's ask ourselves why there was political culture in the first half of the twentieth century and then no more. The reason: there cannot be great political culture without setting out from a collective self, from a non-individual partial standpoint, from a reason or multiple reasons for contrast between two parts of the world, two types of human beings, two social presences, two visions of the future. But here there is a particular problem that no approach to social analysis can resolve. Not even political philosophy is able to do so. We do not know whether it is insoluble. It is certainly a problem that remains unsolved. The dichotomous view of society, of the world and of humanity either is or is not political. It either acts and thinks politically, and hence is present; or it does not act and does not think politically, and then is absent. It is not a case of visibility but of existence. Those who generously maintain that the division into classes

49 In French in the original. [Trans.]

50 The reference is to Jullien Benda, *La trahisons des clercs* (Paris: Grasset, 2003[1928]). [Trans.]

51 *The God that Failed* was a book of essays by Louis Fischer, André Gide, Arthur Koestler, Ignazio Silone, Stephen Spender and Richard Right, first published by Harper Collins in 1949. [Trans.]

is not visible but continues to exist console themselves and their friends with a faith in glorious tomorrows. It's true, the working class is not dead; on the contrary, it is probable that at the world-scale it is destined to expand quantitatively. But the workers' movement is dead. And the class struggle did not exist because there was a working class; the class struggle existed because there was the workers' movement. That is to say, struggle and organization, that of the trade unions and the party, a class consciousness that—as someone counselled—had to be brought from the outside; and, finally, a State, or States that—even if only formally, in language—were a symbolic reference point. The class struggle is not a noumenon to draw upon through a moral law that is within me or through a well-directed aesthetic judgement, as in the case of our—nonetheless beloved—Simone [Weil]. The class struggle is a phenomenal reality that can be seen in the space-time of organization, can be known through the categories of the political and can be acted upon—this is the leap from Kant to Lenin, passing via Hegel–Marx—with the praxis of revolutionary will. Without this, there is only social conflict. But that there has always been, before the workers as there will be after them. The long history of the subaltern classes, which is anything but finished today, has begun again on a large scale, because it unified again at the world level. Only the eruption of the consciously organized working class broke with this history. The workers were the first class of dependent workers that did not claim but won social power; they did not imagine, they exercised political power. For this reason, they have never needed positive utopias, religions of salvation, eschatological millenarianisms. Unfortunately, these are all things that—not coincidentally—we are forced to rediscover today to keep the 'fire in the mind' alight.[52] Here we see again the heroic alliance, *Heldenpaar*, of factory workers and modern

52 Reference is to James H. Billington, *Fire in the Minds of Men: Origins of the Revolutionary Faith* (New York: Basic Books, 1980). [Trans.]

politics. This event of human liberation was able to win and to do so over a long period, and to do so not only in the revolution but also in militant preparation, in active anticipation, in the living significance that it so singularly produced against the being-towards-death that traversed the twentieth century. With the defeat of the workers' movement, the history of the subaltern classes resumes its eternal course. A history without struggle. What seems to represent itself when the second world is reabsorbed into the first and articulated across various levels of development, is an opposition with the world of so-called underdevelopment, in reality of non-development. It is not so. There is no organized force that expresses here this duality, no theory unites this world, no collective consciousness of struggle allows for a voice of antagonism to be heard. There is no politics. Hence, there is no real contradiction. The Western empire will not fall under the shock force of barbarian invasions, it will live by integrating, with some difficulty, the flows of migrants. And so, between the secular pathos for difference and Christian caritas for the lowliest, the damned of the earth will continue to serve the masters of the world.[53]

Diversity and difference, we know, are distinct. Diversity is multiple, difference is of only one kind. Of gender alone. This is a formidable [theoretical] gain, which alone undermines entire worlds of thought. And it rebounds upon practice, or sets out from practice, naturally, with ease but also with potentially explosive consequences. Here the dichotomous model assumes a classical standard of measure. This is the substantial reason for its refusal, not by many but by all. It is the fear of two. The one is the reassuring remaining within itself of all that is. The three is the reassuring arrival point of the synthesis of contradiction. The two

53 'The Damned of the Earth' is the Italian translation of Frantz Fanon's *Les Damnés de la terre*. Available in English as *The Wretched of the Earth* (Constance Farrington trans.) (London: Penguin, 2001). [Trans.]

presupposes insoluble polarity, opposition or, rather, contraposition. And it is always a positive and a negative. Knowing how to take upon oneself the immense power of the negative, in elevated forms, nobly destructive, allows one to recognize the force capable of contending with the destiny of changing the world. Within the Christian horizon, there is a political theology most proximate to this problem. We do not need to choose between monotheism and trinitarianism, between Schmitt and Peterson, one must assume the terrible opposition between Father and Son. In the end, the God who becomes human and the human who becomes God failed to meet. God's defeat, of which Quinzio spoke, lies here.[54] Consider his beautiful expression: 'The cross is the true source [*matrice*] of nihilism, and resurrection is the possibility of seeing it.'[55] The Jewish legacy in Christianity continues to be unaddressed and unresolved. A religion of the Father and one of the Son are two different ways that the divine is present in the world. Different too is the contrast with the powers of evil. In the following years, we shall roam around studying this Manichean gnosis. In other words, the thought of difference has found itself caught in the furrow of a metaphysical issue. So this practice of feminism has had to have recourse to philosophy, to mysticism, to the science of language, to psychoanalysis among other things, in the attempt to get to the bottom of it. It has not succeeded so far. Because what is missing is politics. And no dichotomous model works other than politically, which is to say, in accordance with the categories of modern politics. Women's politics, the official kind, whether in opposition or government, is a politics of piecemeal demands, a practice of emancipation, historical reformism. An arrested rearguard for an extremely advanced front-line where, at best, difference is chosen to be the voice of the impolitical. But only as the voice of modern politics

54 Reference is to Sergio Quinzio, *La sconfitta di Dio* (Milan: Adelphi, 1992). [Trans.]

55 Sergio Quinzio, *La croce e il nulla* (Milan: Adelphi, 2006[1984]).

might it not only have fought but also won. With the end of modern politics, difference will remain a culture, merely a theoretical standpoint on the world and humanity. Better than nothing. But the one that divides into two will not be reassembled, will not explode, we can predict that it will live, will survive, without changing anything essential, either in humanity or the world.

It's true, there is always a first time again, even when one experiences things in one's mature years. Up to now, I always thought that everything could have collapsed, but one thing I would never have let drop: the eleventh thesis of Marx on Feuerbach: 'philosophers have always interpreted the world in various ways; the point is to change it.'[56] For the first time, doubt falls heavily upon this dogma of praxis. There was one final desperate expression of this principle, in the 1980s, but before '89. The standpoint of the political reprised the developmental patter of the workers' point of view: internally coherent yet it did not cohere with the subject who had to practice it, the party, orientated towards class struggles then and towards institutional systems today. The two standpoints astutely grasped how to exploit the remaining phase, but the strategic course of things provided no support. They were revolutionary thoughts of contingency. As revolutionary thought can always perhaps be and must be. Thought for the state of exception. It needs, there and then, an exceptional political personality and the historic subject of collective mobilizing force. If one misses the occasion, not only does it not return, it also turns into its opposite. The failure to grasp the cycle of workers' struggles politically resulted in a new capitalist economy, where the multiple rhythms of intensification of productivity called upon ever-decreasing quantities of productive labour. The failure to grasp the opening of the autonomy of the political during the conflict over mechanisms

56 Karl Marx and Friedrich Engels, *Collected Works*, VOL. 5 (London: Lawrence & Wishart, 1976), p. 5. [Trans.]

and powers of decision, served the establishment of a decisionism directed towards conservative modernization. The great century of alternatives, antagonisms, contestations and liberations was, in the 1980s, smothered in the arms of a right wing that was driven by history to an unforeseen modern victory. Long before the shrivelled bourgeoisies of the world began collecting bricks from the Berlin Wall, stones rained down daily upon the workers and upon politics. When the socialism of the East collapsed, the workers' movement in the West had already been defeated. And it was not a battle. It was a war. More precisely, it was the age of wars. The eleventh thesis began to falter. Hegel's phrase, *Die Welt ändern*, 'change the world', which Marx claimed for himself and bequeathed to us, was taken up the by other side. It was the masters of the world who changed it. Changed it compared to when the workers counted too much; when there was too much politics. A strategic problem arose: can one still wager on politics without the backing of the workers? The answer to that question instigated the search for a unique duplicity: no longer the one internal to theory and within practice, but between theory and practice, between ends of enquiry and form of action. Philosophy and praxis no longer in correspondence. It was a case now of radicalizing thought to its utmost sustainable limit and of moderating politics to the utmost sustainable limit. Enquiry had to claim back possession of the long term, with one's back turned to the future;[57] action had to grapple with the here and now, possessing once again the present. Expending great ideas over the short term meant leaving the hands of thought free. This was an operation of supreme subjective foresight. Where force is lacking, ability provides succour. But whereas Togliatti maintained his duplicity with the force of his charisma, in this case a double operation was required. On the one hand, a highly charismatic

57 The allusion is to Benjamin's description of Paul Klee's 'angel of history' in thesis IX of 'On the Concept of History'. Walter Benjamin, *Selected Writings*, VOL. 4, p. 392. [Trans.]

collective authority that had to operate hegemonically in politics as a responsible nucleus of constructors of socio-institutional architectures. On the other hand, separate and contrasting, a culture of crisis for the late twentieth century, which is to say, a negative thought for the end of the millennium: a 'For a Critique of Modern Civilization' focused on all the consequences of human alienation; a theoretical moment that was destructive of everything inhuman that had been deposited in the world by the bourgeois-capitalist way of life. Neither the one nor other took place: neither a culture of antagonism, nor a leading class in government. The neo-revolutionary experiment, heroically holding together the two aspects, was not even attempted. We have already seen that irretrievable defeat results from the conclusion of the peace, not of the war.

Revolutionary thought/reformist politics: this path too was interrupted. And no longer because of inability or the impossibility of duplicity. But for a deeper reason. Missing was the one thing that might have held together the form of thinking and the mode of action, which did not coincide and was even in contradiction. Missing was the point of view, which is to say, the essential condition for a strongly partisan viewpoint, one that would be able to bear a universality that is not formal and that would be in-itself a transvaluation of all here-to dominant values through an overturning of real relations of domination, of wealth and culture. This point of view was more than that of a class, it amounted to a world, another totality that was in its own way complete but opposed and alternative to that which officially entered the history books. It was a partisan standpoint, not because it is one of the many parts from which one can observe the whole, but because it is one of the two parts into which the whole is divided. It was not an ideological invention. Modern history had led to this because of the needs of capitalism. This was the expression of modern politics. The working class had become conscious of this, organized its struggles in light of it, taking risks through its attempts. It was from this that this world was born: practices, thoughts, interests, values, faiths, myths, reasons, science. Might the work of inheritance pay off? It is in grave doubt. It was a case of shouldering the entire weight of the past, including its terrible falls to carry it to safety, as Aeneas with Anchises outside of the walls of the destroyed Troy so as to build a new city; or rather, so as to go like Moses, like Paul, to establish 'a new people'. The inheritance—this is the non-tragic end of the late twentieth century—was not left buried beneath the ruins. This would have permitted, in the future, through a good political archaeology, to bring the remains to the surface so at least to reconstruct the memory of the old city. Instead, the inheritance melted away into the motionless air of a virtual epoch. They have remained words without roots, talk without thought. The end of history, no, but the end of *this* history, yes—if we understand this history as 'modern'. In truth, the absolute spirit of capitalism is realized. Modern history has won because it can claim to have reached completion, having fulfilled its function. Modern politics lost because, at a certain point in its destiny, it encountered and crossed the path of the workers' movement. This was the historic error of modern politics. But an enthralling error, which makes us love politics as destiny. The adopted destiny was the insane one that was, moreover, inscribed in its beginning: to fight against history. Had there not been the political attempt of the proletarian revolution within the capitalist war of the early twentieth century, perhaps by the end of the century the workers' movement would still have been alive. Better dead, than alive but soulless. We must with all clarity touch the bottom of the abyss. Only after this, if not everything, at least something might once again become possible. Without this preliminary intellectual operation—a political neo-nihilism of a working-class type—there is no form of action worth attempting. Now only thought can give us the order to say: despite it all, we continue.

Interlude

THE PARTY AND ITS DESTINY

'It is precisely that which we cannot speak that must be written.'

—Marìa Zambrano

There are two scenarios or backdrops in which to properly situate the problem. The political party was the protagonist of great history: that common sense has, for justified contingent reasons, come to see it as the night demon from which one should flee while reciting mantras; this is a situation that intellectual research should try to correct, rather than tag along behind.

First scenario. The destiny of parties is the destiny of politics. Of modern politics. Not in its long arc: the one that leads from the early 1500s to the end of the 1900s. But in the medium arc of the last two centuries; let's say from the so-called bourgeois revolutions onwards. It is there that politics divides, formally, almost institutionally into camps. When in the parliaments the representatives of the people line up on the opposite benches; that's where the parties are born. That is not to say that the political party has a parliamentary origin. The party had already formed during the dissolution of the old society and in the work of reassembling new social relations. Read Chateaubriand's *Mémories d'outre-tombe*:

I have recast, mixed and adapted anew two discussions (or 'polemical' essays) that I developed within the unfinished Italian transition. One appeared in *La sinistra nel labirinto* (Massimo Illardi ed.) (Genoa: Costa and Nolan, 1994). The other in *Il destino dei partiti* (Enrico Melchionda ed.) (Rome: Ediesse, 1996).

> The sessions of the National Assembly offered a spectacle of interest that the meetings of our Chambers are far from approaching. One had to get up very early to find a seat in the crowded gallery. The deputies arrived eating, talking, and gesticulating; they formed groups in different parts of the room, according to their opinions. The minutes were read aloud, and then a prearranged subject was discussed or an extraordinary motion was set forth. It was never a matter of some insipid article of law. The order of the day rarely lacked a scheme of destruction. Deputies spoke pro or contra, and everyone, for better or worse, improvised their speeches. These debates grew tempestuous. The galleries joined in the discussion, applauded and cheered, hissed and booed at the speakers.[1]

Let us begin from the phrase: 'The order of the day rarely lacked a scheme of destruction.' Memoires, precisely, from beyond the grave. Those times in which one destroys, are beautiful. To reconstruct almost always means to conserve. Just behind us, unfortunately, are the inappropriate destructions. And so, the immediate necessity: to reconstruct, in any case, parties and politics, with the meagre materials available to us.

Second scenario. In 1984, the journal *Laboratorio politico* organized a conference with the title 'The End of politics?'. Some of the participants already proposed at the time that the question mark should be removed. Among them was Jean Baudrillard, whose talk was titled: 'The Political Showman in the Space of Advertising'.[2] This was spot-on of the 'it happened tomorrow' kind.[3] I found myself frequently citing as the same

1 François-René de Chateaubriand, *Memoirs from Beyond the Grave* (Alex Andresse trans.) (New York: New York Review of Books, 2018), p. 223.

2 'Showman' in English in the original. [Trans.]

3 Reference, via an allusion to René Clair's film *It Happened Tomorrow* (1994), is almost certainly to Silvio Berlusconi—cruise-ship crooner and, at the time Tronti

young Hegel, speaking in *The Positivity of the Christian Religion* (a 1796 fragment from his period in Berne)—between the era of the glory of Greece and the greatness of Rome—of the so-called decadence of the Hellenic epoch:

> The picture of the state as a product of his own energies disappeared from the citizen's soul. The care and oversight of the whole rested on the soul of one man or a few. Each individual had his own allotted place [. . .]. Usefulness to the state was the great end which the state set before its subjects, and the end they set before themselves in their political life was gain, self-maintenance, and perhaps vanity. All activity and every purpose now had a bearing on something individual; activity was no longer for the sake of a whole or an ideal. Either everyone worked for himself or else he was compelled to work for some other individual. All political freedom vanished also; the citizen's right gave him only a right to the security of that property which now filled his entire world.[4]

This will have taken place. That is, in the last two decades this scenario has taken hold, has occupied our days, introduced itself into our work,

was writing, owner of AC Milan football club and the massive media and advertising empire Mediaset—who 'took to the field' of politics in 1994 (which is how he describes his turn to politics—as president of the all-conquering football club, the allusion was clear) with his party Forza Italia, the name taken from Italian football fans' cry 'come on Italy!'. In 1994, Berlusconi won the election, and although he lost power soon afterwards, he was in and out of power and continued to strongly influence Italian politics for the next two decades. It should be noted that Berlusconi's fortunes were largely thanks to the help of the late former prime minister and crook, Bettino Craxi, who, with the onset of *Tangentopoli* (see p. 100n12 below), fled to Tunisia, finding protection under his friend, the dictator Ben Ali, where he died of a tumour soon after among considerable luxury. [Trans.]

4 Hegel, *Early Theological Writings* (Richard Kroner ed., T. M. Knox trans.) (Philadelphia: University of Pennsylvania Press 1975), pp. 156–57.

has created the social imaginary and produced civic conduct. And the tyranny of the majority forces us to acknowledge this as right.

There you are. We do not need to think that the process of the end of politics begins today. One might say, if anything, that today it expresses itself symbolically and hence becomes visible. The last form of conservative revolution, the mediocre one of the 1980s, is the real subject of this process. If we reappraise for a moment the problem, we will see that the end of politics means the primacy of politics in crisis, that is, the crisis of the autonomy of the political. This primacy and, at the same time, this autonomy, mark the century. In this sense, the twentieth century is the century of politics. Politics takes root in the masses of the people who become its active subject, thereby imposing the supremacy of public affairs, of the general interest. Between 1914 and 1917, the essential takes place, from which everything else follows. At that point, the traditional forms of expression of the individual subject have crumbled. The spirit of time changed its horse.[5] Some will say: but this had already happened during the great bourgeois revolutions. But not like this, with this level of dual-consciousness, that of the great masses and great individuals. In fact, it was precisely the ingenious, anticipatory revolution in forms in the years straddling the end and beginning of the century that marked the change in quality. The English revolution, preceded by the Thirty Years War; the American Revolution within a war of Independence; the French Revolution followed by the Napoleonic Wars—these, it is true, are early anticipations of the primacy of politics; and insofar as they are, they are great contemporary events for us, men and women of the twentieth century. It is no coincidence that, over the course of years, the collective imaginary and the battle of ideas in the

5 The implicit reference is to Hegel's famous description of Napoleon: 'I saw the Emperor—this world-spirit—riding out of the city on reconnaissance.' *The Letters* (Clark Butler and Christiane Seiler trans) (Bloomington, IN: Indiana University Press, 1984), p. 114 (translation modified). [Trans.]

field of political theory and of historical readings continue to return to these events. There one can find, for example, the emergence of only one of the subjects that will become a protagonist of the public action of this century: the nation state. Missing is the other subject that, alongside the former, would make the history of the twentieth century: the political party organized at the level of the masses.

Masses and power:[6] once again the place of political action determines the historical epoch that lies immediately behind us. How can you fail to feel the breath down the neck of your own thought? Not that there were not real masses before, or that they had only been masses directed from above by bourgeois elites. It is always a case of elites and masses, whether we speak of those who beheaded Charles I or Louis XVI, or those who eliminated Tsar Nicholas and family. And always directed by leading groups, with a claim to understanding the laws of action. In this century, what has changed is the organization of the masses. In fact, the primacy of politics became the primacy of organization. And the autonomy of the logics of the one fed into the autonomy of the apparatuses of the other, in a perfect correspondence. In this way, the workers' movement anticipated the very interests of its rival, for its own internal reasons, to oppose masses and State. But then on, any interests, including the dominant ones, had to organize themselves in actually autonomous or potentially hegemonic forms. The sociology of political parties gave birth to organizational sociology. Weber before Robert Michels, but classical social democracy before Weber's classic analyses. Mass and class; party and State; the political dialectic of the twentieth century complicates itself at the level of the complexity and intensity developed by the entire culture of crisis. And the historical experiences, including the attempts and failures, all necessitate the primacy of politics over a society that does not accept it, other than as a

6 *Massa e potere* is the Italian title of Elias Canetti's *Crowds and Power*. [Trans.]

provisional exit from a self-destructive emergency—be that a great war or a great crisis; hence a breakdown of equilibria, whether political or economic. Historical experiences in parallel convergence: the authoritarian ones, the totalitarian, the democratic, all summed up in the figures of great individuals—Stalin, Hitler, Roosevelt. Behind the action of each was the same intention of organizing the masses in the form, very differently conceived, of the political party. In Europe as in the United States. Not as is said, with or without apparatuses, with or without machines, but with reference to typologies of political systems, dictatorial, parliamentary, presidential. The political party is, in its own way, a universal model, at least as far as the universe of the Western province is concerned. It is the case of distinguishing between masses of militants, members, electors; between total mobilization, capillary political work, capture of majoritarian consensus. Vanguards and masses, leader and people, political class and citizenship, all of which configure the same type of relationship mediated by the functional presence of an organized form that, since it is a political party, sanctions and to some extent legitimates the political force.

It has not always been like that, just since the victory of the aforementioned bourgeois revolutions. In eighteenth-century England, in nineteenth-century United States and continental Europe, it was a case of laissez-faire, of the full liberty of the invisible hand that moves the market economy. Politics followed. Or rather, it assumed exclusive, privileged access to the relationship between states, to the foundation of colonial empires, the repression of popular unrest, the self-government of administrative bureaucracies. The State took a step back. And politics was subordinate to the economy. Governments really were business committees, as Marx saw clearly.[7] The central place he accords to political

7 The reference is to Marx's famous phrase in the *Manifesto of the Communist Party*: 'The executive of the modern State is but a committee for managing the common

economy stems from this set of circumstances. Moreover, despite the north American anomaly, the primacy of the State and the autonomy of the political had already existed at the time of mercantilism, of early protectionism, of capitalist primitive accumulation—when the legitimate monopoly of force in the hands of the sovereign who decides was needed to govern the violence of the processes of the formation of the wealth of nations. Only after this was liberal capitalism able to take off. The political revolutions were necessary for this. And it will be, according to the happy expression of Karl Polanyi, the hundred years' peace,[8] from the Restoration to the First World War.

The twentieth century will be born in opposition to all of this, which had been anticipated, foretold by the philosophical certification that 'God is dead', by the breaking of all forms, the cry of the vanguards, the crisis of all exactitude of physical laws, of all determinacy of economic laws and all logics of the laws of action. The *Renaissance*[9] of politics begins with the revolution. Whereas it was with war that *Weltpolitik*, world-politics, again set off, under tragic twentieth-century signs. [Friedrich] Meinecke and Otto Hintze, German historicism and State power politics had seen all this coming. The 'primacy of foreign policy' was the expression of this passage. The paradox is that the twentieth century, the century of the great wars between great nations, privileges the primacy of internal politics, politics par excellence. If it is a case of world civil war, then conflict passes between states, it divides peoples. The old order of the old empires, in the First World War and, even more, the new Nazi-Fascist order, in the Second, call upon and organize the

---

affairs of the whole bourgeoisie.' Karl Marx and Friedrich Engels, *Collected Works*, VOL. 6 (London: Lawrence & Wishart, 1976), p. 486. [Trans.]

8 This is the title of the first chapter in Karl Polanyi, *The Great Transformation: The Political and Economic Origins of Our Time* (Boston: Beacon Press, 1957[1944]). [Trans.]

9 In French in the original. [Trans.]

democratic hatred of all social forces and all political classes of modern society. There is an increasing ideologizing of war that rebounds upon politics. Germany in the 1920s, United States in the 30s, Europe in the 40s—these are territories for the friend/enemy hunt, conflictual fields of polarized forces, the opposition of militarized ideological apparatuses. It becomes evident that there is a substantial division characterizing the structures of modern society, one that expresses parties within states, that defines alternative political systems, that imposes conflictual styles and ways of life, which defines the private sphere and the public dimension always and only under the sign of an either/or. When there had been open class struggle on a world scale, the autonomy of the political and the primacy of politics attained their highest level of expression.

Here's a truth that cannot be spoken and so must be written: it is with the end of the age of wars that the decay of politics begins. This is a statement of fact. It has nothing to do with a judgement of value. A gaze takes in the landscape of modern politics. Once again: what is politics, which is to say, not what is Humanity but what is the world of men and women? The thinking of the workers' movement hesitated to pose itself this question during its history; now that we have seen its outcome, it is time for the workers' movement to pose itself the question. Much is required to begin to narrate oneself, to find oneself within the context of events, translating past actions into the language of current problems. It is necessary to periodize, not to deconstruct but to decipher. In universal history, which includes the history of one's own side, there is an enigmatic, mysterious aspect that does not require a transcendent origin. It is to be found there, in the indecipherable, obscure meaning of human things; in the contrast between means and ends; in the disproportion between will and its conditions; in the irrational drives of subjects when they assume collective consistency. To know—that processes are slow, long, murky, indecisive and blind. This is a theme that one must lucidly explore in depth to understand when this subsidence in the political terrain begins; this at first gradual, then precipitous crumbling of the sense of public action. Great politics can be recognized by the quality of the political class that expresses it. What must be understood is when the process takes place of the levelling down of political personality to the stage of generalized smug limitation that ultimately renders useless, unproductive, and hence fatally and easily replaceable the presence of vocationalism-professionalism in the exercise of public activity.[10] What, in this context, is the turning point of the century? The search is open. And a long way from even a provisional conclusion. Let us adopt the convenient writing of history in sequential decades. In the years straddling the 1970s and 80s, politics entered a deep coma, from which it has still not emerged. It is no coincidence that then politics became corrupted, a corruption from which it shows no sign of emerging. Events within nations assume an unwarranted importance. Italy, with its un-tragic dramas, *docet*. Both blocks implode. But one does so more than the other. That is the decisive fact. 1989 marks the peaceful victory of the west over the—at least European—east. A war won by non-military means is unprecedented. It is the symbolic moment that truly marks the death of politics. The collapse of the USSR and the unification of the world under the hegemony of a single power, illustrated by the subsequent Gulf War, offer the possibility of a new hundred-year peace.

The parties: we shall first take stock of them by focusing on historical context. Distinguishing between birth phase and organizational phase. A birth not from historic personalities but from bodies of ideas, combinations of real interests, emotive drives, irrational moods, concrete ends. Behind us lies the general crisis of universalism that presupposed, maintained, linked feudal particularities. The project: a new political universalism able to free the different sides [*parti*] by rendering them reciprocally autonomous and, hence, potentially opposed. At bottom, it

10 The allusion is to Max Weber's *Politics as Vocation*. [Trans.]

is this that the generic human rights of the Revolutionary Constitutions affirmed. They abolished the immobility of the old divisions [*parzialità*], the shell of ancient privileges. Claims to equal rights served only to realize a suppression. This was how bourgeois interest had conceived them. To have confused means with ends, to have adopted a functional moment as a choice of values was a pathetic humanitarian error. To modulate instrumental reason in accordance with the forms of universal reason is impossible, or rather, it is not possible for the bearers of a standpoint opposed to those who promoted such an operation. The tactical instrumentalization of politics must be capable of independent actualization. Each time that one inscribes one's action in the sequence of one's adversary's moves, one remains fatally subordinated to them. Contrary to what is believed, strategies can even become blurred, since in any case they do not count one bit, it is the political choices that must remain distinct. In short: for the same reason that the revolutionary method of the Hegelian dialectic could not be used to criticize the reactionary content of the system, so one could not adopt universal human rights to fight the class contents of nascent capitalist power. There was no clash of contradictions, there was reciprocal functionality. The young Marx had understood this in his critique of politics, but it slipped the clutches of the mature Marx's critique of political economy. And from then through to today, within the workers' movement and after, the real division was the following: between the critique of politics and the critique of political economy. Not which of the two, but which should have primacy. This is to lay it out in the noblest terms. Because now we're in a phase in which the two camps unwittingly speak in prose. One appears to be speaking of something else. But the problems are more or less the same. When feminist thought of difference reopened the file that had been archived under the heading of critique of the philosophy of public law—and it did so precisely by indicting equal rights—the Left failed to even understand the problem. Well, this was it. There is no longer one, there is only two across the entire arc of development and decay of the current form of civilization. The structural political foundation of modernity lies here. To assume this fact; to decipher it in accordance with the specific ways in which it is presented within its determinate historical context; to organize the forces able to support conflict so as to resolve it in its favour—here are the tasks for a party of the Left.

The destiny of political parties is tied to the survival of this political condition. An explicit survival, because the hidden one lies there, ever less visible to the naked eye, and always more obscurely present. When a future school of thought turns its hand to the monumental history of bourgeois ideology—a politically orientated Bouvard and Pécuchet—what will emerge is the eternal philosophical, theological, literary, economic, juridical, psychological, politico-theoretical effort to conceal reality and to represent it by its contrary. It is then necessary to realize that ideological apparatuses are constructive; they produce relations and impose conditions. Today more than yesterday. The total mobilization of ideas that has been organized in recent years, with no shortage of resources, against the dichotomous view of society, has broken through the lines and obstructed the antagonist viewpoint. Instead of grasping the new forms of the division of the world, the actual frontiers of the radicalization of history, the contemporary figures of the spirit of division, and hence the lines and folds within the fractures of human beings, one passively assumes the winning idea of the world, of history and humanity, reunited, and only rendered more complex. I maintain: no serious proposal for a Left political party is possible if one adopts this subordinate horizon of political culture.

The crisis of parties has causes far more profound than those that are typically attributed to it. The Italian case has further diverted the course of the problem. It's been a 'case' that has itself concerned a 'fate'.

In the happy expression of a long-time friend of mine,[11] there is also a *genus italicum* in politics, both theoretical and practical. Indeed: the Italian anomaly strikes again, after the ready and optimistic certification of its death. Although there has been an exaggerated jealous exclusivity of this moral question of ours. We are pedigree chickens in a common hen coup. Here some have cried out what elsewhere, where one is a 'nation', is not spoken of for love of the motherland. *Tangentopoli*,[12] to use this futile name that only the newspapers could have come up with, is everywhere a phenomenon of civil society that is attributed solely to halls of power.[13] Corruption is inscribed at least as much in the logic of the market as it is in that of power. If anything can truthfully be said of our case, it's perhaps this: no political class that has been in power for 40 years of peace can resist corruption. All the more so when without a credible threat of an alternative. Here, in the country of politics, the fall of politics has been more deeply felt and more clearly visible. Indeed, the symbolic imaginary has become direct and explicit. The revolt of

---

11 Reference to Alberto Asor Rosa, and more specifically to his book of literary criticism: *Genus italicum. Saggi sulla identità letteraria italiana nel corso del tempo* (Turin: Einaudi, 1997). [Trans.]

12 This was the name ('bribe city') given to the corruption scandal of the early 1990s that engulfed the Italian political and business establishment—and of organized crime—in which bribery of politicians by business and mafia was shown to have taken place across local and national government. It brought down the historic parties of government, including the Christian Democrats—who had been in power throughout the postwar period—as well as the Socialist Party (which by this time had long lost any obvious relation to socialism). Apart from some minor local exceptions, only the Italian Communist Party was largely untouched by the scandal, although it had by now begun its long-term identity crisis—exemplified by a never-ending sequence of names—leading it today to the vacuous name of Democratic Party: which amounts to saying, it's a party and it operates in a democracy. [Trans.]

13 Tronti critically employs expression *il Palazzo* popularized by Pier Paolo Pasolini in the mid-1970s as a synecdoche for elite political power. [Trans.]

the rich against the poor that characterized the 80s in the West, with an allegorical finale in the East, has assumed the figure of the entrepreneur that in a single leap becomes the owner of power, brandishing the weapon of anti-politics. These two things: the firm that becomes party, for a moment even government, and the managers of their business interests in civil society who become representatives of the people in Parliament, do more to critique the results of contemporary democracies than we do with our theoretico-historical whining.[14] This is the stuff presented to us by tone-deaf choruses of the 'Italian revolution'. We are just missing a touch of republican monarchism, which we hope is impossible.[15] The programme of Togliatti and Dossetti was that of a 'Progressive Democracy'. Christian history, socialist tradition, and communist politics could be found there, it was a strategic intersection. It is one of the many

14 Reference here is again to the events of the early-to-mid 1990s, Berlusconi's turn to politics with his Forza Italia, made up of many members from his Mediaset media empire in positions of political power. There are more recent examples in the United States of America. [Trans.]

15 This consciously contradictory name was that given by Maurice Duverger (1917–2014)—a French political scientist who was also a European parliamentarian for the Italian Communist Party—to the French system of direct election of the president. Francesco Cossiga (1928–2010) considered this model suited to Italy after the collapse of the Berlin Wall and the loss of trust in parties following the corruption scandals of the early 1990s. Cossiga, incidentally, was a former prime minister and president of Italy for the Christian Democrats, as well as minister of the interior during the time of the 'strategy of tension', when agents of the Italian, the Unites States, and, reputedly, NATO's security services used far-right groups to plant bombs and carry out attacks, with the aim of undermining the Italian Communist Party. The two 'ss' in his name, were frequently depicted in the Nazi SS style during this time. It is, perhaps, not entirely irrelevant here that Cossiga admitted to being actively involved in Gladio, a stay-behind paramilitary organization established in Italy (and elsewhere in western Europe) after World War Two by the Western Union, then overseen by NATO and the CIA, which was designed to stop the spread of communism. [Trans.]

paradoxes with which the impetus of history enjoys disrupting the ranks of politics. Those popular elements came together only once they found themselves without a people. That which was once blocked by the 'great and terrible world' divided into two opposing camps,[16] is now permitted by the dazzling news that little Italy [*Italietta*] had returned to its eternal vices: the corruption of the powerful, the municipalism of the simple folk, the self-promotion of leaders and the common sense—or, worse—the good sense of intellectuals. From here followed the call to improbable new constituent assemblies. But how can one reform in the courtyard of *such a* politics a constitution, the Italian one, that was born in the arena of *that* history? It can't be done. We have seen an entire political class crumble around us: 'democracy without a leader'; that is, 'rule by the "professional politician" who has no vocation'.[17] We see emerging, in the sketchy figures of pre-political personalities, a minor form of 'leader democracy'; not vocation but ambition without profession.[18]

---

16 The expression, 'the great and terrible world', is from Antonio Gramsci, *The Prison Notebooks*, VOL. 1 (New York: Columbia University Press, 1992), p. 2. [Trans.]

17 Max Weber, 'Politics as a Vocation' in *Political Writings* (Peter Lassman and Ronald Speirs eds, Ronald Speirs trans.) (Cambridge: Cambridge University Press, 1994), p. 351. Tronti does not explicitly reference Weber's essay here. [Trans.]

18 With the notion of 'leader democracies' (*Führerdemokratie*), Tronti is again in dialogue with Weber's account of charismatic leadership, specifically as a type of 'plebiscitary democracy'. What is being advanced with this notion is an elite conception of democracy: i.e. democracy as a form of devotion to charismatic leaders, so as to overcome the risk of bureaucratization supposedly characteristic of party government, where such 'leaderless democracy [. . .] favours horse-trading amongst notables for the allocation of places on the lists, but also [. . .] because it will in the future make it possible for pressure groups to force the parties to include their officials in the lists, thereby creating an unpolitical parliament in which there is no genuine leadership' ('Politics as Vocation', p. 351; see also Weber, *Economy and Society* [Berkeley: University of California Press, 1978], pp. 266ff, 1111–55). Joseph Schumpeter, a later champion of leadership democracy, would argue that one should reverse the classical notion of democracy, which contended that the primary purpose

A few years ago, before the notoriety of many misdeeds, a theory of 'political exchange' spread here too. It had noble fathers, such as Schumpeter, and serious sons, such as Gian Enrico Rusconi. It was not a political conception of the market, but a mercantile conceptualization of politics, which was precisely the notion that won out after the crisis of parties had already begun and was advancing. It was this idea that smouldered beneath the ashes throughout those 1980s. The last serious project of the government of society, which in any case was mistaken, was that of so-called national solidarity. The 'historic compromise' was worth attempting simply to ground the political and institutional conditions for a democracy of alternation.[19] In 1976, the two poles of the

of democracy was to 'vest the power of deciding political issues in the electorate' and instead view its primary purpose as that of 'the election of men who are able to do the deciding [. . .] the democratic method is that institutional arrangement for arriving at political decision in which individuals acquire the power to decide by means of a competitive struggle for the people's vote'. Joseph Schumpeter, *Capitalism, Socialism, and Democracy* (London: Unwin University Books, 1974), p. 269. [Trans.]

19 The 'historic compromise' was declared by the then general secretary of the Italian Communist Party (PCI), Enrico Berlinguer, following the coup in Chile on 11 September 1973. He called for a 'new great "historic compromise" between the forces that gather together and represent the great majority of the Italian people' (cited in Guido Crainz, *Il paese mancato* [Rome: Donizelli, 2003], p. 450). The fear, expressed in the Directorate of the party already the day after the Chilean coup, was that the peaceful path to socialism—which had been party policy in the postwar period—would increasingly appear closed to its followers, encouraging adventurism and direct actions, the outcome of which might have been foretold by the events of Chile. Thus, the compromise suggested that an external support to a centre-left government—a broad political alliance—was necessary to stabilize the system. Views of this decision among left intellectuals have diverged radically. They range from Luciano Gruppi's defence of the compromise, which situated it within a history of Italian communism from Gramsci to Togliatti and Berlinguer (*Il compromesso storico* [Rome: Editori riuniti, 1977]); to Antonio Negri's angry denunciation in 1975, according to which it did not even amount to classical reformism, but was rather

alternative were much more distinct than they were in 1996.[20] But it is easy to understand what it was that the Christian Democrats (DC) and the Italian Communist Party (PCI) were unable to do. And not because the US veto was still in place, or because the distancing from the USSR

---

merely a tool in the service of capitalist restructuring (see 'Proletarians and the State' in *Books for Burning* [London: Verso, 2005], pp. 118–79). The kidnapping and execution of the then leader of the Christian Democrats (DC), Aldo Moro, by the Red Brigades in 1978, is the most extreme objection to this course of action. Moro, the figure behind the strategy of compromise with the PCI, was kidnapped on his way to the Chamber of Deputies to support the formation of a new government that would, for the first time, have received the external support of the PCI. That the US, NATO, and the Soviet Union all had strong reasons to prevent the formation of such a government has resulted in a proliferation of conspiracies easily able to rival those surrounding the Kennedy assassination. [Trans.]

20 The elections of 1976 took place under the watchword of 'national solidarity' at a time when 'the country was economically unstable, [and] street violence had reached new levels of savagery' (Paul Ginsborg, *A History of Contemporary Italy* [Harmondsworth: Penguin, 1990], p. 376). While the DC won with 38 per cent of the vote, the PCI received 34 per cent, with the socialist PSI far behind with 9 per cent. What national solidarity amounted to was that the largest opposition parties (PCI and PSI) would agree not to bring about the fall of the government, while it in turn would fully consult with the opposition on the programme of government. While the elections of 1976 ended in the tragedy of the Moro kidnapping and execution in 1978, those of 1996 ended not so much in farce as in stalemate. The new voting system combined 75 per cent of seats distributed on first past-the-post basis and 25 per cent through proportional representation. In a system that was used to proportional representation, it was clear that coalitions would need to be formed. The two coalitions were, on the centre-left, the Ulivo (Olive Tree Alliance), which included alongside the Democratic Party of the Left (PDS–ex-PCI), Greens as well as Catholics such as Romano Prodi and even Lamberto Dini, who had been Treasury Secretary in the previous Berlusconi government. Berlusconi, on the other hand, stood with the neo-Fascist National Alliance, rooted in the centre and south of Italy, and Northern League separatists from the North. The centre-left scraped by with a measly percentage point over Berlusconi's 'Pole of Liberties'. [Trans.]

had not yet taken place. In a bipolar world, rightly, which is to say realistically, the two parties referred to two distinct camps. One might, however, have manoeuvred with agility so that, in that context, a future of democratic bipolarity might have got through the folds of the rival blocks. It would perhaps have passed more easily than the idea of governing together. For this latter idea, what was missing were the conditions of a collective political culture. Moro had been ready. Perhaps Berlinguer as well. But the DC State-party and the moderate block on the one hand, and the PCI party-form and the people of the Left on the other, were unwilling. These unspoken historical findings remain solid: the DC died with Moro; the PCI died with Berlinguer. The crisis of the great parties came much earlier; recognition of it came extremely late. The judicial actions and the revolt of the Northern League[21] made the phenomenon visible. But what caused it to explode was the end of the bipolar international order. Until 1991, the house remained precariously standing. Then it crumbled. The problem today is not why those parties passed away. The problem is why they did not deliver a historic inheritance. For political formations, the theme of epochal shifts is always one of inheritance. Far more than a question of innovations. Those able to advance their position in the balance of forces, compared to their rivals, through a necessary destruction of their own past as well, are engaged in great politics. And they navigate the shift with this prospective in mind. The

21 The Lega Nord was a right-wing federalist party that called for the separation of the mythical land of Padania, covering much of the wealthy territory of the Po river and basin from the rest of Italy that it identified with a supposedly centralizing Rome and—with strongly racialized overtones—with a lazy south, the latter being historically the most impoverished area of Italy. The Lega Nord (now, simply the Lega), was frequently in and out of government with Berlusconi. In 2022, one hundred years since Mussolini's fascists took power, the Lega entered government with Fratelli d'Italia, the heirs of the Movimento Sociale Italiano, the postwar party composed of the remnants of Italian Fascism. [Trans.]

use of crisis for development is the principal paradigm against which to measure the quality of the political. There is no system, whether of ideas or states, that is so dilapidated that it can be peacefully overthrown, other than by tragic subjective errors. The different response to crises of capitalism in 1929 and of socialism in 1989 should give us pause for thought. This is a vast history that remains unthought by the Left. There is no ignorance worse than that of those who think they have always known. And yet it sometimes feels as though it would be enough to find the thread to begin weaving once again. A change of form is one thing, quite another to renounce the very reasons for one's existence. These lie in living history and cannot be abolished by a decree from above. It is not true that they will, in any case, continue to make themselves felt in new guises. The truth is that one can lose them. The tragedy is that these reasons have been lost. And so it happens that one ceases to be and then one knows not what to do. And certainly, it becomes hard to recreate the party if there is no longer a side [*parte*] to organize.

Here lies the true point of desperate difficulty. While the problem is clear, all solutions appear confused. Without question, one side [*parte*] must be reconstructed. Otherwise, there is no party. And even more importantly, there is no politics. But which side [*parte*]? How is it to be structured? With reference to what? What organizational form should it take? That of a social actor, certainly. Centred on the world of work. To which there is generic consent, almost indifference, ritual verbal assent that ultimately fails to produce even symbolic facts. There is a failure to confront the bitter subject of the political consequences that the revolution in work has produced in society. The fracturing of the social block of the Left begins with the loss of centrality of the worker, which in turn has been technologically undermined. The theme of the tragic impact of technology on being in the twentieth century was only tackled by the great conservative philosophical consciousnesses and narrated by late-bourgeois art. Whereas the workers' movement, even from the heights of its magnificent experiences, has stuttered on this, has equivocated, deluded itself and, in the end, surrendered. It failed to grasp the demonic aspect of technology, just as it failed—as we shall see—to grasp the demonic aspect of power, these two forces that bent the century to their wills.

Today, work, for the Left, from being a political resource, has become a historic contradiction. Why? Because the political concept of work has weakened; it has almost crumpled. Empirically, it is right to say 'work' in the plural.[22] The differentiation of activities and of the modalities of work is a fact. The multiplicity of labour relations is also a fact. Not to speak of the wage differentials. One says 'flexibility' with a fixed smile. Only to find oneself with increasingly rigid and rising levels of unemployment. And that's without turning to futuristic questions regarding the so-called end of work. Politics, however, does not describe facts. It unites them, or tries to do so, both conceptually and practically. For the Left, politically, work is a symbolic frontier: an idea/value of belonging, recognition, conflict and organization. One can push back the frontier of the simple reproduction of employee labour to the point of the expanded reproduction of self-employed labour, but only in the sense that it too is now indirectly employed labour, which is in turn subordi¬nated to market regulations, to the control of financial flows, to compatibility rules of supranational organisms and to the shifting orientation of government policies. And politics, politics in general, always originates from the contrast with dependence upon the interest of another. From the mere cultivation of one's independent interests are born partial political acts, those of a body, a group, a class. And so, as the total social quantity of work increases, its specific political quality

22 Whereas the Italian *lavoro* has singular and plural forms, that is not the case for English. Tronti's point is that capitalism has gone from a dominant form of work or labour, typically associated with the industrial working class, to numerous types of work, none of which can claim a position of monopoly. [Trans.]

falls. The political party that formally adopts this social labour referent must be well aware of the weakness it betrays. It lacks strength. Because strength stems from its concentration. Only a concentrated force can be endowed with potentially dominant organized forms. The golden age of the workers' movement came when the industrial working class united the world of work with its struggles, and it is no coincidence that only then did the opportunity arise to bring the long history of the subaltern classes to an end.

I know that the left ear has, for some time now, become hard of hearing. This is the reason why, unfortunately, going against our nature, we must raise our voices. But here too it is unnecessary to resort to judgements of value. We need but acknowledge facts. The nature or form of the workers' movement has, until very recently, lumped together all the Left parties with their respective experiences of government and the state. The Italian Communist Party defined itself as the party of the working class. It was not. It was a powerful mobilizing intellectual and popular myth. 'To go to the school of the working class' was, in the twentieth century, the one answer equal to that provided by the conservative revolution, that is, of the anti-modern path of those who went to the school of the State and the Kingdom. Today, a bloodless Left with no past, no history, entirely engaged in trying to make others forget what it was, advances. Making verbal tributes to the world of work and then turning to 'concrete' issues. But difficulties are not overcome by ignoring them. Labour as social actor [*parte sociale*] cannot feed itself on weak thought.[23] It cannot be described as a place of dispersal: light,

23 *Pensiero debole*, or weak thought, was a distinctively Italian conceptualization of what Jean-François Lyotard termed the 'postmodern condition'. Drawing on Nietzsche and Heidegger's account of nihilism as the weakening of the foundations of Western notions of being, truth and the subject, Gianni Vattimo, one of the principal philosophers of this current of thought, argued for an always open, pluri-vocal (rather than univocal), and ever reinterpretable hermeneutics of the central categories of Western thought. [Trans.]

mobile, pragmatic, non-ideological without paying a heavy price, losing ground, weakening interests, forfeiting power and crisis of one's organization. Those who say that this side [*parte*] can no longer simply be represented, it must first be rebuilt, are correct. This is what Bruno Trentin argues.[24] I, who for some time now come from a diametrically contrasting position, recognize that his approach is the only one worth debating with. At least in part, that engagement takes place among the pages of this book. This side [*parte*], reconstructed. Or even when it had, for the first time, been constructed. The world of work under the centrality of the worker was a materially existing structural reality, strategically placed at the heart of capitalist production. It needed a tactical-organizational armature to become conscious or to operate as dissolver of given social relations or even to engage in a sagacious reformist politics. And so, it was something entirely different from the contemporary form of labour as a social partner. The instance of change is not that of the progressive fragmentation and corporatization of the different labour segments, and the contradictory articulation of interest groups among workers. Were it only this, the field could be reunified by effective trade-union action. The trade union as political subject of general interest of the workers was attempted but failed. Now both the one and other standpoint are in crisis: that of the organic relationship between trade union and party, evident in British labourism and German social democracy, and that of trade-union autonomy as in the Italian case. This is because the phase change is profound. It is untrue that the conflict of the theoretico-economic categories identifying the two camps has disappeared. Even less can one say that the two camps have disappeared. But wage and profit no longer confront one another directly. Between the one and the other a terrain of mediations has imposed itself, one that is not neutral but is managed by whichever of the two contending

24 See, for instance, *La città del lavoro. Sinistra e crisi del fordismo* (Milan: Feltrinelli, 1997). [Trans.]

parties holds the levers of power. As usual, to grasp the real problem, we must reverse the prattle of today's public opinion. Because the truth is that the Left in government is without power—if by power we understand, as in the classic conception of the workers' movement, not domination but force, realized hegemony, a will able to direct processes, organize subjects, shift relationships and direct change.

Those mediations that since the 1930s have been in the hands of the State, since the 1960s pass into those of government. Because what the ruinous collapse of politics produced in the passage to the final acute phase of the world civil war and the dangers to the system that it had ominously triggered, meant ever less State, increasingly more government. You can see this piece of twentieth-century history reflected in the regression of the political class: increasingly few statesmen; evermore men of government. The number of mediations has increased exponentially, although their quality has dropped to a minimum. Mediations are between numbers not between forces. Compromises not between powers but between weaknesses. The activity of government is in the hands of different rungs of management. Because government is now a non-place, an ephemeral passage for ideas regarding society that, like the *flaneur* in the metropolitan *passages*, no longer finish there. Why is this? Because there are no longer party-led governments. 'Party government'[25] was a highpoint in modern political history. On this topic, see the studies by Mauro Calise.[26] At times and in places, it has become interwoven with the only serious political history of the last centuries, that of the modern State. This is not, as is often trivially believed to be, that of the nation-state, which is instead already a minor history. There is an earlier founding from which everything else follows. In the passage between absolute

25 In English in the original. [Trans.]

26 Mauro Calise, *Governo di partito. Antecedenti e conseguenze in America* (Bologna: Il Mulino, 1989); *Dopo la partitocrazia* (Turin: Einaudi, 1994). [Trans.]

monarchies and revolutionary regimes, Bonapartist dictatorships and aristocratic restorations, up to the first forms of liberal bourgeois institutions, the State becomes political regulator of capitalist accumulation and social guarantor of the industrial revolution. The political party assumes this hegemonic history of the State and advances it with other means. All the great parties do this, the American and the European, those of the continent or of the isles. The parties of the workers' movement exist within this history, all of them, the reformist and the revolutionary, the mass and the vanguard parties, those that construct Welfare States as well as those building Socialism in One Country, despite the gargantuan contradiction that marked the century. If this one history is not reconstituted; if one continues to look at it with the cockeyed gaze of the political alternative of the twentieth century, on the one side beautiful forms and on the other the accursed crimes, one will merely produce edifying tales for unwitting epigones unable to firmly grasp the logic of public affairs.

In other words. The destiny of the party is the same destiny as that of the State and of modern politics. It is improbable that the State will return on the grand scale in its traditional format. And so impossible too is the return of the party-form in the shape it assumed in the period straddling the nineteenth and twentieth centuries. The crisis of politics lies here. The centrality of governments is the consequence. They occupy empty spaces and perform given functions. It is not only in Italy that, with or without a democracy of alternatives, governments are increasingly technical and ever-decreasingly political ones. Parliamentary political majorities elect and support the boards of the country-corporation.[27] Competent bureaucrats seeking to manage the public realm, which is to say, to balance the budget and repay one's debts, respecting social and international compatibilities, allowing entry into the European Union,

27 The idea of an *azienda-paese* was a leitmotif of Berlusconi's politics. [Trans.]

exiting from emergencies. The first stage of government action: put one's accounts in order; second stage of politics: we'll see. How long has it been since one formed a political government with a plan for society? How long since alternative ideas of the state were advanced? How long since the different sides were distinguished by the different senses given to politics? We need to understand that something has gone profoundly awry, something difficult to set right because it is not only the question of the form of the party that is in question, and that it is not enough to seek or to propose reforms. The entire axis of political action is in question, from the summit of power to the depths of the people, and vice versa. Hence the reason why there is no prayer so vapid as the one that continues to repeat the democratic litany, as if the gods, *demos* and *kratos*, were still with us, conversing, and had not—for some time now—definitively fled to distant and opposed worlds. The State is no longer the concentration of power and the monopoly of violence. It lacks the form for the one and the other. The politicized masses organized in the party that made up the political category of the people [*popolo*] have become apolitical people [*gente*], privatized and manipulatable non-individuals. The General Will has been entombed with Rousseau. The structural transition is expressed well by the semantic mutation. The historic idea of 'masses in the State' gives way to the electoral slogan 'the Left in government'. And so it should be. Here we're in the heart of the question of the party. The party as organized form of social conflict is an ingenious idea of the workers' movement. The Left in government is ashamed of coming from here. But between the Left in government and the government of the Left there exists a difference in quality. In the middle lies precisely the question that calls for a decision: what party for the Left?

The answer is not at all simple. It is doubtful there even is an answer. The fundamental reason for the crisis of politics, of its degeneration and corruption, lies in the overthrow of the meaning of politics. The law of oligarchy that Michels had already discovered at the outset of European social democracy and the concept of political market that Schumpeter developed from observing American democracy, together give us the picture of the critical existence of contemporary political parties. Everything else seems to descend from here, and from the other phenomenon that arrives here, issuing from other causes, the loss of the social justifications for the political party. The centrality of the electoral market within the political system, this reduction of political action to winning consent is the dark disease of modern democracies. Along this path, democratic regimes become expanded oligarchic regimes. Interclass party and electoral party are two figures of the same political form, which have triggered a degenerate logic of development that everywhere reaches the extremes: the oligarchic party of the elect becomes the party of the leader to be elected; the party of all becomes the party of nobody, a non-party that is chosen for a day but that does not ask—must not ask!—for everyday participation and belonging. The party is the vote. The real powers are the opinion polls. There is only one other power that counts: the performance of the stock market. So-called communication then turns these into idols sitting atop altars. The opinions of trade unions and business lobbies, the role of social partners and, it must be said, even politico-cultural actors serve merely to write the footnotes, the commentary and explanation. The muddling of political party and the electoral coalition, the temptation to turn the latter into a political subject stems from an idea of the party as subordinate and a hegemonic idea of public opinion, which is to say, a passively neutral idea of politics. Whether neutral, complex, secular, systemic, functional or polyvalent. The neutralization of politics is a process that has traversed and marked the second half of the twentieth century. It was the true, pacific, victorious answer to the age of war in the first half of the century. A systemic response. And, indeed, never has there been such a solid stabilization of the current system of world domination as there has been since the crisis of politics. Capitalism needed politics to be born, and then to save itself from death at the hands of crisis and collapse. But it was great politics, with an abundance of public aims, albeit unrealized. Due to the fear of those ends, the choice became always for the little politics of governments, useful but not dangerous, inevitable and controllable. Nothing more is designed to kill modern politics so much as little politics. Even the corruption of public power through the parties is little politics, at once cause and consequence the one of the other. In this way, the ethical de-legitimation of parties leads to the de-politicization of public action.

The destiny of parties received the seal of this context. From here on there is only decadence and crisis. The idea of party reform is a weak one. And the great party of the Left is a minimum programme. The Left is badly implicated in the fall of the party form, far more than the Right. Because in a phase of capitalist stabilization, the Left has much more need of politics than the Right. And without the party, there is no politics. And we have seen what 'the new way of doing politics' consists of. If the parties don't do it, the judges do, the journalists, the great communicators, finance, the law, the talk shows, this proactive civil society, not the impotent one of citizen volunteers. Party politics, for the Left, stood between the masses and the State: these two figures of the century that, if not extinct, are on the way to extinction. The Left must establish a paradigmatic relationship with the party, one that takes up a position towards the world. One cannot put ones' hope in how things progress, as once was possible. Left to themselves, they do not tend towards the better—understood as the side [*parte*] that wants to advance a project of great social transformation through the political organization of all alternative subjects. It is not a case of defining the magnificent and progressive fate of the party and following it. I repeat, it is a case of fighting against the destiny of decadence and crisis that sweeps over and overwhelms the very idea and practice of politics. A theoretical question drops into view here that, being political, needs an answer capable of embracing the sense of collective human action. Must the party represent its own social referent [*parte*] just as it is, which is to say, bearing the interests, needs, drives, the demands as they are objectively expressed within a historical phase, or should it rather orientate, stimulate, choose, decide within its own analysis of society and on the basis of a political project of its own? The best party experiences, those of the workers' movement, held together these two functions, accentuating sometimes the one, sometimes the other, based on politico-organizational options filled and formed by living thought. The organizational solutions of social-democratic or communist-type existed within the same partisan [*di parte*] choice of party. Mass party or vanguard party, both were present in the PCI. This is a tradition that, right down to the very definitions, needs to be overcome, not refused, moved beyond without being abandoned. The present phase, marked by a totalizing hegemony of the capitalist way of life at the level of the world-economy, demands a return to an autonomous political form that can oppose it, subjectively and critically. The problem is not: to be a force of opposition or force of government. There is no question that, today, this opposition can be more effectively exerted at the level of government. But one must know how to do so, and to want to do so. And so also the question of political will returns. This must be rediscovered in the terms of the autonomous qualities of one's own political culture, one that can judge, intervene, deconstruct and attack. A crisis of the party form carries with it a drop in the quality of the political class. Despite appearances, the Left suffers from this more than the Right. In a schema that is not politically but socially correct; the Right is not identified with the sum of parliamentarians of the *Polo delle libertà*,[28] but with the current ruling class of the nation: banks and

28 The 'Pole of Liberties' was Berlusconi's centre-right coalition for the 1994 election, which included his Forza Italia and the separatist Lega Nord in the north, and in the

industry, private and public management, large- and medium-sized business, high civil-service administration, specialized academic knowledge. Either one rediscovers a political force, a politics endowed with force able to lead—I repeat—in opposition to this complex world of domination, so as to shift the balance of power. Or one is fatally reduced to act as a subordinate, operating as a subject-instrument, the only one possible in a particular phase to escape a situation of emergency and to lead the country back to the norm—before then receiving one's marching papers. Not all, but many of the experiences of the Left in government have fallen during such an operation of voluntary servitude to systemic compatibilities. What is in question is not the need of social and political compromise in such phases; but the more there is a need of great compromise, the more is there a need of a great politics. The Left certainly does not need to pull back from governing in the state of exception, but in the phase of exception it must not renounce the function of the sovereign who decides.

I know that it's difficult, if not by now impossible, to convince people of something not already inscribed within the logic of the dominant ideas; but here it is not the imagination but reality that tells us that the environment is one in which non-political forces effectively administer power, to which politics is unable to oppose its own context of force. A politics that is so acquiescent as to incorporate the ideology of anti-politics not only fails to win, it fails even to compete. And yet, the essential aspect of the new conflictual dichotomy lies here. The crisis of politics, through the crisis of parties, right through to the crisis of the party regimes, has secured for an incalculable time the privatizing, that is to say, non-political and anti-political, global framework. It is true that behind it lie processes that are, if possible, deeper still. To take up again

south a coalition excluding the Lega and including the former fascists, Alleanza Nazionale. [Trans.]

the leitmotiv of the discussion. In the second half of the century, politics lost, almost at the same time as did the two historic subjectivities capable of deploying their own force: the masses and the State. How and with what can one substitute these two powerful subjects, these subjective forces? This is the real task that confronts the Left. And that the Left has a future depends substantively on its ability to return subjectivity and force to politics. My idea is that this task can be fulfilled by adopting and conjugating the two great legacies: that of the struggle of the workers' movement, as the high point of the long history of war of subaltern classes, unfortunately not the last one; and the tragically Weberian figure of modern politics, including the history of autonomy and hence sovereignty of the modern State. From here, and only on this basis, can one and must one then go on to innovate profoundly and radically the ideas, forms, places, programmes and means and ends of the action of the Left.

Constitution, organization, collective action. The interweaving of these levels must be advanced politically from above and from outside contemporary civil consciousness, which alone, spontaneously, after centuries of capitalism is no longer capable of producing any serious alternative, dividing itself between animal spirits and good intentions. We do not know which of these two things is the more damaging to the concrete utopia of 'making society' of finally free persons. Can the Left, *on the eve of the third millennium*, give up on adjusting this idea in a form beyond that dramatically exhausted over the twentieth century, drawing the bow to discharge an arrow towards other possible forms, seeking still to shift the balance of power away from the socially dominant ones? Certainly this perspective must be set back on its feet, it must be achieved with the weapons of political realism, taking care of compatibilities—yes—but of historic ones, surveying the geopolitical situation, showing the capacity to convince with the message not with the medium, wining consent—democracy as a method not as a value—without forcing history but guiding it with a wise and secure hand. And so, the present opportunity offered by the centrality of government must be grasped and administered. The Left must draw up a governing force capable of presenting a power to contract with both the objective laws of movement of production and the so-called self-regulating operations of the market, as well as with the neo-corporative fragmentation of interest groups and diffuse social bodies and classes. A European Left should operate analogously in what is now a decisive supranational terrain. Institutional power should be made to weigh politically on the equilibria imposed by the concentration of financial power, by the iron cage of alignments and by the momentum of the locomotive of the economy. How long do we have to wait for a common struggle to be initiated by the Left at the level of Europe? Or is international social conflict no longer even contemplated in the political vocabulary of a Left that calls itself European? A Left fit for government, certainly. But for the Left, is not government not also—I say *also*—the advanced outpost, the most capable, most favourable for the organization of its struggles? Government and opposition are not distinct politics, but two forms of the same politics. And yes, of course the most suitable of these forms today, after the wars and peace of the twentieth century, after that socialism and this capitalism, is to oppose from the height of government. This is not a slogan. It is a strategic programme. To win and retain consent to fulfil this task; this is the Left, after the workers' movement. Only from here, from this politics of responsibility and of conviction might the nobility of doing be revitalized and find expression. To pass back through the Red Sea from political thinking to political action, it is necessary that the waters part before a new exodus and close again over the pursuing army of dominant ideas.

Constitution means to slate for thought and action the great problem of what comes after the State? I repeat, not after the nation-state, that is a problem of the connection between national political power and supranational institutions, which are like duplicates of the world market. Neither is it simply a problem of the State-form as it is posed by the latest developments in the case of Italy.[29] But here too, an anti-historical idea of secession has only been able to appear due to organic weakness, that is, due to the loss of authority of the idea of the State. Still, these are technical problems resolvable with the little politics of today. A problem, on the other hand, whose theoretico-historical solution is difficult—given the wretchedness of current institutional ideas—is that of the search for a supranational State-form. The Europe-State: here is a potentially powerful idea for the Left. European *Kultur*—not *Zivilization*—which becomes State.[30] The rules governing the world economy will not be written by the socialist International of the second millennium or, worse, by the planetary Olive-form.[31] They will be written by the central banks alone on behalf of national capitals, organized according to great spaces, USA, Europe, Pacific. The authorities across the rest of the world will follow. The world Left can realistically attempt to rewrite the rules of political governance only from within and from the base of European civilization. *Socialism*—what this word signalled can be achieved, if it can *still* be achieved, only in one continent. The Left should look courageously at the European world. If there is to be any further political civilization for the world, it cannot but still come from here. Hence, only politics can save us. But the strategic theme is: after the crisis of the modern State, which is the real public consequence of the passage of world civil war, what today is power and what now is politics? The second half of the century was given an inheritance from the first half to which it gave no reply. Surrounding this there is a deafening silence. Neither capitalism nor socialism gave a reply. And naturally, this provoked the

29 The reference is once again to the Northern League's desire to secede from Italy to form the mythical land of Padania. [Trans.]

30 The distinction between a living, organic Kultur and a sterile, mechanical *Zivilization* was a mainstay of early-twentieth-century German thought and is central to Spengler's *The Decline of the West*. [Trans.]

31 Reference is no doubt to the centre-left 'Olive Tree Alliance'. [Trans.]

collapse of socialism rather than of capitalism. This for a series of reasons that we need to understand and that will engage our thinking over the coming years. One point, however, has reached a place of relative clarity: capitalism has been able to limit, control and defeat the totalitarian breach implicit within the nature of the modern state. The liberal tradition understood the Leviathan better than Marxist theory. Conversely: the communist attempt to build socialism bore within its own corpus the theoretical problem of the overcoming of the State. Without a practical solution, or without initiating it, and even with the—forced—overthrow of that viewpoint, the attempt could not succeed. Today the Left poses this problem again in typically minimalist form. Reform of the Welfare State, going beyond the social state without impinging on the universality of rights, privatizing everything while guaranteeing services to the weakest social groups: progressive parish sermons. One thinks one is speaking in new ways about politics by expelling the theme of power. Result: the power that used to be exerted without politics is now exerted against politics. Converting power back into authority or, rather, authority *versus* power: this is the thinking that comes to us from an attentive feminine thought. At least here the problem is confronted. From the idea of difference to the concept of authority is quite a path, especially if one acknowledges that the idea of universal human rights has never been able to drive into crisis the practice of the exclusivity of power. If anything, it has had to reckon with different, authoritative forms of power. The search must be to find political organizational forms that render practicable the passage from the violence of power to the force of authority. The Left must rediscover and provide politics with authority, as well as with subjectivity and force. Governing force is ultimately this: winning in the field of the natural capacity for consent via an elevated form of action; and to enable a shared efficacy of decision to be born here. Not the charismatic personality, but charismatic leading classes. Leaderism imposes itself today via the barbarous civilization of the image more than through the plebiscitary impulses of the mass. The latter are weaker today than they were in the 1920s and 30s, but the primacy of the media over life swells the rivers of dirty water. One should gently withhold from the experts in communications the chance to speak of politics. An authoritative government of human things should no longer need to appeal to a television audience. It could speak simply through the free mediation of different alternative cultures. It is between these that one should instead be called to choose.

Organization and collective action should be tied to constitution, like the form to the idea, the instrument to the objective. When we say, 'constitutive of the new party of the Left', we mean the following: that all the elements are to be put back in their place via a labour of reformulation of both means and ends, with a view to producing a divergence in the collocation of one's own movement and in the situation of one's adversary. The practice of organized politics is yet to be defined. The meaning of organization, of a 'doing together', needs rediscovery, because it is not a potential that is there and needs merely to be given form, as was once the case in the passage from factory to society to politics. It is not simply that the party needs reforming, for the party was but is no longer. If anything, it is to be constructed as if for the first time, along with its forms—structures, militants, leadership—through an intelligent capacity for holding together continuity/discontinuity, which is the duty of all historic movements. The novelty is that these forces must be constructed before they can be represented. Not idealistically created. There is a social material for which the party represents the subjective condition of a political consistency. That is the significance of the phrase: no politics without the party. Here lies the nexus: constitution—organization—action. The idea of a weak party is quite literally inconsistent. If one says that it needs to float on the rippling waves of social complexity, then one may as well give up on the idea of party and think of something else. The party that wanted to exist in society's folds did so in reality as an organized force. The task of the party today is to politically simplify the complexity of society. To simplify means to mobilize. It is not by complexifying society that one produces political action. Complexify to understand, not to act. Never as today is it necessary to distinguish the two planes, that of culture and that of politics. We must retain the richness of cultural diversity's complexity: gathering it, expressing it, describing it, horizontally, empirically—for politics. Politics needs it like it needs the air to breathe, that is, to gauge its own quality, its ability to adhere, to fit its epoch. Let us speak no more of cultural politics. But of political politics in new forms and in the great sense: return/restoration/construction of Politics—of this we must speak again.

It will never happen, perhaps never again, if we do not come back to dividing the one in two, beyond all systemic appearances. In these last two decades of meagre history, feminist political practices are the only ones to have introduced linguistic novelties. We owe to these the creative proposal of a theoretical frontier. After all, it is the same thing to passively accept the fragmentation of subjects as an ineliminable datum and to renounce political subjectivity. The irony: those who enthusiastically sing of a finally achieved majoritarian democracy of alternation, closing the door on the Italian case,[32] are the same who claim that, for the good of all, the end of all social dichotomies has been

32 By the Italian case, Tronti is no doubt referring to what in Italy is known as the *anomalia italiana*, i.e. that of a large, nominally liberal, democratic, industrial nation, which for much of the postwar period was under international 'tutelage'. The effects of this were perverse: constant changes of government, where the same figures returned again and again, and where the second biggest party—the PCI—was never permitted to form part of the multiple coalition governments; where politics was everywhere, yet political change never happened at the level of the control of the state; a nation that contained not one state, but three: the national government, the Vatican, and organized crime—yet none of these domestic powers having a free hand on the peninsula. [Trans.]

achieved. Those who discover political conflict are the same who hide social conflict. Those who condemn consociationalism between parties are the same who celebrate class conciliation. This is the royal road to the destruction of politics. And, I believe, the path to a new corruption of politicians, one that is more subtle, internal, of conscience. And not only in the 'bad' Italy, but also in the 'beautiful' Europe. Not to speak of the great powers, where finally the new has arrived, or of great powers in vogue where this new is centuries old. Two political camps either mobilize around two great partisan interests competing over who is better able to care, from their differing standpoints, for the general interest and stand in conflict over this; or each is a formal fiction, and together they establish a merely virtual alternative. True political alternation rests on great alternatives in the modelling of society. The definitive breakdown of the political centre calls upon the political decomposition of the social centre, of that viscous aggregation of daily compromises of corporative interests, which in their concord produce a humoral consent to those who represent them as they are. Should one pursue and represent that same moderatism just as it is, or should it not rather be dissolved and radicalized in the form of alternative democratic choices? The plebiscitary drive has changed: the so-called ordinary people[33] ask for a

33 The term *la gente* (or *la gens* in French) has no obvious translation other than 'people' in English. This of course would make the distinction between *la gente* and *il popolo* impossible in English. As Tronti goes on to argue, the idea of *la gente* is best understood in contrast to the concept of 'the people'. The latter has a much longer and more significant conceptual and political genealogy, linked to the period of the bourgeois revolutions but also to anti-colonial struggles (although it also has its reactionary uses; see Asor Rosa, *The Writer and the People*). Where 'the people' is a noble idea, one of popular struggle from below, national liberation and the like, *la gente* (folk, ordinary people) are merely scattered individuals, atomistic and self-orientated. The 'masses', on the other hand, are most obviously those that emerge from the twentieth-century processes of industrialization, mass production and consumption, and of urban concentration. To mark the distinction, I have opted to

leader not so that he alone can decide, but so he can represent them. To decompose the idea of ordinary people, to divide *le pensée unique*, to relate bodies, classes, individuals to their substantive interests and reassemble society into two poles, that is what politics does, what it must do. That is an example of true reform. It is only possible to recover the authority of politics on this basis. The subject of an authoritative partisan politics and a future party of the Left are for me the same thing.

In contrast to what many believe, the totalitarian societies of the twentieth century have little in common, perhaps only one thing: the conception of politics as total mobilization. The form of 'one party [state]' is self-contradictory. The model lay in the relation between the nation-state and its people in the face of the world war. But, by definition, the party cannot be of all the people, of the entire nation. Unless, as today, there is the phenomenon of religious fundamentalism. This seems to be the only residual form of totalizing politics. But it is not the sole one and it is not a residual form. Today, voluntary total mobilization expresses itself best in the political outcomes of contemporary democracies. And it is not simply a question of plebiscitary temptations, of preferences for leaderism or decisionist short cuts. These are *consequentia rerum*. For when competing political currents in government come together to agree that there is one, only one possible form of social organization, what is this if not a totalizing solution to the problem? Prior to the decision on the merits of single issues, when it comes to the formulation of the deceive political order of the day, the Agora's acclamation has already taken place in the halls of power [*il Palazzo*].[34] For politics, what needs to be overthrown is not the concept of mobilization but that of totality. The model of the organized working class was that of partial [*parziale*]

---

translate *gente* as 'ordinary people', as in 'the ordinary man or women in the street'. [Trans.]

34 See p. 100n13 above. [Trans.]

mobilization in the figure of the political party that comes at the end of a long series of associative, cooperative, mutual aid and trade-union experiences. Mobilization of a non-minoritarian part [*parte*] of society, first in defence of one's conditions, then in solidarity with other struggles, followed by a claim to autonomy, and finally as a project to win power. This was an uphill struggle in all senses. One could find there a prophetic energy, now lost, towards the human condition in a society pervaded by egotism and exploitation, standing against it and ending up giving a new meaning to modern politics, one no longer composed of power, the law courts, the prince, the domination of the few over the many and over all others. This created popular support and conviction, a culture of alternative elites and common sense among antagonistic masses without which there was no bridging past and future. The social and political Left cannot traverse the present and change it, other than by presenting itself symbolically in its party as a historic movement. This is its strongest weapon. Within the *longue durée*, capitalism must be seen as contingent, as emergent, an occasion to be overcome or to be used, it comes to the same. To expend great ideas over the short term is fine. To expend small ideas over the long term is not. In the first case, great politics takes the form of tactics; not in the second. The general secretary of the PCI in opposition could allow himself to be *totus politicus*: behind him was political force, a world of ideas, a people of believers and, something that doesn't hurt, a powerful block with military force. And to those who say that from sometime back the PCI should have broken with this, I say: please, take up something else, take up charity work. Certainly, however, the general secretary of the Left party of government cannot be *totus politicus*; behind and surrounding him is a dangerous vacuum.[35] People say: but there's electoral support. There is, a modest amount.

35 At the time of writing, Italy had for the first time in its history, parties that were the heirs of the PCI in government (while the PCI had renounced its communist affiliations). These legislatures ran from 1996 to 2001. [Trans.]

Well, modest electoral support never made history on its own. It never did anything but provide alternation in governments, with no other consequences. If this is the end, then there is no longer any need for there to be any follow up to modern politics, better to break with it and move on to game theory. The responses of history have rightly charged us with winning back the reality principle. But my impression is that already we are beyond this and find ourselves urgently needing to bend the stick the other way. Furthermore, political contingency, i.e. having finally entered government, demands that we look for a different spread of possibilities, of thought, if of nothing else. It is the reason why some of us need to play Jiminy Cricket. Or, while one often calls for thinking over the long term, one ends up providing only short-term actions. Forceful ideas are necessary. They are needed to render visible possibilities, to set passions in motion, to provoke, to motivate and direct hope, exodus to somewhere else. A Left without myths will be a poor, colourless, distant, cold and in the end useless Left. Degenerations, failures, breakdowns did not stem from the fact that the impossible was attempted, but that at a certain point the impossible was abandoned.

The 'lofty spirit' and 'far-reaching aims' are two qualities that Machiavelli ascribed to the Duke Valentino.[36] Perhaps today the Gramscian image of the party as collective intellectual is no longer appropriate: because of the unsalvageable political function of culture and, moreover, the impossibility of giving it a social inflection. Intellectual work persists as inner testimony of time, as speaking truthfully about one's own side [*parte*] and the world, as in *cultiver son jardin* to one's best ability in a hostile society. Gramsci's other suggestion, however, that of the party-as-Prince seems to me to assume contemporary relevance: even though everyone is willing to find signs to the contrary

36 See Machiavelli's discussion of Cesare Borgia, known as Duke Valentino, from Chapter 7 of *The Prince*. [Trans.]

and, perhaps, precisely for this reason. The lesson of political realism tells the Left that it must now row against the tide of the epoch. The long 'progressive era'[37] is long gone. Everything, thoughts and actions, the sensitivity of the masses and the unconscious of the individual, all are marked by a widespread counter-revolution. If one reads the destiny of the political party, one finds the word: *end*. The end of the idea of party risks carrying with it the idea of the Left. It is against its very destiny that the Left must struggle.

37 In English in the original. [Trans.]

Five Movements

POLITIK ALS BERUF: THE END

Let us start with this quotation: 'Politics is founded on the fact of human plurality. God created *man*, but *men* are a human [. . .] product.'[1] This is a thought of Hannah Arendt's. It is the beginning of a posthumously published lecture fragment from 1950, *Was ist Politik*?. Political thinking at the time had behind it the Holocaust and the Bomb, around it the Cold War, ahead of it two great illusions, Democracy and Communism. Politics was trapped in this iron cage. There was no crisis of politics. On the contrary, it was to it that one turned to resolve the big problems. With trust that it could resolve them. This is the reason for Man and *men*.

Arendt says: philosophy and theology, and science too, are always concerned only with Man. Were there only one man, or only identical men, it would be the same. Philosophical, theological or scientific discourse would all stand on their own feet. Schmitt's and Peterson's debate on political theology was also about this. I don't doubt that both political philosophy and political science, while using different methods, reduce men to man. For this reason, they are incapable of answering the question: what is politics? Who then answers this question? Politics itself does. Once again: *die Politik* and *das Politische*. It is not only the

In German and English in the original. *Politik als Beruf* is the original title of Max Weber's 'Politics as a Vocation' lecture in 1919. [Trans.]

1 Hannah Arendt, 'Introduction *into* Politics' in *The Promise of Politics* (New York: Schocken Books, 2005), p. 93. Throughout this chapter I have retained Arendt's gendered language of the lecture. [Trans.]

distinction between political praxis and a criterion of judgement, between political practice and a category of the political. For me, this distinction is the way in which the twentieth century has adjusted the relationship between tactics and strategy, between necessities dictated by immediacy and the freedom won for the long term. The contemporary idea of the autonomy of the political is not the same as the modern idea of the autonomy of the political. But on this point I abandon all hope of being understood.

Let us begin again with two statements by Arendt. The first: 'Politics arises *between men*, and so quite *outside* of *man*.' There is no *zoon politikon*: it is false to say that there is within man, as part of his essence, a political element. 'Politics arises in what lies *between men* and is established as relationships. Hobbes understood this.'[2] The second statement reads: 'At the center of politics lies concern for the world, not for man.'[3] To posit man at the centre of present preoccupations and to maintain that he must be changed to redress the problem is a 'truly apolitical' attitude.[4] 'The aim of politics is to change or conserve or establish a world.'[5] So what is politics? It is to put men into relation with one another, with reference to a preoccupation with the world. Politics–relation, politics–world. Still a question of politics and the political? Yes, partly. Practice and project: action with its laws, and the horizon with its objectives. Contingency and freedom: perhaps, at the end of the century, the sense of politics should be inflected thus. For if the problem is how to expend great ideas over the short term, the search for a solution sends us back to the history of time, the long arc of the twentieth century and the narrowing of its end.

2 Arendt, 'Introduction *into* Politics', p. 95.

3 Arendt, 'Introduction *into* Politics', p. 106.

4 Arendt, 'Introduction *into* Politics', p. 98.

5 Hannah Arendt, *Was ist Politik? Fragmente aus dem Nachlass* (Ursula Ludz ed.) (Munich: Piper, 1993), p. 191.

We must free politics from the weight of necessity. It is this weight that has introduced into politics the elements of crisis. Over the course of the century, politics not only assumes the burden of the history of men but also of the life of man: man, who has seen his life flung into total war, the victim of menacing, dark, overpowering forces, is also forced to become the subject of great ideological undertakings, only to then have to weigh up within them the harsh reality of quotidian relationships. We must say that, unfortunately, within the century, politics has also concerned itself with man, the one with the capital M; and with the single man, the solitary one who grapples with himself, independently of his having wanted to participate in the history of the world, of having freely decided to enter relations with men. A tragic condition, because driven by powers that were, in their own way, superhuman: the human condition of the twentieth century. The dialogue in Malraux's *La Condition Humaine*: ' "What political faith can account for man's suffering?" asks the pastor. And the answer of the revolutionary: "I am more anxious to diminish it than to account for it." '[6] Between this question and this reply, politics left and returned, it left itself and returned to itself, to the point of loss that now strikes and kills it. The twentieth century has revealed the two faces of politics: the demonic face of power, and the sacralized one of commitment. This time, *Macht-Gewalt* on one side, choice of life and commitment on the other. Monsters and saints have entered politics, pushed there by history. It has been possible to read, and it was possible to write, *Mein Kampf* and *Lettere dei condannnati a morte della Resistenza*.[7] The same nation produced Goebbels and Bonhoeffer. It was a great century of great contrasts.

6 André Malraux, *Man's Fate* (Haakon M. Chevalier trans.) (New York: Modern Library, 1934), p. 177.

7 *Letters of the Condemned to Death of the Resistance* (Piero Malvezzi and Giovanni Pirelli eds) (Turin: Einaudi, 1945[1952]). This is a collection of the last letters Italian Resistance fighters, dated between 8 September 1943 to 25 April 1945, written to friends and loved ones shortly before facing Nazi or Fascist firing squads. [Trans.]

Politics and contingency. Two communicating and incommunicable worlds. The daily clash of contradictions that ask to be repaired. The capacity to dominate the short term during its disordered flow. Contingency is the real place of politics. The problem that breaks in and the solution that presses forth: there lies the measure of political action. Of its quality. The politics of the day-to-day is great politics. The quotidian crushes the qualities of politics only when it is the mediocre politician who acts. That is, nearly always. Hence, it is true that, typically, what one sees is the dialectic of small actions and the blind daily acts that are prisoner of the here and now. It is true that one tends to load each moment with epochal meaning. It is true that the easiest thing to do is to lose the thread of history while doing politics, and so it is the most frequent. But when from the contingent situation there emerges the need for great action, when from necessity arises decision, then one has true politics, that which it is worth being there for. The reverse is not true: to have a project, to prepare it, cultivate it, to be conscious of it and not to deem it worthwhile measuring it against events. To claim one possesses political truth, to own it and misunderstand it is the original sin of all revolutionary attempts. And it is the internal fault that has always led to the failure of those attempts. Absolute politics is modern politics. The twentieth century raised it to its unbearable limit and to the emphatic tragedy of the final solution or to forced emancipation. Then the absolute of politics nosily collapsed, overwhelming with the fall of the walls the very meaning of politics as well as its relational character, the relativity of inter-human relations which always rest upon the dubious consistency of the human quality of subjects that practice it and of those who suffer it.

Open parenthesis. François Furet says: 'A mysterious evil was at work in the political ideas of the twentieth century.'[8] However, this is so

8 François Furet, *The Passing of an Illusion: The Idea of Communism in the Twentieth Century* (Deborah Furet trans.) (Chicago: University of Chicago Press, 1999), p. 29.

in both the first and second half of the century: in the shape of a greater evil that we fought, and a lesser evil that we endured. Why do historians write that the history of the century stopped in 1945? Why do they lack the courage to say that what followed is morally worse than what took place before, since it included fewer, increasingly fewer, conscious acts, fewer life choices and assumptions of responsibility? Better Nolte than Furet. At least, the former has a strong thesis that can be opposed: the equivalence of Nazism and Bolshevism; or rather, the revisionist thesis that justifies Nazism as reaction to Bolshevism. In contrast, Furet's 'democratic' thesis goes as follows: 'Fascism was born as a reaction against Communism. Communism prolonged its tenancy thanks to anti-Fascism.'[9] As far as quality, his statement is one for textbooks of civic miseducation; as for its substance, it is the tale of his illusion and his 'unfortunate engagement', or better, of his 'erstwhile blindness'.[10] After all, Eric Hobsbawm's 'short [twentieth] century' (1914–1991), closes with T. S. Eliot's: 'this is the way the world ends / Not with a bang but a whimper'.[11] By taking on this prescient sentiment of the poet, the historian can say:

> The destruction of the past, or rather of the social mechanisms that links one's contemporary experience to that of earlier generations, is one of the most characteristic and eerie phenomena of the late twentieth century. Most young men and women at the century's end grow up in a sort of permanent present lacking any organic relation to the public past of the times they live in.[12]

---

9 Furet, *Passing of an Illusion*, p. 24.

10 Furet, *Passing of an Illusion*, p. *xi*.

11 *The Age of Extremes: The Short Twentieth Century, 1914–1991* (London: Abacus, 1994), p. 12. T. S. Eliot's poem is, of course, 'The Hollow Men' (1925). [Trans.]

12 Hobsbawm, *Age of Extremes*, p. 3.

But can politics forgo the history that produced it? Here lies the difficulty of the problem. Politics' loss of meaning and the ruinous collapse of historical consciousness are as one. The empty emphasis on the new sinks its extremely fragile roots here. Indeed, politics wanders confusedly in a way not seen at other times. The exception—Schmitt was wont to say—is more interesting than the normal situation. And today, politics does not need to respond to a state of historic exceptionalism. It is politics itself that finds itself in its own state of exception. This exceptionalism must in turn be inflected. For example, there is nothing tragic about it in its conduct, in its discourse. And this is a grave limit. The great politics of the twentieth century is dead. Many revel in this because they impute the tragedies of the century to that idea of politics. But that was not great politics, it was bad politics. I know this involves a debatable ethical judgement. But the world civil war and its results, the Holocaust and the Bomb—which led Arendt to present anew the question: what is politics?—justify this judgement. The great politics of the century was the other one. It was the two revolutions, the workers' revolution and the conservative revolution, between which was the 'Great Crash', the period of its incubation from 1914 to 1929 and the capitalist response of the 1930s. Here contingency and politics, chance and action, state of exception and decision encounter themselves again, refer one to the other and are fused. The opposite of today. The century is extinguished in the victory of little politics: a long decadence, an interminable drift, a collective human inconsistency of political classes, institutions, programmes; actions without thought, without future, and a present transfixed before the empty image of itself.

If sovereign is he who decides on the exception,[13] then who decides today, not within politics but about politics? It is precisely this that is

13 This is an unreferenced quotation from Carl Schmitt's *Political Theology* (Chicago: University of Chicago Press, 1985), p. 5. [Trans.]

unknown. Politics no longer has sovereignty over its territory. It has been invaded, conquered, subjugated. He who does politics today—who governs or wishes to get into government—knows that hardly anything in his decision lies in his hands. Economic compatibilities are like an iron cage around political action. The rules of the supranational market and the logics of international finance close all space of movement for the life of the nation-state. Geoeconomics replaces geopolitics. The technologies of communication void of all significance the attention for the public interest and management of the public sphere. 'How to say' replaces 'what is to be done'. The decay of the political classes, reduced to masks without brains; the crumbling of political personality, without profession or vocation; reducing conflict and agreement to private chatter. Dramatically, although not tragically, the subject of 'politics and destiny' returns at the end of the twentieth century. In the mid-1990s, the problem Karl Löwith posed in the mid-1930s returns resolved: 'is the manner in which the political gets understood by one of its active participants defined by "fate", or is this manner of understanding perhaps regulated by *factical occurrences*?'[14] Problem solved: because at this point those who actively participate, the political class in the figure of the political personality, are no longer inclined to conceive of the 'political' as 'destiny' but simply guided by what de facto takes place. If from Marx to Schmitt—as Löwith argues—what happened was that faith in a conceptual discussion had given way before a theory of direct action and there had taken place an 'inversion of philosophical insight into the essence of politics, so that such insight became an intellectual instrument of political action', what happens post-Schmitt and to this day? That is, not since the 1980s but since the 1950s. On this, the discussion remains open, the analysis still imprecise and reflections extremely underdeveloped. The

14 Karl Löwith, 'The Occasional Decisionism of Carl Schmitt' in *Martin Heidegger and European Nihilism* (Richard Wolin ed.) (New York: Columbia University Press, 1995), p. 156.

dissolution of the great readings of the present, that of Western Marxism, that of political Catholicism and even that of classical liberalism, have created a vacuum of thought at the heart of Europe which has resulted in a general crisis of political culture. The practices that referred to these currents have persisted, even sometimes successfully, but without intellectual self-awareness, lacking a presentable strategic framework, incapable of producing a future, and ultimately victims of traditionalist revanchism camouflaging as apparently irresistible novelty. With the overthrow of all the accounts of what should have happened, only mediocre images of what in fact happened remain standing.

Today it is not a case of concluding the parabola of the modern. Neither is it a case of readying oneself to passively represent the so-called postmodern. The problem—not the project—is rather to establish the labour of consciously overcoming modernity. Leo Strauss wrote to Karl Löwith on 15 August 1946: 'We agree today that we need historical reflection—only I assert that it is neither a progress nor a fate to submit to with resignation, but is an unavoidable means for the overcoming of modernity.'[15] And Löwith replies to Strauss, 18 August 1946: 'You say, one cannot overcome modernity with modern means. That sounds plausible but seems to me only correct with qualifications [. . .]. After all, the discontent of modernity with itself exists only on the basis of historical consciousness, of the knowledge of other and "better" times; and where this consciousness is lost—as with the generation born after 1910 in Russia and the one born after 1930 in Germany, modernity is also not perceived any longer as something to be overcome—on the contrary.'[16] Today we are dealing with different generations: either the one born after 1945 in Italy, or after 1968 in the West more widely. But

15 Leo Strauss and Karl Löwith, 'Correspondence concerning modernity', *The Independent Journal of Philosophy* 4 (1983): 107.

16 Strauss and Löwith, 'Correspondence concerning modernity': 110.

the matter remains the same, or rather, it is still more serious. Subordination to modernity has become public opinion, widespread and prevalent, intellectual common sense. All that which seeks to present itself as a critique of modernity falls into the category of the ancient. The new is exclusively in the hands of the old forces that have dominated the modern age. So, who now remains repository of that historical consciousness on the basis of which one is able to rebuild and launch the notion of 'other and better' times?

The distinction between epoch and phase falls here. And it does so at a point that is certainly not only that of political language. If the epoch, let's say the twentieth century, experienced the primacy of the masses in politics, the phase—and the present one is one of the many that the epoch traverses—sees the primacy of ordinary people. The emergence, prevalence, the incursion of this term is relatively recent. It is a generic term, like the politics that enunciate it. It lacks theoretical depth, analytical force or definitional capacity. It is a propaganda terrain for marketing objects, not a terrain for action by political subjects. 'Ordinary people' does not mean classes, not masses, not even 'the people'; it is closer to the idea of a television 'audience'[17] than to that of public opinion. This century of ours has been, among other things, the century of the entrance of the masses into politics. Active masses, organized masses, manipulated masses. 'Mass' not 'pack'. Man—says Canetti in *Crowds and Power*—'was a beast of prey, though one which never wanted to be solitary.'[18] 'Men have learnt from wolves.' The 'word "pack" [. . .] best expresses the joint and swift movement involved, and the concreteness of the goal in view.' A behaviour very similar to that of

17 In English in the original. [Trans.]

18 Elias Canetti, *Crowds and Power* (Carol Stewart trans.) (New York: Continuum, 1978), p. 108. It is important to note that the Italian is translated as *Masse e potere* (*Masse und Macht*, in the original). I have therefore kept 'mass' and 'masses' where the English speaks of 'crowds'. [Trans.]

so-called people. 'The pack wants its prey. [. . .] In order to attain what it's after, it must have speed. [. . .] It urges itself on with its joint clamour [. . .].'[19] In fact, the most natural and genuine pack is the hunting pack. Immediately after that comes the one that depends upon another pack that it stands against, the war pack. For Canetti, 'mass' is many things. Where this concept most approaches the concept of class is in the description of 'prohibition masses'. This is an example of a negative mass: 'a large number of people together refuse to continue to do what, till then, they had done singly.'[20] The example is that of a strike. In the exercise of productive activity, the equality of workers is insufficient to determine the formation of the mass. It is the interruption of this exercise, the refusal to continue to work that triggers this process. 'The moment of standstill is a great moment, and has been celebrated in workers' songs.'[21] Because here their fictitious equality becomes suddenly real. 'But, when they stop work, they all do the same thing. It is as though their hands had all dropped at exactly the same moment and now they had to exert all their strength not to lift them up again [. . .] Stopping work makes the workers equals.' These hands that drop influence those of others by contagion. 'Their inaction spreads to the whole of society.' To continue usual activities becomes impossible even for those who to start with did not think to interrupt it. 'The sense of a strike is that others should do nothing while the workers are idle.' It is in this way that from the mass itself 'rises up a mass organization'.[22]

In the second half of the century, the democratic mass-human won out: a historically unprecedented figure born in the American heart of the West, as the European Tocqueville had glimpsed with some disquiet. For that historic figure to win definitively, it had to win three world

19 Canetti, *Crowds and Power*, p. 96.

20 Canetti, *Crowds and Power*, p. 55.

21 Canetti, *Crowds and Power*, p. 56.

22 Canetti, *Crowds and Power*, p. 57 (translation modified).

wars, or, more correctly, one single civil war running from 1914 to 1989 in World-Europe. The democracies unified themselves under the centrality, hegemony, the cult, or rather the religion of this type of average individual. From this followed a macroscopic process of decadence of politics, the consequences of which confront us today in their entirety. Corruption, in the pathological forms that this eternal phenomenon has assumed, is not the cause but the consequence of that process, one of its consequences. The anti-political common sense which dominates so-called civil society, sanctions not the reactionary reduction of 'the people' to ordinary people so much as the suicide of modern politics. There is no longer a Prince, which is to say, in the terms of contemporary history, there is no longer a collective political subject. For this reason, all institutional solutions are unable to resolve the problems of government, and political systems are unable to rediscover authority and have lost power. Instead, lacking personality, they entrust themselves to the search for *a* personality, while political programmes are subordinated to the efficacy of the message and political currents must reckon with public opinion no longer, for they obey a public without opinion. Parties, like governments, no longer win consent but concede it, and they do so either to non-political powers or to privatized masses. Ironically, the classical historical division between governors and governed has not been overcome by communism but suppressed by democracy: in this sense, today, even the governors are governed. For example: the Left that goes into government is not the governing but the governed Left. Democracy is no longer a value to be affirmed, because democracies have suppressed politics, which is to say, the way humans relate to one another; and they have done so without dealing with Man again but, on the contrary, by reducing men and women definitively to atomistic technico-economic entities. *Homo democraticus* is *homo oeconomicus* in the age of neutralization and depoliticization.[23]

---

23 Tronti's reference is to Carl Schmitt's 1929 essay, 'The Age of Neutralizations and

Let us say man, men, and the word, the concept is now unsayable. Politics has used these terms, then it has ideologically, democratically, abused them. Politics has been killed in their name too. The non-recognition of the complexity of human beings, of their inner conflictuality, of their differentiated duality, has impoverished the forms of intra-human relations; it has denied them of the symbolic order essential to their very existence, which is lived life, incarnated thought, experiences and practices. Luisa Muraro spoke of the current impracticability of *caritas*, as the problem that 'concerns the shared practices, those which alone make their mark on living together and that form culture.'[24] The 'suffering of the social body' expresses this need to do, in the sense of being able-to-be-for the other and in the sense of wanting to-be-in-common. These two social dimensions are currently beyond possibility and will. We have built a society that permits these practices and these desires for the Sunday heroism of the individual, not for daily collective practice. Muraro goes on to say: '*caritas* is the Christian name, the Western name of pity, which is to say, of the intersection between human history and its surplus, its excess, its hope, its "searching further", its god [. . .] you choose the word.' Politics, in what way can it begin again to concern itself with the beyond here and now? 'Once again', because in the past, even in the twentieth century, this tension has existed, this inner drive to go beyond the necessary context of action, bearing subjectively into contingency the occasion for a reading of historical destiny. And even if it were the case of taking up a path of this type, why not attempt it? Politics now needs to take a wager upon itself. *The Politics of*

Depoliticizations', which was a lecture then published in the second edition of *The Concept of the Political*. An English translation, 'The Age of Neutralizations and Depoliticizations', can be found in the journal *Telos* 96 (1993): 130–42. [Trans.]

24 This and the following Muraro quote: Luisa Muraro, 'Quello che ci trova impreparati', *Bailamme* 17 (1995): 284–92.

Desire, reads the title of a book by Lia Cigarini.[25] And the introduction by Ida Dominijanni reads: 'The Desire of Politics': 'becoming petrified, we know that it is from the male side that desire has given way, and it is on that side that the unnamed delicate but tenacious thread that links it to politics [. . .] Political work will consist in this for the foreseeable future: propelling female desire anew, bringing into play male desire and self-consciousness.'[26] If politics has to this point been the form of male action, is the crisis of forms that puts its destiny in question perhaps the occasion for the overcoming of the modern Political? Let us leave this question open and reflect on it. Dominijanni continues: 'Once sexual difference has put in question the notion of the individual and of the subject that supports the constellation of the Political in the West, all the other categories of this constellation—equality, representation, majority, decision, power—are challenged, one after another.'[27] That is where we are. The concepts of the political no longer answer to the command of politics. The machine lacks a subject to drive it. Current history is at the mercy of itself. What can be done to continue to think politics?

25 Lia Cigarini, *La politica del desiderio* (Ida Dominijanni introd.) (Parma: Nuova Pratiche Editrice, 1995).

26 Cigarini, *La politica del desiderio*, p. 38.

27 Cigarini, *La politica del desiderio*, p. 26.

THE PRINCE AND UTOPIA

Modern history is founded upon stellar political coincidences. On 10 December 1513, Machiavelli wrote to Vettori about the pamphlet he had composed called *De principatibus*, a 'whimsy' on 'what a principality is, of what kinds they are, how they are acquired, how they are maintained, why they are lost'.[1] In December 1516, in Louvain, Thomas More published *Libellus vere aureus nec minus salutaris quam festinus de optimo reipublicae statu, deque noua Insula Utopia authore clarissimo viro Thoma Moro*. But the first years of *De principatibus* ran precisely from 1513 to 1516, as is apparent by—among other things—the change in the dedication from Giuliano to Lorenzo de' Medici.[2] Hence, Machiavelli's *The Prince* and More's *Utopia* are contemporaneous. Together, they are modern politics. The man who at the time was secretary of the Florentine Republic and the future chancellor of England presented two faces to the newly reborn political body. Between the Oricellari Gardens[3] and the Tudor court, the issue was how to recompose the relationship between

1 See Giorgio Inglese, *Introduzione a 'Il Principe'* (Turin: Einaudi 1995).

2 A translation of this famous letter is available at: https://bityl.co/OXOu (last accessed 18 May 2024). [Trans.]

3 These were the famous gardens of Bernardo Rucellai that formed a sort of sixteenth-century intellectual salon that proved so important to the development of the Italian language, literature and thinking of the Renaissance. See Felix Gilbert, 'Bernardo Rucellai and the Orti Oricellari: A Study on the Origin of Modern Political Thought', *Journal of the Warburg and Courtauld Institutes* 12 (1949): 101–31. [Trans.]

men in society, through what political means, under what forms of state. In both cases, the discourse was propositive. The sixteenth century opened the modern era with its own 'what is to be done'. It is the same thing to speak of what is or what ought to be, of actual reality or of the place that is not. It serves to say what must be done. And so, from here on, this is how it would be for political thought: implicated in the immediate practice of action, using and bending to this practice the examples of the past and images of the future, paying a price on both levels—that of the existence of the thinker and the consistency of thought. Machiavelli and More would end up two condemned men. And the work: in the end, it must sacrifice rigour to effectiveness, profundity to style, the truth of the enquiry to the utility of the argument. The greatest political thinkers are those who are aware of this destiny and do not fear realizing it.

It's a good exercise, to read these two texts together. A comparative reading? No. Complementary? Yes. Novel insights follow from this complementarity. Opposed concepts come together and conflict without uniting. Human figures of thought are expressed. Parallel lives of the modern. From here a path flows and spreads that also arrives at an end without a beyond, traversing phases of advance and retreat. Here we find the example of how one spark is lit in the contact between the beginning and end, with the time in-between left to scholars to explore. There is nothing more illuminating than the *incipit* of modern politics for grasping the drabness of its death. The nexus between realism and utopia is built at the start of the sixteenth century. It is untrue that Machiavelli alone, from *The Prince* to *The Discourses*, dictated the paradigm of modern politics as a whole. The other dimension, the island of Utopia, is essential for the completion of this design. The daring description of modern political action immediately called alongside it for the imaginary prescription of another world. Then the two aspects became separated in the dichotomous schema that presided over the construction and conservation of modern societies: realism to the ruling classes, utopia to the subaltern classes. The proof that the workers' movement was a great subject of modern politics lies in the fact that, within it, at least from the time of Marx's scientific oeuvre onwards, the two separated, contradictory aspects, the realist grasp of reality and the utopian impetus towards the future, held together. The two sides [*parti*] had each attempted a mediation and a synthesis, in the epoch of the bourgeois revolutions and the epoch of the proletarian revolutions. Liberally using the meaning that Mannheim gave to the terms 'ideology' and 'utopia', we can say that ideology and ideological apparatuses, the knowing false consciousness produced for the masses and the intellectuals, was the attempt to unify realism and utopia, to dialectically overcome the contradiction. It showed thought at its worst. The rights of man as the disguise for bourgeois interests and the idea of general class foisted onto the workers to mask the practice of a neo-oligarchic power are midway episodes to be studied and then forgotten. Better to return to the divergence and coexistence of the beginnings.

Burkhardt and Meinecke explained how the idea of the Reason of State took a path that was relatively autonomous from its origin in Machiavelli, as it adapted to the two Reformations: Protestant and Catholic. Giovanni Botero (1589) says that reason of state tells of the means for the conservation and then the expansion, but only in the last instance of the foundation of dominion, for the 'reason of state presupposes a prince and a state'.[4] The ways of founding presuppose a will to conquer. And political reason precedes the reason of state. This is Machiavelli. But the more daring the means, the more noble the end. And against the politics of states as they are, one must construct the model of an island that does not exist. This is More. The interlacing is

4 Giovanni Botero, *The Reason of State* (Cambridge: Cambridge University Press, 2017), p. 4.

profound. Book Two, with the story of the laws and behaviours of the Utopians, was thought out before Book One, with its critique of events in England. After 1510, while More narrated the noble gestures of Utopus, Machiavelli was describing the wicked activities of Duke Valentino—each doing so with admiration for his hero. 'I would not know of any better precepts to give to a new prince than the example of his deeds'.[5] 'They say that from the beginning the whole city was planned by Utopus himself, but that he left to posterity matters of adornment and improvement.'[6] This is the double Prince of modern politics: the one is to be found in the manner of killing of Vitellozzo Vitelli, Oliverotto da Fermo, Messer Pagodo and the Duke Garavina Orsini; the other lies in the tale of the voyage of Raphael Hythloday concerning the form of a state 'that is not only very happy, but also [. . .] likely to last forever'.[7] 'Having wiped out these leaders.'[8] The 'structure of that commonwealth which I consider not only the best but indeed the only one that can rightfully claim that name.'[9] And the distinction is not the simple naive one between the practical actions of the prince and the justification given to the people. Were it only that, Savonarola's sermons would be sufficient to throw light on the deceit. In reality, it is a case of two practices or, rather, two theory-practices developed and realized for the same ends. Those are not yet the words chosen, the concepts are not yet mature. It will be necessary to go through the rupture of Christianity, through the civil wars of religion to come to the season of the great political seventeenth century, with the problem that Europe takes upon itself for the West: how to draw order from chaos, political order from social conflict.

5 Machiavelli, *Prince*, p. 25.

6 Thomas More, *Utopia* (Cambridge: Cambridge University Press, 2002), p. 46.

7 More, *Utopia*, p. 106.

8 Machiavelli, *Prince*, p. 26.

9 More, *Utopia*, p. 103.

A Prince, therefore, must not have any other object nor any other thought, nor must he adopt anything as his art but war, its institutions, and its discipline; because that is the only art befitting one who commands. This discipline is of such efficacy that not only does it maintain those who were born princes, but it enables men of private station on many occasions to rise to that position. On the other hand, it is evident that when princes have given more thought to delicate refinements than to military concerns, they have lost their state. The most important reason why you lose it is by neglecting this art, while the way to acquire it is to be well versed in this art.[10]

They utterly despise war as an activity fit only for beasts yet practised more by man than by any other animal. Unlike almost every other people in the world, they think nothing so inglorious as the glory won in battle. Yet on certain assigned days, both men and women carry on vigorous military training, so they will be fit to fight should the need arise. But they go to war only for good reasons: to protect their own land, to drive invading armies from the territories of their friends, or to liberate an oppressed people, in the name of compassion and humanity, from tyranny and servitude.[11]

Among the other bad effects it brings with it, being unarmed makes you contemptible [. . .] Between an armed and an unarmed man, there is no comparison whatsoever [. . .] never take his mind from this exercise of war, and in peacetime he must train himself more than in time of war.[12]

10 Machiavelli, *Prince*, p. 50.

11 More, *Utopia*, p. 85.

12 Machiavelli, *Prince*, p. 51.

> The Utopians are not only troubled but ashamed when their forces gain a bloody victory [. . .] They boast that they have really acted with manly and virile bravery when they have won a victory such as no animal except man could achieve—a victory gained by strength of understanding.[13]

From the sixteenth to the twentieth centuries, modern politics displays both these aspects of war. War as the continuation of politics by other means can be carried out, and has been, in either of these ways. Criminal war and *bellum justum* are forms of politics. Forms perfectly suited to the stage of modern development of the human social relationship. They do not exhaust the horizon of the public sphere, nor do they encompass the full complexity of human existence in the history of modern society. But they constitute an ineliminable, and indeed uneliminated, part of it. If one goes from the Machiavellian art of war to the explosion of armed conflicts, they always occurred with the aim of civilizing war. The *jus publicum europaeum* presided over the civilizing of war between states. Only the civil wars escaped these civil forms of legalized violence between states. The twentieth century broke with a tradition and destroyed and dissolved forms. It radicalized the two options of war, improperly setting them in opposition, as only war or only peace. The crescendo of the world civil wars, the reduction of civil war to world war or celebration of it as world war, and vice versa, cancelled all forms of civilizing of war, starting from the theatre of total confrontation through to the scene of daily life. Terrorism inherits the criminality of war. To pacificism remains the residue of the just war. In 'peacetime he must train himself more than in time of war', is the notable condition of the Cold War. The Gulf War is instead the classic philanthropic war. Thomas More is only bearable alongside Machiavelli, and perhaps Hobbes. Hexter places More the 'realist' alongside other writer-politicians engaged in both practical

13 More, *Utopia*, p. 86.

and theoretical politics, and often charged with high roles of office: 'Sir John Fortesque, Lord Chief Justice of England, Philippe de Comynes and Calude Syessel, one diplomat and one advisor to Louis XI, the other Louis XII, and Niccolò Machiavelli, secretary to the Florentine Republic', were all animated by 'a vivid and profound sense of political realities that is one of the most significant traits of the age of the new Monarchies in Europe'.[14] Moreover, Machiavelli won because the reason of state of the Jesuits was mediated by More and perhaps Erasmus. In Erasmus, wrote Huizinga, there is 'more boldness than in Machiavelli, more ruthlessness than in Montaigne. But Erasmus will not have it credited to him: it is Folly who speaks. He purposely makes us tread the round of the *circulus vitiosus*, as in the old saw: A Cretan said, all Cretans are liars.'[15] This is a perfect synthesis of modern bourgeois common sense. Needlessly serious. To be attacked with the spirit of irony, with the play of thought, the happy jest that strikes things at the root. Erasmus, with the *Institutio principis christiani*, becomes the moral counsellor to the prince, as Machiavelli had been his political counsellor. But without believing in it any more than necessary. Let's not allow ourselves to be misled by severe depictions of the paintings of the time, that of Quentin Metsys' Erasmus, that of Hans Holbein's More from which Rubens drew freely a century later. At the beginning of the modern, there was an engaged disenchantment, just as there must be for us at the end. A 'whimsy' is what Machiavelli calls *De principatibus*. And Huiziniga recalls, for *Moriae Encomium*, Rabelais:

---

14 J. H. Hexter, *More's Utopia: The Biography of an Idea* (New York: Harper Torchbooks, 1952), p. 64.

15 In the English the first line reads quite differently: 'This is bolder and more chilling than Machiavelli, more detached than Montaigne' (Johan Huizinga, *Erasmus and the Age of Reformation* [Princeton University Press, New Jersey, 1984], p. 71). It is unclear whether the discrepancy is in the translation or the mistake is Tronti's. [Trans.]

> '*Valete, plaudite, vivite, bibite.*' How could one take the *Moria* too seriously, when even More's *Utopia*, which is a true companion-piece to it and makes such a grave impression on us, is treated by its author and Erasmus as a mere jest? There is a place where the *Laus* seems to touch both More and Rabelais; the place where Stultitia speaks of her father, Plutus, the god of wealth, at whose beck all things are turned topsy-turvy, according to whose will all human affairs are regulated—war and peace, government and counsel, justice and treaties.[16]

Treatises, faith, men:

> [One] sees from experience in our times that the princes who have accomplished great deeds are those who have thought little about keeping faith and who have known how cunningly to manipulate men's minds [. . .] A wise ruler, therefore, cannot and should not keep his word when such an observance would be to his disadvantage [. . .] If men were all good, this precept would not be good. But since men are a wicked lot [. . .][17]

> In Europe, of course, and especially in those regions where the Christian faith and religion prevail, the dignity of treaties is everywhere kept sacred and inviolable. This is partly because the princes are all so just and virtuous, partly from the awe and reverence that everyone feels for the popes. Just as the popes [. . .] [t]hey think, and rightly, that it would be shameful if people who are specifically called 'the faithful' acted in bad faith.[18]

16 Huizinga, *Erasmus and the Age of Reformation*, p. 76.

17 Machiavelli, *Prince*, pp. 60–61.

18 More, *Utopia*, pp. 83–84.

> A prince never lacks legitimate reasons to colour over his failure to keep his word. Of this, one could cite an endless number of modern examples to show how many pacts and how many promises have been made null and void because of the faithlessness of princes [. . .] But it is necessary to know how to colour over this nature effectively, and to be a great pretender and dissembler. Men are so simple-minded and so controlled by their immediate needs that he who deceives will always find someone who will let himself be deceived.[19]

> Thus people are apt to think that justice is altogether a humble, plebeian virtue, far beneath the dignity of kings. Or else they conclude that there are two kinds of justice, one for the common herd, a lowly justice that creeps along the ground, hedged in everywhere and encumbered with chains; and the other, which is the justice of princes, much more majestic and hence more free than common justice, so that it can do anything it wants and nothing it doesn't want.[20]

Faithfulness and liberty, sadness and justice, deceit and credulity: to read this splendid dual prose leaves one believing that everything has been said. Modern politics has thrown open the ways to paths untravelled in the secret recesses of human nature. In this, it has proven to be a great driver of liberation. Modern philosophy has needed modern politics to place humanity at the heart of the world. The subject of action and the subject of knowledge present themselves, once again, as two faces of the human being inasmuch he is a social being, which is to say, a man in relation to other men. Faces at once united and divided, co-present and non-coincident—like Machiavelli and More. Ultimately, every utopian dimension is a choice of new forms of knowing. The 'dream of a thing'

---

19 Machiavelli, *Prince*, p. 61.

20 More, *Utopia*, p. 84.

is needed more for knowing the world as it is via an imaginative contrast, a negative consciousness, than it is to change it. For this reason, the 'place that is not' can be provided. It is the realistic grasp of reality that constitutes the true basis of the will to the radical transformation of things, which is to say, of the relations of human domination and subjection. Machiavelli's endeavour to set out from the 'nature of the times',[21] investing them more with 'impetuousness' than with 'caution', is revolutionary. It is the prince or, more precisely, political decision-making that resolves the conflict between the elites [*ottimati*] and the people, except for where the people are not united with the elites [*non essere le code unite co' capi*[22]]. In contrast to the criterion of modern politics is 'a natural defect of men: first, to want to live day-by-day; the other, to not believe what has not been might be'.[23] More's motives are optimistically reformist. To the objection: '[t]here is no place for philosophy in the council of kings', the answer is: '[b]ut there is another philosophy, better suited for the role of a citizen, that takes its cue, adapts itself to the drama in hand and acts in part neatly and appropriately.'[24] Not to forcefully introduce unusual and extravagant discussions that have no weight for those who have opposing ideas, '[i]nstead, by an indirect approach, you must strive and struggle as best you can to handle everything tactfully—and thus what you cannot turn to good, you may at least make as little bad as possible.'[25]

Two books, two authors, two intellectual paths to view the world of men with the eyes of politics. They mirror each other. With a difference,

21 Machiavelli, *Prince*, p. 85.

22 From Machiavelli's letter to Vettori, 10 August 1513, in *Tutte le opere*, 2nd EDN (Florence: Bompiani, 2018), p. 2852. The phrase in square brackets literally means: where the tail is not united with the head or leader. [Trans.]

23 Machiavelli, *Tutte le opera*, p. 2853.

24 More, *Utopia*, pp. 34–35.

25 More, *Utopia*, p. 35.

which is one of quality. Revolutionary realism can hold the two aspects together, impetuosity and respect, audacity and caution, force and prudence, to 'set up a pope he wanted' or 'at least he could act to ensure that it would not be someone he did not want'.[26] That is not unimportant. But one cannot deny the intellectual superiority of the first option. It alone binds the complexity of the historical process to political action. Utopia is subordinated to realism. Only alongside it can it exist. Thomas More is already in part in Niccolò Machiavelli. Whereas the inverse is not true. The real tiger's leap into the future is Bloch's 'concrete utopia' that Niccolò, with 'greatness of spirit' and 'lofty intent'[27] assigns to the *Exhortatio* of Chapter 26: *ad capessendam Italiam in libertatemque a barbaris vindicandem*.[28] The utopia is 'as a true basis for every enterprise, to provide yourself with your own soldiers'[29] and not tell tales *de optimo reipublicae statu*.[30] And yet. With both elements, we still have modern politics. When only one remains, no longer.

More's and Erasmus' Catholic reformism will be swept away by the revolutionary drive of Luther's Reformation. I think those interpreters (Edward L. Surtz and Jack H. Hexter) are right who understand *Utopia* within the milieu of Christian humanism of an Erasmine type, in theological rather than rationalist form, moved by religious impulse rather than built upon a naturalist foundation. Here we find a more general point of interpretation of the early modern period, which needs exploring

26 Machiavelli, *Prince*, p. 29.

27 Machiavelli, *Prince*, p. 29. The Italian phrases '*l'animo grande*' and '*l'intenzione alta*' are translated rather differently as 'great courage and high goals' in the Oxford edition. [Trans.]

28 Machiavelli, *Prince*, p. 87. 'An exhortation to seize Italy and to free her from the barbarians'. [Trans.]

29 Machiavelli, *Prince*, p. 89.

30 'On the Best State of a Commonwealth', a phrase drawn from the full title of More's *Utopia*. [Trans.]

further. Alberto Asor Rosa understands Francesco Guicciardini's *Ricordi*, which he situates between Erasmus and Paolo Sarpi, to be 'a singular amalgam of materialist analysis and Stoic-Christian preoccupations'.[31] From it he draws a category and a figure from which, for some time now, I have adopted a certain disposition of the soul: they are the political category of 'Italian pessimism' and the human figure of the 'sceptical politician'. For instance, Asor Rosa writes of Guicciardini: 'the intrinsic politicality of his reasoning borders an area where a different form of thought begins: where reflection on the uncertainty and problematic nature of knowing begins and develops, as does the overpowering dominance of evil over good in history, of nature over reason, and over the contingency and precariousness of human destiny'. This is the 'product of the "catastrophe" or at least incessant chain of "mutations" ' that strikes Italy at the very start of the modern. Precisely in the tale of the *Storia d'Italia* one becomes aware—and Asor Rosa is right to detect a Leopardian accent here in Guicciardini—'of how much instability, like a sea agitated by the winds, is human reality subjected to'.[32]

Between Machiavelli and Erasmus, not only Guicciardini but More too. In contrast to the entirely modern break Machiavelli provokes, the latter thinkers demonstrate a sense of continuity to assure a moderate transition to new times. For instance, the religions of the Utopians are various, although principally of a deistic form accompanied by a practice of tolerance. 'But after they heard from us the name of Christ,'[33] they inclined towards it with affection, since they rediscovered in it the precepts of one of their natural religions. In *The Prince*, one finds the

31 See Alberto Asor Rosa on the '*Ricordi* di Francesco Guicciardini' and the 'Istoria del concilio tridentino' in *Letteratura italiana. Le Opere, II. Dal Cinquecento al Settecento* (Alberto Asor Rosa ed.) (Turin: Einaudi, 1993), pp. 3–90 and 799–863, quotation at p. 89. Both essays have been reprinted in Asor Rosa, *Genus italicum*.

32 See Asor Rosa, *Genus italicum*, pp. 340–41.

33 More, *Utopia*, p. 93.

anticipatory echo of what politics will become in the age of the wars of religion. No trace of this in the island of *Utopia*. One discovers more excavating the past than by scrutinizing the future. Even more so by starting from the 'the knowledge of the deeds of great Men'[34] rather than from the 'laws and institutions'[35] of an imaginary State. It is still the case that one discovers the secret of politics as thought and action in 'the long experience in modern affairs and a continuous study of antiquity'.[36] But at the end of the twentieth century, only the first of these paths remains open; the second is practicable only with great difficulty. The experience of modern things is for us the lived experience of the century, where history was grasped through heretical, isolated, prohibited, and accursed characters; or in figures redeemed by their oeuvres, posthumously welcomed into the wretched Olympus of bourgeois feeling. Each can take their pick of names here. But for us, the lesson of ancient things embraces all of modernity, from its beginnings to its later developments and on to its results. The modern as a political passion more than as a historical discipline: it assumes the risky exercise of thought, walking along an unstable borderline between what has been and what might have been, between the hated necessity of actual reality and the beloved contingency of subversive will. Passion is to look at the body of history with the eyes charged with desire of politics. The vocation of the political is to possess history, which is not woman in the sense of fortune, and even if it were, certainly there's no reason 'if you want to keep her under [. . .] to beat her and force her down'.[37] At least this is something that the late twentieth century offers us that is novel. History is sovereign before politics and does not permit itself to be beaten or knocked about. And the desire is for what, differing from me, posits itself with respect

34 Machiavelli, *Prince*, p. 5.

35 More, *Utopia*, p. 107.

36 Machiavelli, *Prince*, p. 5.

37 Machiavelli, *Prince*, p. 87.

to me, simply and comprehensively, as another history. It is a relationship mediated by the depths of twentieth century European *Kultur*. It can only be comprehended and engaged from within. Political action might be the masculine before the feminine of history. That is how I feel it can be expressed. But politics can be the feminine before the masculine of historical events, as it has been and as it continues to be. This is how it expresses itself, setting out from woman. In both the one and other cases, politics can be the armed Prince of a concrete utopia, even when, especially when, it expresses itself in collective forms such as state, as party, as movement. Without this, it is not that we inaugurate another way of doing politics, it is just that the modern epoch of politics comes to an end. That these are our ancient things is a research choice opposed to the anti-modern motivations subtly hidden in so many rediscoveries of classical politics. This is the choice of Machiavelli, who took as reference point for his teaching, for his *Discourse*, the politics of the Romans not that of the Greeks, the history of the Republic, not the myth of the *polis*, the Roman civil struggles not Athenian democracy. In politics, realism is Rome, utopia is Greece. Of Greece there is nostalgia. How can we sever from our souls the living flesh of *deutsche Romantik*? Could we breathe without Hölderlin? But since the time that the worst postmodern politics bowed before the anti-modern utopia of Greek politics, Pericles can only be read as recounted by Thucydides. Instead, 'the Romans did in these instances what all wise princes must do [. . .] recognizing dangers from afar, the Romans always found remedies for them.'[38] This anticipating and knowing 'from afar' is one of the categories of the political. Because, as 'physicians say about the ethical [*etico*]' (I know well it reads *tisico*, but *etico* sounds right to me),[39] bad politics is

38 Machiavelli, *Prince*, p. 12.

39 Tronti is playing with words: where Machiavelli writes *tisico*, i.e. 'consumptive', Tronti chooses to read *etico*, thus suggesting a none-too-subtle critique of the reduction of politics to ethics characteristic of contemporary thought. [Trans.]

easy to cure but difficult to diagnose, 'but as time passes', it becomes easy to diagnose but difficult to cure. The Romans never did 'approve of what is always on the lips of our wise men today—to reap the benefits of time. Instead, they reaped the benefits of their virtue and prudence; for time brings within it all things, and it can bring with it the good as well as the evil, and the evil as well as the good'.[40] To the 'wise men' of our times, I suggest another text. Augustine in his *De civitate Dei* opposes the seriousness and moderation of the Romans to the frivolousness and lasciviousness of the Greeks. *Gravitas* against *levitas*. This is a decidedly 'untimely' opposition. Like the other one that opposes the 'greedy arrogance of the contemptible Greeks' to the 'humble clemency of the barbarians, uncouth as they were'.[41] Hence,

> [a]ll the devastation, butchery, the plundering, the conflagrations, and all the anguish which accompanied the recent disaster at Rome were in accordance with the general practice of warfare. But there was something which established a new custom, something which changed the whole aspect of the scene; the savagery of the barbarians took on such an aspect of gentleness that the largest basilicas were selected and set aside to be filled with people to be spared by the enemy. No one was to be violently used there, no one snatched away. Many were to be brought there for liberation by merciful foes; none were to be taken from there into captivity even by cruel enemies. This is to be attributed to the name of Christ and the influence of Christianity.[42]

---

40 Machiavelli, *Prince*, pp. 12–13.

41 Augustine, *The City of God* (Henry Bettenson trans.) (Harmondsworth: Pelican, 1972), p. 10.

42 Augustine, *City of God*, pp. 12–13.

Allusive language, allusive citations: this alone permits pieces of truth to pass through the mesh of opinions today. This is the restriction that a dull, grey, indifferent, filled and empty, ever-moving and static epoch, a time of Enlightenment, yes, but with the lights out, a middle age without transition. No, it is not the fourth or fifth century. On the horizon, there is no encounter with the name of Christ and clement uncouth barbarians. The third and fourth Rome have already fallen, without history noticing. The great beginning of the sixteenth century and of the twentieth speak to each other. Signalling the *Miserabilismus* of this millennium's end.

KARL UND CARL

'Listen, Jacob [. . .] you have to admit, if you've learned anything at all, you learned something from Schmitt.'[1] A statement to be read alongside the story of when after a walk in the vicinity of Plettenberg, having returned home together, over a cup of tea Schmitt said to him: 'All right, Taubes, let's read Romans 9:11.'[2] Taubes himself provided us with the definitive formula of the correct relationship to Carl Schmitt: *Gegenstrebige Fügung* (divergent accord).[3] Jacob the friend (1923–1987), the German Rabbi in exile, ready to speak, not to write. In the folds of the twentieth century lie hidden the miraculous existence of these invisible characters. Extremely rare and very real presences. You meet them in books, spiritual brothers, like old fated natural acquaintances. By now the value lies only in the obscurity, separateness, reserve, refusal to show themselves of these solitary existences. What was impossible then, in the century of great contrasts, has today become necessary, in the years and months and days of minor confusions. When you find that Taubes says of Schmitt: he is an apocalyptic prophet of the counter-revolution,

---

1 Jacob Taubes, *The Political Theology of St. Paul* (Dana Hollander trans.) (Stanford: Stanford University Press, 2003), p. 101.

2 Taubes, *The Political Theology of St. Paul*, p. 2.

3 This is the subtitle Taubes gave to a book of correspondence between the two thinkers, published by Merve Verlag, Berlin, 1987. This has been translated into English, minus the subtitle, *To Carl Schmitt: Letters and Reflections* (Keith Tribe trans.) (New York: Columbia University Press, 2013). [Trans.]

to say of himself: I am an apocalyptic prophet of the revolution—then you see that the target of the problem has been struck with the arrow of thought.

> The science of apocalypticism presupposes a passive attitude toward the happenings of history. There is an absence of action. The fate of world history is predetermined and there is no sense in trying to resist it. The passive voice predominates in the apocalyptic style. In the apocalypses, no one 'acts' but rather everything 'happens.' [. . .] The passive style of apocalypticism, which is prevalent in the writings of Karl Marx, is motivated by a lack of faith in mankind. The long period of suffering, the repeated disappointments, the crushing power of evil, the enormous colossus of the demonic kingdom of the world all contribute to the despair apocalypticism felt about redemption, if redemption were at the mercy of mankind. It is from this point on that the largely misunderstood concept of 'determinism' can be integrated into the thinking of the Marxist apocalypse. Marx also sees higher powers at work in history, which the individual is powerless to influence, and he dresses them up in mythical garments of his time as 'productive forces.'[4]

A truly original way to read Marx. At that point, after two world wars, after the Holocaust and the Bomb, he had his reasons. Does he still? Viewed through the politics of the twentieth century, the horizon of Marx's thought has suffered an apocalyptic catastrophe. We should not allow ourselves to be misled by the farcical way socialism collapsed. The tragedy of this history was in its beginnings, its developments, in the desperate anti-deterministic struggle against the immense power of the productive forces that was mythologically evoked by the depth of

4 Jacob Taubes, *Occidental Eschatology* (David Ratmoko trans.) (Stanford: Stanford University Press, 2009), p. 34.

processes beyond human control. Here lies the decisive reason for the, impossible and yet necessary encounter of Marx and Schmitt. Both see rising above them the unassailable force of a historic enemy and seek the tools for conflict at that level. The more they draw the tragic greatness of the task from the realistic analysis of the epochal situation, the more they are forced to radicalize the extremes of political decision. Two forms of agonic, 'polemical' thought: not only practical action but also theoretical research as war. Two standpoints from opposed positions, with different ends, with the same method, against the same problem: capitalism-modernity, the history that bears it, the politics that contrasts it. The one, Prometheus, the other Epimetheus. After which are the nineteenth and twentieth centuries. Behind Marx, Hegel; behind Schmitt, Weber. Marx is the Weber of the Proletariat in the same way that Weber is the Marx of the bourgeoisie.[5] And of Weber, Taubes said that he was the synthesis of Marx and Nietzsche. Here, it is from this synthesis that we must begin again. From within this all-German intellectual quadrilateral, composed of Marx-Nietzsche-Weber-Schmitt, for *Ein feste Burg ist unser Gott*, to put it in terms of the chorale cantata 302 and 303 BMV.[6] From the height of these walls the attacks of the alien artificial intelligences of 2001 must be repelled.

With Carl Schmitt: in divergent accord. With Karl Marx: in convergent discord. This is the inner sense of a theorist of politics, a son of the workers' movement, at the end of the twentieth century, after the defeat of the revolution. Between Marx and Schmitt, a relationship of natural,

5 It was Albert Salomon who famously called Weber the 'bourgeois Marx.' See Wolfgang J. Mommsen, 'Max Weber as Critic of Marxism', *The Canadian Journal of Sociology / Cahiers canadiens de sociologie* 2(4) (Autumn 1977): 373–98. The quotation appears on p. 374n1. [Trans.]

6 'A Mighty Fortress is our God' is a hymn composed by Martin Luther between 1527–29 and put to music by Johann Sebastian Bach. It is a paraphrase of Psalm 46. [Trans.]

historic complementarity. In the twentieth century, it is impossible to read Marx without Schmitt politically. But reading Schmitt without Marx is historically impossible because Schmitt would not exist without Marx. Taubes writes: 'He was the anti-Bolshevist [. . .] He could have become a Leninist, but he had what it took to become the only relevant anti-Leninist'.[7] He became it only in thought.

It is not only his destiny to become something political only in thought. Together, Marx and Schmitt gave us back *das Kriterium des Politischen*, from the moment that, after Lenin, such a criterion had been gradually lost. Indeed, together they make up the new name of the friend-enemy. Our Marx alone *contra hostem* [against the enemy] survived in the century. He had need of this new public enemy to discover what in the nineteenth century could not be discovered: the autonomy of the political. The twentieth century is politics realized, modern politics accomplished, lacking now the possibility of a beyond after itself. Perhaps only the workers' movement, as custodian of its own legacy of struggles and organization, by going beyond itself might, have been able to bear politics to safety away from the forces of history. An equal social power endowed with strategic thought and material force was needed. The possibility of continuity lies on in the social. Classes that die are never entirely extinguished. Roots sinking deep into the centuries cannot be cut in day days or years. The aristocracy has, in its own way, survived capitalism. And in England, once the mother and now the grandmother of the modern, it was the aristocracy that carried out the bourgeois revolutions, as authoritative studies have shown. The young bourgeoisie, as custodian of the spirit of capitalism in the human soul, played no small role either: it was enough for it to sink weak roots into ancient nations for it to resist the violence of politics with its own historic grounds, and to demonstrate that it did not deserve to die while those that were killing

7 Taubes, *Political Theology of Paul*, p. 102.

it did. Instead, politics is tied to contingency, to the occasion, the moment, the passage. Society is extended history. Politics is short history. And yet, the *longue durée* can be interrupted or bent or diverted by the interruption of the leap into the instant of the short period. This is the force of politics, its subjectivity-will, which is always one and only one irrational happening within history's many rationales.

The age of wars, of direct confrontation, of polar contrast, the divided world, divided society, politics-as-conflict has forced us to come to terms with and test ourselves against the thought of the enemy in an intense involvement that included belonging and refusal, exclusions and exchanges. I believe this to be an unprecedented condition of intellectual research, in any case: a state of exception for political theory. Those who did not live through this time are missing something. And it is not the tragic sense of struggle that is lacking. One can acquire that, for those who have mettle in the soul from experiences of disappointment. What is lacking is instead that polemical form of thinking that leaves you within the unsolved contradiction, in direct and naked contact with the unabsorbable negative polarity that in the end becomes a part of you against which you must fight and bargain. Marx incorporated Schmitt into himself in the twentieth century. Because revolution and counter-revolution, revolutionary and counter-revolutionary apocalypticism, proletarian revolution and conservative revolution, that is, the great politics of the century not only occupied the entire landscape of possible action, radicalizing the possible life-choices available, but so directly referred to one another that that which lay in the middle, liberal democracy, was for a lengthy period rightly culturally subordinate. Historical revisionism, like all coherently reactionary standpoints, contains a core of truth which it is necessary to reveal. It should have been accompanied by a philosophical revisionism. But this could only come from the Left, like the historical could only come from the right. Political thought had the chance to overcome the rigidified schema of the orthodox Marxist tradition. The Marx-Schmitt operation was, essentially, this. What was lacking was the courage to adopt it, to test its practical consequences. The unresolved problematic knot is the relationship to modernity. This is the bequest of the intellectual research that the history of the workers' movement deposited for possible improbable neo-revolutionary prospects. It is not only today that modernity is, as is believed by the vulgar common sense of the epoch, a door thrown open onto a virtual future. Modernity is also the accumulation of material from the past, buried civilizations, cities wiped away, scattered stones. It is not only futuristic innovation but also elapsed history. We exist in late modernity, where the drive of technological futures coexists with the need for an archaeology of the modern. If one fails to recognize this ambiguity of modernity, its being *Welt von gestern* in addition to being the *future of the world*,[8] one cannot establish a relationship to it as a problem. The workers' movement had confronted and resolved it in its own way: through a Marxist approach, it had declared itself a part of the modern, its offspring and heir, capable of using historical change in a partisan way for a process of human emancipation. These were its struggles, these are what its forms of organization wanted, what the taking of the Russian Winter Palace intended—and it was so from its origins. This is the project that has failed. But with it too the idea of development as progress, this anti-politics of modernity that triumphant capitalism adopted as it took up the flags the working class dropped in the dust. In the opposite camp, the solution was to demonize the modern through the essentializing of technology, where Roman Catholicism and the metaphysics of the death of God of Protestant hue came together in a holy alliance against the century. Anti-modernism was not that of the totalitarian solutions. On the contrary, these were an explicit expression of a part of the soul of the structural reality of modern civilization. Anti-modernism was rather

8 In English in the original. [Trans.]

that of the cultures that initially hoped those solutions would be decisive weapons against the enemy. This explains the initial endorsement by figures of an aristocratic standpoint for the plebeian, fascist and Nazi eruption. This, like the other, was a failed project. This is the century of failure of intellectual and moral reforms, from whichever side [*parte*] they came. The final winning solution was that of objective material processes: whether they were demonically totalitarian or angelically democratic, it matters little now. Modern history won out in the end, because while its ambiguous dual face existed, it went unrecognized; it worked for itself without being used for anything else. The defeat is of politics, for having been unable to adapt its duality to the ambiguity of modernity, by practising it as its terrain as well as combatting it as an adversary.

This aptitude in theoretically grasping the sign of this dual modernity existed, separately, equally shared in Marx and Schmitt. Carlo Galli is right to extract Schmitt's work from the chance context of 1920–30s Germany to the epochal contextualization of the genealogy of politics, of the origin of modern politics. Analogously, Marx's work cannot be traced back to mid-nineteenth century Manchester capitalism but to the genealogy of political economy, to the origin of the modern conception of the economic. Only the complementarity of these two frameworks provides us with the ambiguous complexity of the modern. Together they allow us to decipher the results of the first and the second half of the twentieth century, and rewrite in the language of the century the great founding theme of the modern, that of conflict and order, as: revolution and form. 'Schmitt's genealogy is an ascending or descending to the origin of modern politics. It is in the specifically modern political concepts and institutions that Schmitt sees at work, as moments of origin, as much the perception of radical disorder as the compulsion to the production of artificial order; as much contingency as the need for form.'[9] Janus-faced modernity: on the one side the process of secularization, on the other the point of catastrophe—at the start and at the end. As it was for Marx: capitalist development in the middle but at the start there is the violence of original accumulation and at the end the *Zusammenbruch* of the system thanks to unresolvable fundamental contradictions.[10] Moreover, according to Marx, history is made by men in determinate conditions, men not man, which is to say, classes in their internal battles, and the parties as nomenclatures of classes and governments as committee for managing the affairs of the classes. 'For Schmitt, political action [. . .] is only by the sovereign, the point where the modern *logos*, the strategic thought of the rational order, concentrates so intensely as to negate itself: from the individual and his strategies one can expect nothing but disorder or, in any case, ineffectiveness, whereas the energy of the masses must be given form.'[11] While the differences listed by Galli remain,[12] the operation of Marx plus Schmitt gives a sum of thought superior to that of the two scientific endeavours that share, incidentally, an immediate political misfortune, which is to say, an abyssal

9 Carlo Galli, *Genealogia della politica. Carl Schmitt e la crisi del pensiero politico moderno* (Bologna: Il Mulino, 1996), p. *xii*.

10 'Original accumulation', sometimes also rendered as 'primitive accumulation' is a notion drawn from Marx's *Capital*, VOL. 1, in which he describes the bloody historical process of the formation of the 'original' capital that constitutes the grounds for the cycle of capitalist production to get off the ground in the first place. It emerges through a process of 'conquest, enslavement, robbery, murder, in short, force'; a 'historical process of the divorcing the producer from the means of production' and so can be described as the 'pre-history of capital, and of the mode of production corresponding to capitalism'; a history 'written in the annals of mankind in letters of blood and fire' (*Capital*, VOL. 1, pp. 874, 875). Whether original accumulation is a one-off process or is continually repeated in new forms has spawned a huge literature and is by no means a settled dispute. [Trans.]

11 Galli, *Genealogia della politica*, pp. *xxiii–xxiv*.

12 Galli, *Genealogia della politica*, pp. 52–56.

disproportion between their theoretical contributions and their practical experimentations. But to reject Ernst Niekisch's contention that 'Schmitt's is the bourgeoisie's answer to the Marxist concept of class struggle' and to assert in contrast that 'Schmitt's is a reinterpretation of the class struggle within a categorical framework far from the Marxist one',[13] is to say that Karl und Carl can only together provide that 'tragic hermeneutic of the modern', the only one able to account for the epochal crisis of class struggle. The crisis of modern political reason is part of this context. Schmitt crosses the path of a certain twentieth century heretical to Marxism, one lying between Lukàcs and Korsch, but above all one finds in his formative works the battering ram that is Lenin. Galli's reading of this is wonderfully put:

> What in Lenin's thought fascinated Schmitt is certainly not that of the withering away of politics, which for Schmitt betrays the influence of the modern power of technology, so much as the moment of revolution and of the political command of the proletariat, of a form of politics that, despite everything, is constituted by the extreme polemical intensity that underpins it. The dictatorship of the proletariat—the hyper-political move to the withering away of politics—appears to him to contain (much more than bourgeois discursive mediation) an embryo of awareness that politics is marked by an intensity that is independent of every other area of existence.[14]

Hence, that the Italian operaismo of the 1960s crossed paths with Schmitt's work in the 1970s has much deeper grounds than those that Galli attributes to it. We shall have to return to this issue elsewhere. It is true that to begin with there was the practical ambition to extract from Schmitt the secret of the autonomy of the political to hand it as a weapon

13 Galli, *Genealogia della politica*, pp. 54–55.

14 Galli, *Genealogia della politica*, p. 47.

to the party of the working class. But this was the naive occasion for the encounter. *Et a hoste consilium*[15] means much more than distinguishing between revolutionary form and reactionary content of a thinking. No, the relationship we wanted to establish with Schmitt was not the same as that of Marx to Hegel. As, step by step, the crisis of class struggle and that of modern politics advanced together, and the two processes—the end of the workers' movement and the end of modern politics—became more evident, so too the relationship with Schmitt became tighter, more intense, more internal.

Schmitt wrote, 'Only he who knows his prey better than himself can conquer.' To know the one that one is fighting better than he knows himself is not so much the way to beat him so much as to become independent of him. Introject him to not become subordinated to him. '[D]o not speak lightly of the enemy. One categorizes oneself through the enemy.' Do not aim to annihilate him. 'But all destruction is only self-destruction. The enemy, by contrast, is the other. Remember the great sentence of the philosopher: the relation in the other to itself, that is the real infinity.'[16] *Der Feind ist unsre eigne Frage als Gestalt*:[17] this is the

15 This Latin phrase, which translates as 'And from the enemies, wisdom', often considered to be a paraphrase or allusion to a line from Ovid's *Metapmorphoses*, '*Fas est et ab hoste doceri*' ('I can learn from my foe'), Book 4, line 428. These are also the final words of the first chapter of Galli's *Genealogia della politica*, in which he claims that, despite similarities, Schmitt's categorical framework is in the final analysis alien to the Marxist one (p. 56). [Trans.]

16 Carl Schmitt, *Ex Captivitate Salus*: *Experiences, 1945–1947* (Matthew Hannah trans.) (Cambridge: Polity Press, 2017), p. 35, p. 71 and p. 71, respectively.

17 Depending on the translation of *Gestalt*, this can be rendered as in the Matthew Hannah translation for the English edition of *Ex captivitate salus*, as 'The enemy is our own question as form'; or, as in Neil Levi's renditions in 'Schmitt and the Question of the Aesthetic', *New German Critique* 101 (Summer 2007): 27: 'The enemy embodies our own question,' 'The enemy is a figure for our own question,' or finally, as in the Italian version, 'The enemy is the personification of our own question.' [Trans.]

cipher by which not only Schmitt's but Marx's thought too can be recognized. Marx, who with the modern instrument of the class struggle discovered the laws of movement of capital. Schmitt, who against the *Behemoth* of the world civil wars rediscovered the political decision of the modern *Leviathan*. Schmitt, even though he did not know the entirety of Marx's work, understood the essence of his position. To it he opposed his own. Revolution/counter-revolution is the great conflict, the great epochal war that lies immediately behind us, the passing not of an illusion but of a reality. That the conflict never existed or, worse, that it should is the soothing illusory idea. In that context, Marx gestured forward to twentieth-century nihilism; Schmitt harked back, to nineteenth-century traditionalism. Two great seasons that complemented each other. They were rich not so much in evoking understanding of what has been so much as in visions of the future that tear through our present. Through the philosophy of the counter-revolutionary state—de Maistre, de Bonald, Donoso Cortés—Schmitt understood the twentieth century better, especially as far as its outcomes are concerned, than social democracy and liberal democracy together. Understanding the opposite is the profoundest way to understand oneself. Understanding the extreme opposite serves to define the radicality of one's standpoint. Radicalness serves to foresee what will come far beyond one's own time. Donoso Cortés and Tocqueville—these two extraordinary figures who incredibly coexisted during a crucial passage of modern history, before and after the European civil war of 1848—should, following Schmitt, be read together. Two great anticipators, together hurled from the nineteenth into the twentieth century, connote the greatness of the two opposed and yet complementary forms of political thought. The one, with which Book One of *Démocratie en Amérique* (1835) ends:

> There are two great peoples on the earth today who, starting from different points, seem to advance toward the same goal:

> these are the Russians and the Anglo-Americans. [. . .] The American struggles against the obstacles that nature opposes to him; the Russian grapples with men. The one combats the wilderness and barbarism, the other, civilization vested with all its arms: thus the conquests of the American are made with the plowshare of the laborer, those of the Russian, with the sword of the soldier. [. . .] Their point of departure is different, their ways are diverse; nonetheless, each of them seems called by a secret design of Providence to hold the destinies of half the world in its hands one day.[18]

And the other form of thought, that of Donoso Cortés, can be found in the 'Discurso sobre la situación general de Europa' of 30 January 1850.[19] One finds there the great prophecy that the revolution was more likely to erupt in St Petersburg than in London. Donoso was returning from a sojourn in Berlin, but his talk concerns Russia not Prussia. It is from here that the new enemy of European civilization emerges from the possible encounter of revolutionary socialism and Russian politics. Schmitt, in an essay from 1927, summarizes as follows what for him was the most disconcerting of Donoso's 'interpretive predictions':

> first, the revolution will dissolve all standing armies; then, socialism will destroy feelings of patriotism and reduce all antitheses to that between the haves and the have nots; then, after the socialist revolution, all national feelings will be destroyed, the Slavic peoples will be united under Russian leadership, and all that will be left in Europe will be the antithesis of the exploiters

18 Alexis de Tocqueville, *Democracy in America* (Harvey C. Mansfield and Delba Winthrop eds and trans) (Chicago: University of Chicago Press, 2000), pp. 100–101.

19 *Obras de Don Juan Donoso Cortés*, VOL. 3 (Madrid: Imprenta de Tejado, 1854), pp. 303–26.

> and the exploited. Then, Russia's great hour will have come, and with it the great chastisement of Europe.[20]

This chastisement will be a long one and will not end only with, for example, the fall of England.

> But that will hardly be the end of the chastisement, because the Russians are not like the Germans, who renewed European civilization during the *Völkerwanderung* [migration of peoples]. Russia's aristocracy and government are just as corrupt as their counterparts in Europe; after her victory, Russia will carry the poison of old Europe in its blood, and eventually will die and rot from it.[21]

Et voilà! This ambiguous, contradictory process of centralization and democratization of humanity that is not simply progressive a *finis Europae*, the decline of the West, seen from two contrasting viewpoints: from that of an anticipatory liberal critique of democracy and from an unexhausted and inexhaustible Christian conception of history. Both the Frenchman and the Spaniard, interpreters-anticipators of that *Kritik der Zeit* that in the specifically German understanding of the word 'critique' from Kierkegaard and Burckhardt to Troeltsch, Weber, Rathenau and to Spengler is formed in the second half of the nineteenth century and traverses the entire first half of the twentieth before coming to a halt, crumbles in the face of the great crisis of politics with which our century sadly terminates. In 1971, Schmitt wrote:

> Karl Marx could still admit that the ideological superstructure (of which the concepts of right and legality form a part) develops sometimes more slowly than the economic-industrial base. Contemporary progress no longer has as much time and

20 Carl Schmitt, 'Donoso Cortés in Berlin (1849)', *Telos*, 125 (2002): 97.

21 Schmitt, 'Donoso Cortés in Berlin', pp. 97–98.

> patience. It evokes the future and encourages growing expectations, which it then surpasses with new ever-greater expectations. But its political expectation arrives at the end of the 'political' as whole. Humanity is understood as a substantially pacified unitary society; there are no more enemies; they become conflictual *partners* (*Konfliktspartners*); in place of world politics a world police must be established. [22]

Karl Marx and Carl Schmitt exemplify the political archaeology of the modern even more so than Niccoló Machiavelli and Thomas More. The latter, modern eternity has welcomed as innocuous into the paradise of culture. The former it has damned and plunged into the hell of politics.

---

22 Carl Schmitt, *Le categorie del politico* (Giovanni Miglio and Pierangelo Schiera eds and trans) (Bologna: Il Mulino, 1972), p. 25. This was an extremely influential Italian language collection of writings by the German jurist, which is in print to this day. The cited passage comes from Schmitt's preface to the Italian edition, dated August 1971. [Trans.]

POLITICS AND PROPHECY

Let us seek, behind the words, the thoughts of Sergio Quinzio.[1] Reading and re-reading, one does not escape the strong impression that some or many of his past thoughts would soon become ours. Quinzio had the voice, the guise, the physicality of the prophet. A modern prophet, implicated in history: as always with the prophet, who is inserted within the history of his time and whose gaze is cast beyond. Not like the utopian, who is outside history, wants to remain outside it, who does not 'gaze' beyond but 'remains' beyond. Quinzio did not disdain from laying out his writing in the pages of a daily newspaper, in daily conversations with others, in the daily debates over the unsolved problems caused by the clash of the phase with the epoch. He was a militant critic of an eternal, lived, endured, meditated-upon and opposed time.

Mine is a dual gaze on Quinzio. First: I learn from him what 'Christianity' is. Something that one learns again continuously, always from the beginning. At this point, his Christianity might also be mine. Might. Second: I recognize the tragic in the religious because I recognize the tragic in the political. The two dimensions have that in common. we

---

This essay was originally published in *Bailamme, Rivista di spiritualità e politica*, 20 (1996), *in memoriam* of Sergio Quinzio. I think it fits well into the subject of discussion. I dedicate it to the prophetic voices of the 'monks' don Giuseppe Dossetti, Father Benedetto Calati, and Pietro Ingrao.

1 I have been unable to trace this quotation to the great theologian who was a profound influence on the later Tronti. [Trans.]

would like it to not be so. But it is. It is of this second gaze that I shall speak here. Of the first, I am not yet capable. Quinzio's is not a 'political' discourse; even less is it 'impolitical'.[2] However, politics feels itself to be more than merely interrogated by his thinking, it feels itself to be forcefully provoked and called to a different agenda. If politics is the production of the future, prophecy and utopia are two ways, different and contrasting, of seeing the future. 'Seeing' is the right word. In politics today, one no longer sees: one looks, observes, analyses, then one acts, competes, fights, always and only subordinated to that which is, one accepts what has been till now, one forsakes thinking of what might be; both the hither side and the beyond of the present appears cancelled—if ever there had been history, now there is no longer.

Pro-feteía: prediction of a future event by divine embassy. *Pro-feteúo*: I speak in the name of, on behalf of, *Teoú*, of the Deity, of God. Matthew 1:22: 'All this took place to fulfil what the Lord had said through the prophet'; 26:54: 'But how then would the Scriptures be fulfilled that they say it must happen this way?' This is what the Scriptures say: 'it must happen' in that way. It takes place because it was predicted. Thus, to predict is to make it so that it will happen. Isaiah 41:22: 'Let them bring them forth, and shew us what will happen: let them shew the former things, what they be, that we may consider them, and know that latter end of them; or declare for us things for to come.'[3] Quinzio writes on Isaiah:

2 I take the reference to be to Thomas Mann's *Reflections of an Unpolitical Man* (in Italian, *Considerazioni di un uomo impolitico*), a book to which Tronti often refers, rather than to the work of the Italian philosopher Roberto Esposito (such as in *Categories of the Impolitical*). [Trans.]

3 I have used the New International Version or the King James Version of the Bible, depending upon which rendition was to closest to Tronti's on a case by case basis. [Trans.]

> The prophet does not write books but makes gestures and says words inseparably that belong to the immediate primary reality in which one suffers or rejoices, wins or loses, lives or dies, not to the reflected and secondary reality that is constituted by liturgical forms or those imbued with wisdom that evoke the past so as to bring comfort and render the present acceptable [. . .]. Prophecy announces the future, not because it is the mirror or formula of a reality that is already given, but because it is the seed of the things that the prophecy itself elicits in that moment [. . .]. For this reason, the speech of the prophet is a single cry, condemned to repeat itself, and in repeating itself it turns itself into oratorical exertion until what it invokes is granted. The rhythm of prophetic language comes from the break that [in turn] stems from the need to draw breath; it is crudely and monotonously cadenced by the parallelism of conforming and deforming, of the already accomplished and the not-yet accomplished, of the shouting and the remaining silent, of desperation and consolation.[4]

Salvation and damnation, hope and fall, messianic message and apocalyptic passage, a chaotic entanglement of events that 'follow one another again and again' in an eternal circular return. The prophetic word sheds light on this tragic narrative of human history. The epochs who joyously do without this word sketch times blind to the future. For fear of the unfolding of the harshness of history, one lives in the violence of the daily news. One of the fruitful 'untimelinesses' of Quinzio is that he is an anti-Enlightenment and hence anti-progressive thinker. He writes in *La croce e il nulla*:

> It is infinitely too late to fight Voltaire's battle, the evils into which we are now sinking really cannot find even partial and

4 Sergio Quinzio, *Un commento alla Bibbia* (Milan: Adelphi, 1979), pp. 257–59.

> temporary remedy in tolerance. Despite the extravagant appearances, we are not threatened by the fanatical presumption of possessing truth, as occurred in other epochs, but by the paralysing certainty of the radical doubtfulness of everything, which leaves space for nothing but indifference—and hence to a disguised but ruthless conflict of interests, or to a vain and painful turmoil to fill the void.[5]

From here stems his consistent, debatable view of the modern as an 'enormous illness born in the space of the missed eschatological event'.[6] There is in Quinzio an anti-modern vocation that must be contained, controlled, of which he at times is also aware and reverses. It is the charm of his speech in the hostile climate of the contemporary debate. It is a point that marks a more-than-justified limit to his research. Justified in the following sense: that the hoped-for future, both that enunciated in the Word as well as that known through Science, has thunderously failed; and both theological concepts, as well as their secularization in the categories of the political, in their failure, have demonstrated the extent of their impotence. And so:

> Since we remain, despite ourselves, modern historical men, we find ourselves before the wall of the impossibility of any future. None of the historical models that we have developed—first sacred ones, theological, and then profane, secularized ones—hold for us any longer. All the forms in which we have thought the future as meaningful future—up to the idea of the progress of humanity, or of the 'world spirit', or of the classless society—lie behind us. Hence, to escape the loss of meaning, one is driven into not thinking about the future, into dissolving the very thought of it. At most, one grants oneself a 'weak future',

5 Sergio Quinzio, *La croce e il nulla* (Milan: Adelphi, 1984), p. 210.

6 Quinzio, *La croce e il nulla*, p. 211.

> which through 'post-Nietzschean cunning' delivers us to the immutable cyclical eternity of the eternal return. Is another idea of the future possible, desirable, prophetically sayable? 'The future is not inscribed anywhere in the eternal, in the absolute, in the destiny of necessity, but it is the total risk of an empty space to be filled. Inasmuch, the future has a relationship to will, not to knowledge. As a 'hope that is seen is not hope' (Romans 8:24), so a thing believed that is known, is no longer believed. Nothing assures us that a future desired by faith is possible; but neither is the dividing line between the possible and impossible guaranteed, there is no certainty regarding what is possible and what is impossible.[7]

Here is a belief that can be shared, a critical faith open to doubt not in its foundations but its outcomes, macerated in the uncertainty that what is about to happen is different from what should have happened, dramatically exposed to the delusion of present things by its need of future events. Besides, Quinzio, along the final itinerary of this thinking, from *Dalla gola del leone* (1980) to *Mysterium iniquitatis* (1995), by way of *La sconfitta di Dio* (1992), accompanied us in the suffering for other defeated faiths and other abandoned hopes. See 'Il silenzio della Chiesa' in *Mysterium iniquitatis*, when he makes Dostoyevsky's words his own: 'How dreadfully has it tormented me (and torments me even now)—this longing for faith, which is all the stronger for the proofs I have against it.'[8] Because—he said—suffering lies not in 'disbelief' or in 'doubt'. Here there is a banal, elementary, 'psychological' separation between the real and the ideal, 'between the real that is put in doubt and the ideal in whose name reality is put in doubt'. But 'faith, for the believer, is an

7 Quinzio, *La croce e il nulla*, pp. 31–32.

8 Letter to Mme M. D. Fonvision, beginning of January 1854, in *Letters of Fyodor Michailovich Dostoevsky to his Family Friends* (New York: MacMillan, 1917), p. 71. [Trans.]

immediate certainty'. And 'the true problems, the true questions, are those that explode within a horizon of certainty'. Certainty of faith: if anything, it is a case of choosing between the 'hard and weighty *fides quae creditur*' [faith which is believed] and the 'magnificent *fides qua creditor* [faith by which it is believed] that raises us in flight towards the ideal'.[9] There. This final *fides* is that which will then be defined in the movement of utopia and pragmatism, always conjugated 'nobly' together. But the other, the first, the faith that is believed, that is the one that holds, that seeks to hold, desires to hold, tragically together prophecy and realism.

Prophecy is an explosion of truth. Revealed truth. Interpreted for men and women of faith. An ancient human straining towards what is to come in contrast with the laws, rules, the logics of modernity. Two *loci classici* for a necessarily rational view on this obscure backdrop. Spinoza's *Tractatus Theologico-Politicus*, Chapter 1: 'Of Prophecy', Chapter 2: 'Of Prophets'. Why is it that when he poses the great problem of the *libertas philosophandi*, of modern civic human liberty, one sets out from prophecy and prophets?

> Prophecy, or revelation, is sure knowledge revealed by God to man. A prophet is one who interprets the revelations of God to those who are unable to attain to sure knowledge of the matters revealed and therefore can only apprehend them by simple faith. The Hebrew word for prophet is '*nabi*', i.e. speaker or interpreter, but in Scripture its meaning is restricted to interpreter of God, as we may learn from Exodus 7:1, there God says to Moses, 'See, I may have made thee a god to Pharaoh, and Aaron thy brother shall be thy prophet.'[10]

9 Sergio Quinzio, *Mysterium iniquitatis* (Milan: Adelphi, 1995), pp. 92–95.

10 Benedict Spinoza, *A Theologico-Political Treatise* (R. H. M. Elwes trans.) (New York: Dover, 1951), p. 13.

The 'prophets were endowed with unusually vivid imagination, and not with unusually perfect minds'.[11] And Hobbes, *Leviathan*, Chapter 36, 'Of the Word of God, and of the Prophets': 'Prophecy is not an Art, nor (when it is taken for Praedication) a constant vocation; but an extraordinary, and temporary Employment from God, most often of Good men, but sometimes also of the Wicked.'[12] Indeed, one reads in Deuteronomy, 13:1–3: 'If a prophet, or one who foretells by dreams, appears among you and announces to you a sign or wonder, and if the sign or wonder spoken of takes place, and the prophet says, "Let us follow other gods" (gods you have not known) "and let us worship them", you must not listen to the words of that prophet or dreamer. The Lord your God is testing you.' And in 1 John 4:1: 'Dear friends, do not believe every spirit, but test the spirits to see whether they are from God, because many false prophets have gone out into the world.' Spinoza-Hobbes: no utopia, and prophecy, yes, but within reason! To adopt utopia, good intentions are enough. To cleave to prophecy, a calculation of truth is necessary. Prophecy does not imply any certainty and at the same time it cannot communicate doubts. It is knowledge, not of what is but of what is about to be, of what needs to happen for it to be. Revelation is grasped through the signs, and through the signs it is in turn revealed. The prophet composes the signs of God and those for men through the imagination. His destiny is to remain misunderstood. But when there is a deviation from destiny, within the state of exception, then an event of great history is given. Prophetic history is always the result of great politics. Between politics and prophecy there is a fine veil of unfathomable complicity. To grasp the signs of historic times, that is the task of politics. When the signs of the times are missing, there is a crisis of politics. When the signs of the times are there but politics fails to grasp them,

11 Spinoza, *Theologico-Political Treatise*, p. 27.

12 Thomas Hobbes, *Leviathan* (Cambridge: Cambridge University Press, 1996), p. 291.

there is a historic crisis. When there are signs and politics sees them and takes them on, only then is one of the rare epochs of *Veränderung der Welt*, of world-transformation, given. It is easy to understand the conditions we find ourselves in today, where we have been till now, and Quinzio along with us. But we are interested in the lofty historic meeting point of prophecy and politics, the one that Quinzio was unable to see, and us along with him. Let us seeks it in the future past.

The occasion for my reflection is given by the publication of Mario Miegge's *Il sogno del re di Babilonia. Profezia e storia da Thomas Müntzer a Isaac Newton* (1995). He begins with Daniel 2:1–2, the book of the prophet Daniel written in the second century BCE 'And in the second year of the reign of Nebuchadnezzar, Nebuchadnezzar dreamed dreams, wherewith his spirit was troubled, and his sleep abandoned him. Then the king commanded to call the magicians, the astrologers, and the Chaldeans, for to shew the king his dreams.' But first they wanted the story of the dream so that they could interpret it. Only Daniel was able to tell the king what he had dreamt. Because 'there is a God in heaven that revealeth secrets, and maketh known [. . .] what shall be in the end of days' (Daniel 2:28). 'As for thee, O king, thy thoughts came into thy mind upon thy bed, what should come to pass hereafter' (2:29). The king had a 'vision.' There follows the tale of the statue, the head of which was of pure gold, with feet of iron and clay, and of the stone that became detached from the mountain, and the kingdoms that succeed one another from the pieces of the fractured statue (2:31–45). Miegge reads this powerful myth as an interpretive key to the beginning of the modern era, between the religious civil wars of the sixteenth century and the English revolution of the seventeenth century, when the nexus of prophecy and history turns into the nexus of prophecy and politics. Koselleck and Dubois have read this passage theoretically and historically.[13] (We

13 The reference is almost certainly to Claude-Gilbert Dubois, *La conception de*

might add here Michael Walzer's *The Revolution of the Saints.*) Prophetic explosion and great transformation. The anticipation of the final event and the perception of the novelty of the present. *Vergangene Zukunft*:[14] that equilibrium between the 'space of experience' and 'horizon of expectation', *zwei historische Kategorien*—as Koselleck calls them; an equilibrium built and broken in a brief, intense and violent political moment between the Reformation and the peasant war. My idea is that prophecy explodes in the periods of complete change, of leaps and upheavals. Behind it lies mysticism and politics, speculative mysticism and revolutionary politics, between Meister Eckart and Thomas Müntzer two extremities that touch, two radical standpoints on man, on God and towards other men and women. *Justi vivent in aeternum* [the just live eternally], preached the Meister or, as in another sermon, *Justi in perpetuum vivent* [the just live in perpetuity]. But who are the just? Here they are, in a text that was not incidentally subject to the papal bull, *In agro dominico* (in the Lord's field):

> Those who have entirely renounced themselves, and who do not in the least seek their own in anything, whatever it may be, whether great or small, who do not look below themselves, or above themselves, or at themselves, who love neither goods nor honours, nor comfort nor joy, nor advantage, nor devotion, nor holiness, nor reward, nor heaven, but have renounced all this, and all that is theirs.[15]

---

l'histoire en France au XVIe siècle (1560–1610) (Paris: Nizet, 1977) [Trans.]

14 The reference is to Reinhart Koselleck, *Futures Past: On the Semantics of Historical Time* (New York: Columbia University Press, 2004), especially Chapter 14, '"Space of Experience" and "Horizon of Expectation": Two Historical Categories', pp. 255–75. [Trans.]

15 *Meister Eckart: An Introduction to the Study of His Works with an Anthology of His Sermons* (James M. Clark ed. and trans.) (Edinburgh: Thomas Nelson and Sons, 1957), p. 185.

Miegge tells us that a reply comes from the chief prophet of the peasant rebels—*An Exposition of the Second Chapter of Daniel the Prophet, preached at the castle of Allstedt before the active and dear dukes and rulers of Saxony by Thomas Müntzer, servant of the word of God*, 1524—whom Ernst Bloch cites at length in his *Thomas Müntzer: Theologian of the Revolution*:

> I have tried to blow the [Lord's] loud, moving trumpets, so that they resound with zeal for the knowledge of God, and to spare no man on earth who strives against the word of God.[16]

> For the stone torn from the mountain has become great. The poor laity and the peasants see it much more clearly than you do. [. . .] Indeed, the stone is great! The foolish world has long feared it. The stone fell upon the world when it was still small. What then should we do now, after it has grown so great and powerful? And after it has struck the great statue so powerfully and irresistibly that it has smashed down the old pots of clay?[17]

Modern apocalyptic literature has its own history, specific forms, and figures. Not only narration/vision, intentionally falsified characters, pre- or post-dated epochs, symbolic-allegorical language, the *imagination* that defeats *ratio* but, in addition, a direct relationship with revolutionary exegesis, earthly eschatology, a worldly beyond, political messianism, a tale not of the end of the world but of the subversive hand of God over history so as to overturn its direction, and finally the powerful arm of

16 Thomas Müntzer, 'Letter to Frederick the Wise. Allstedt, 4 October 1523' in *Sermon to the Princes* (Wu Ming introd., Alberto Toscano pref. and annot., Michael G. Baylor trans.) (London: Verso, 2010), p. 101. Bloch's quote from this letter begins with the lines 'There is need for a new John to rise in the spirit of Elijah' but these appear to have been interpolated by Bloch or one of his sources. [Trans.]

17 Müntzer, 'Sermon to the Princes (or an Exposition of the Second Chapter of Daniel' in *Sermon to the Princes*, pp. 28–29. [Trans.]

the Magnificat that truly raises the humble and defeats the powerful. Yes, it is the hidden, minoritarian, marginal, heretical face of modern politics. If its words were symbolically violent, against it actions, repression was materially violent. There is nothing to be recovered but much to be understood. And perhaps something to avenge.

Koselleck: 'The genesis of the absolutist state is accompanied by a sporadic struggle against all manner of religious and political predictions. The state enforced a monopoly on the control of the future [by suppressing apocalyptic and astrological readings of the future]'.[18] The absolute state, the first form of modern state, is concerned to repress all apocalyptic interpretations. In line with its anti-ecclesiastical activity, it assumed what had been a task of the Church. Historical time passed into the hands of modern politics. Human expectations were scaled down, minimized, became worldly. The state, in struggle with the Church, became a secular Church. Not only the absolutist state but everything that followed the modern state, from the liberal to the democratic, including the intervening authoritarian solutions, held together the monopoly of force and the monopoly of history, or at least proposed doing so. When at the start of the modern era politics became state, it acted with different forms of violence. And violence has as many forms as there are forms of domination. The aims of domination and violence—i.e. the forms of power—are to suppress the future, to manage the immutability and the repeatability of the present. To look back from the present results of late modernity to the beginnings of the modern and its developments, one can see that only one force has found itself in position to break a link of the chain. It was a class social force, the heir of the long history of subaltern classes that was able to become the dominant class. But the working class did not adopt a prophetic voice; it

18 Koselleck, *Futures Past*, p. 16. Tronti leaves the section in brackets out of his quotation, but as it seems relevant to his point, I have reinserted it. [Trans.]

tried to provide itself with a scientific one. Perhaps it could have been possible to not see these in opposition. Action and thought in the experience of the workers' movement were able to define for the first time in history, after the great Christian experience, two complementary modalities of free human existence. And while political passion lived alongside the rigour of thought, there was a place for great hopes. When the relationship broke down, everything collapsed. The dream of a thing: that standing behind Thomas Müntzer there were, in the 1900s, not the German peasants but the proletarians of all the world united.

The 'dream of a thing' is prophecy, not utopia. If prophecy erupts in upheaval, utopia intervenes within change. Total overturning for the one, slow mutation for the other. U-topia, the non-place is the search for another place. Utopia is the ideal form of a society built upon the plane of principles and values, not seen but foreseen, not thrown [*gettata*] but projected [*progettata*]. It is again politics that becomes state, *de optimo reipublicae statu*, Thomas More, *Nova Insula Utopia*. And so it is. Even when one spoke of the extinction of the state,[19] to achieve it one had to resort to the highest figure of the state. Now this history of the state has reached its end. And it was great history when compared to the woefulness of today's politics. The state is reduced to government; politics is reduced to administration. The new Nebuchadnezzar has lost sleep, not because he has forgotten his dream but because he never dreamt. Daniel is no longer with us, but there are 'magicians, the astrologers, and the Chaldeans'. It is certain that the great statue, resplendent and terrible, has crumbled. The feet of iron and clay did not endure. And the stone that moved without anyone moving it, it has become a mountain. This new mountain is not the New Kingdom. After the Four Kingdoms, how many others have there been since the fourth century?

---

19 Italian rendering of the well-known Marxist expression usually translated into English as the 'withering away of the state'. [Trans.]

There is always a Fifth Kingdom, as a symbolic prophetic gift. But we live in times such that it appears as the highest form of domination, because its shape is diffuse, interiorized, freely, democratically accepted. Can alternative politics, having traversed the entire history of the state, take up again control of the future? Or will modern politics fall along with the modern state? Doubts. Research.

One thing is certain. We must begin again to speak authoritatively of a part or side, instead of speaking, in a subaltern way, in the name of everyone. Ernst Bloch speaks harsh words, in *Geist der Utopie*, which I think the meek soul of Sergio Quinzio would have liked:

> Sometimes the conquest of evil may succeed more quietly, as the rider on Lake Constance succeeded through heedlessness, and, more deeply, the saint in special situations succeeds through the kiss of righteousness, through a creative disregard; but as a rule the soul must assume guilt in order to destroy the existing evil, in order not to assume even more guilt by an idyllic retreat, a hypocritical connivance in injustice. Dominance and power in themselves are evil, but it is necessary to confront power in terms of power, as a categorical imperative with revolver in hand.[20]

And *Spuren*: 'for humanity is something that has yet to be discovered'.[21] These two aspects can be found together, like acting and thinking, always rigorously from a partisan standpoint: first 'the darkness of the lived moment', the 'Now and its darkness'; then the 'not-yet-conscious knowledge', the not-yet become. Are these concepts paraphrases of the utopian or of the prophetic? They are unified in the category of the 'Not Yet'

20 Ernst Bloch, *The Spirit of Utopia* (Anthony A. Nassar trans.) (Stanford: Stanford University Press, 2000), p. 242.

21 Ernst Bloch, *Traces* (Anthony A. Nassar trans.) (Stanford: Stanford University Press, 2006), p. 18.

(*nocht nicht*), a category that enters the 'realest part of our waking dreams'.[22] Bloch's concrete utopia is prophecy. Also because the two principles, Bloch's principle of hope and Hans Jonas' principle of responsibility, are no longer feasible in present conditions. There are no more principles, which are all reduced to the wretchedness of values. It is not only the religious, but also the political that reduced to the ethical decays and dies. The religious and the political are, in their respective autonomies, the two great existential dimensions of modern humanity. Can they rediscover themselves as what they are, or is their destiny to become subordinated to something else?

Quinzio's lesson returns here. For he reminds us of the mystery of the human condition, not of its immutability but its contingent eternity; this contradiction lacerates and does not console. Revolutionary thought failed to confront this problem. Not all but some of its failures stem from here. And it is from here that new paths must be identified, and new breaches forcibly made. What is Quinzio's should be rendered to Quinzio and nothing more. But one political path today—one, not the only one—is to bind together an apocalyptic vision of the future with a realist reading of the present. A choice that is dictated by the epoch, which we have defined as being without signs of the times. By now great tactics—and great politics is always great tactics—is no longer autonomous because it no longer has great forces to manoeuvre and subjective powers to give voice to. Hence passing through the point of catastrophe cannot be evaded for the vision of upheaval, and if possible, it in turn rises to the most ambitious heights. But after the defeat of God, messianic anticipation runs into contradiction with the apocalyptic transition. 'Behold, I come quickly!' (Revelation 22:7): this prophetic phrase can no longer be uttered. This Sergio Quinzio knew, and he suffered from it. At the same time, he believed and did not resign himself. Quinzio reading

22 Bloch, *Spirit of Utopia*, pp. 199ff., p. 202, p. 253 and p. 247, respectively.

Daniel. The book of Daniel, he says, contains seven visions 'that compose a single apocalyptic proclamation'. The first vision, in particular, that of Daniel 2,

> expresses the regressive character of history. Civilizations, empires, worldly powers that succeed one another through the centuries sink lower and have an increasingly lesser value. The whole history of the world is a repellent hybrid that in the end becomes a chaotic mixture of strength and weakness in which the division, non-homogeneity, the pluralist discord of elements is the sign of imminent decomposition. The sense of the entire course of history consists in proceeding towards destruction so that the kingdom of God is established.[23]

It is our contemporary condition: awaiting without hope, vocation without belief, faith without ethics, or more precisely political faith without ethical values, will without possibility of decision-making, 'speaking on behalf of' *a part* without an ultimate end, but because, at least for us, 'so it must come to pass'.

23 Quinzio, *Un commento alla Bibbia*, p. 319.

KOMMUNISMUS ODER EUROPA

'Es waren schöne glänzende Zeiten'. 'Those were beautiful and magnificent times, when Europe was a Christian land, when *one* Christianity dwelled on this civilized continent and when *one* common interest joined the most distant provinces of this vast spiritual empire.' This is the opening to *Die Christenheit oder Europa*.[1] Up and till a few years ago, an icy chill would fall upon our thoughts on reading these words. And today, how should we read them with our eyes cleansed by the air of the century? 1799: not after the revolution, which was anything but finished within the revolution, certainly after the Enlightenment century. Let us take up for ourselves this romantic revolt against the reformist eighteenth century. Only we, after all, can savour the taste of the 'critique of revolution'. In *Die Christenheit*, Schmitt finds Burke's influence.[2] As Novalis writes: 'Burke has written a revolutionary book against the Revolution.'[3] It's true. Whoever wishes to really understand 1789 should read this book of 1790: 'By following false lights, France has bought undisguised calamities at a higher price than any nation has purchased the most equivocal

1 See Novalis, 'Christianity or Europe: a Fragment' in Frederick C. Beiser (ed.), *The Early Political Writings of the German Romantics* (Cambridge: Cambridge University Press, 1996), p. 61.

2 Carl Schmitt, *Political Romanticism* (Guy Oakes trans.) (Cambridge: MIT Press, 1986), p. 112.

3 Novalis, 'Miscellaneous Observations' in *Philosophical Writings* (Margaret Mahony Stoljar ed. And trans.) (Albany: SUNY Press, 1997), p. 43.

blessings.'[4] For example: it 'has extended through all the ranks of life, as if she were communicating some privilege, or laying open some secluded benefit, all the unhappy corruption that usually were the disease of wealth and power. This is one of the new principles of equality in France.'[5] From here, it has been possible to see 'the medicine of the state corrupted into its poison.'[6] The conservative revolutionary Burke foresaw that in the revolution the 'commonwealth itself would [. . .] crumble away, be disconnected into the dust and powder of individuality'.[7] He tended to dangerously 'consecrate' the state; he recommended to 'never dream of beginning [the state's] reformation by its subversion', but instead to address 'the faults of the state as to the wounds of a father, with pious awe and trembling solicitude'.[8] 'Society is indeed a contract. Subordinate contracts for objects of mere occasional interest may be dissolved at pleasure—but the state ought not to be considered as nothing better than a partnership agreement in a trade of pepper and coffee, calico or tobacco, or some such low concern to be taken up for a temporary interest. It is to be looked on with reverence; because it is not a partnership in things subservient only to the gross animal existence of a temporary and perishable nature. It is a partnership in all science; a partnership in all art; a partnership in every virtue, and in all perfection.'[9]

Tradition and revolution are the great political problems that the end of the twentieth century hands back to us, unresolved and unresolvable. In '89 of our century, the theme was buried. But it was not born in the '89 of that other century. There it had merely exploded in an

4 Edmund Burke, *Reflections on the Revolution in France and Other Writings* (New York: Everyman's Library, 2015), p. 456.

5 Burke, *Reflections on the Revolution*, p. 456.

6 Burke, *Reflections on the Revolution*, p. 457.

7 Burke, *Reflections on the Revolution*, p. 508.

8 Burke, *Reflections on the Revolution*, p. 508.

9 Burke, *Reflections on the Revolution*, pp. 508–9.

event of universal history. The theme lies within the entire arc of modern politics; it is there in its beginning, and so assumes the character of the origin of the modern; and it lives anew in the signs of the twilight of the West. It dies when all of this shows itself to be at once scattered and punctured. The young Hegel, he too standing within the revolution, within its ongoing process between 1799 and 1800, writes: 'The ever-increasing contradiction [*Der Immer vergrössernde Widerspruch*] between the unknown that men and women unwittingly seek and the life that is offered and permitted them.' Consider another *incipit*, this time of the text that Georg Lasson published with the 'misleading title "Freedom and Fate" [*Freiheit und Schicksal*]'.[10] But once a text has been named, it is difficult to think of it as nameless. 'Only then can a limited life, as force, be attacked with force by a better life, when this latter too has become force [*Macht*] and comes to fear violence [*Gewalt*].' *Freheit und Schicksal* are two founding categories of the modern in the lengthy course of its two millennia, from the Christianity of the origins to that of the end. Or at least, let us say that they will be, when we get used to being modern in this sense, which is to say as 'not ancient'. The liberty of the moderns and the fate of the moderns—it is necessary to reconnect these two aspects *in interiore homine*, like two conflictual locations of an irresolvable break, two divergent instances of unsalvageable negation. Only from the depths of this extreme danger can one rise again to that which

10 See Remo Bodei, *Scomposizioni. Forme dell'individuo moderno* (Einaudi, Turin, 1987), pp. 4ff. I am unaware of any English translation of this fragment (and so I have translated it from the Italian). There is an extended discussion of it in H. S. Harris, *Hegel's Development*: *Towards the Sunlight 1770–1801* (Oxford: Clarendon Press, 1972), pp. 440ff. Luporini's translation into Italian referenced by Tronti, with the title 'Un frammento politico giovanile di G. F. Hegel' [A political fragment of the young G. F. Hegel], first appeared in the journal *Società* 1 (1945), and was reprinted in *Filosofi vecchi e nuovi* (Florence: Sansoni, 1947). [Trans.]

saves.[11] Besides, 'freedom' and 'fate' are two new names for 'politics' and 'history'. Politics is freedom in history; history is fate in politics. Modernity has permitted the experience of this human condition, of historico-political contradictory consciousness: the most fortunate lived it; the less fortunate thought it. The epoch of revolutions and the epoch of wars posed the same problem in different forms. Freedom against fate; tragically, the breath of a better life—to say it with that Hegel—touched that time. Afterwards, fate against freedom, under the force of necessity, where 'subsistent life lost its own force and all of its dignity'.

'The age of revolution is particularly most instructive, in contrast to everything older and earlier, on account of the mutability of things, the multiformity of modern life as compared to earlier life, the strong change in the pulse beat, and, finally, through the great notoriety of everything connected with it.'[12] Burckhardt spoke in a situation not far from our own. In the 1870s–80s, he saw the '*ewige Revision*' [eternal revision], that is to say, the revolution, as a long process now behind us, not concluded but interrupted. He did not fear this process, he didn't celebrate it nor judge it. He did not teach it. He knew it. Among the 30 audience members of his set of lectures *Über das Studium der Geschichte*, in Basel in the winter of 1870, was Nietzsche.[13] It seems that Nietzsche's second *Untimely Meditation*: *On the Uses and Abuses of History for Life*, was

---

11 Tronti is again referencing Hölderlin's 'Patmos'. See also Martin Heidegger's influential reading of Hölderlin's 'Patmos' in 'The Question Concerning Technology' (see *The Question Concerning Technology and Other Essays* [William Lovitt trans., New York: Harper Torchbooks, 1977], pp. 28–35) and, for a useful exposition, see William Davis's 'Hölderlin, Heidegger, and Hyperobjects' in *Wild Romanticism* (M. Poetzsch and C. Falke eds) (London: Routledge, 2021), pp. 127–43. [Trans.]

12 Jakob Burkhardt, *Judgements on History and Historians* (Harry Zohn trans.) (London and New York: Routledge, 2007), p. 254.

13 See Joachim Fest's appendix to Jakob Burckhardt, *Considerazioni sulla storia universale* (Milan: SE, 1990), p. 255.

inspired by these lectures. Burkhardt wrote: 'Our task, in lieu of all wishing, is to free ourselves as much as possible from foolish joys and fears and to apply ourselves above all to the understanding of historical development.'[14] The rest of the passage provides us with a particularly effective formulation: 'the age of revolution makes this objective understanding the most difficult for us. As soon as we become aware of our position, we find ourselves on a more or less defective ship which is drifting along on one wave among millions [triggered by the revolution].[15] *Wir sind diese Woge Selbst* [. . .] But one could also say that we ourselves are, in part, this wave.'[16]

Hence, is it only in a later period that the spirit can range freely across the past? After the epoch of revolution, the one-hundred-year peace, then the epoch of war, then nothing; and the late, mature epoch of the free spirit has not yet come. No 'Archimedean point beyond events [. . .] capable of spiritually overcoming things'[17] could be found, and it will be all the more difficult to find it in the sea of tranquillity that threatens us. So, are we once again left with a final 'utmost need' to contemplate those 'entities' that we term historic powers? This, for Burckhardt, 'is our freedom in the full knowledge of the enormous and generous tyranny of things and of the flow of necessity'.[18] After 1789: 'the freedom to postulate all sorts of things, as though the world were a tabula rasa and everything could be enforced through well-devised

14 Burckhardt, *Judgements on History and Historians*, p. 253.

15 This phrase does not appear in the English translation (unlike in the Italian). However, the context makes the reference to the revolution clear. [Trans.]

16 Burckhardt, *Judgements on History and Historians*, p. 253.

17 The English translation is substantially different: 'With its own strength the new church would not nearly have sufficed to create an Archimedean point, a banner to rally round; it would have inclined to nothing but sects' (*Judgements on History and Historians*, p. 120). [Trans.]

18 I have been unable to find any similar phrase in the English translation. [Trans.]

institutions [*Einrechtungen*].'[19] 'The driving force in all this is a great optimistic will which has suffused the times since the middle of the eighteenth century.'[20] After 1815: 'Only now, through the peace, were revealed the consequences of a released colossal real property and an industry hitherto really shackled and only relatively free. With England as the model, the age of absolute ruthless *acquisition and communication* began (Goethe to Zelter: *Reichtum und Schnelligkeit*, wealth and speed); modern industry came into being.'[21] The similarity of the epochs, a harking to, not a returning to. The always the same does not return but the different resembles. After the epoch of revolutions or after the age of wars, with the revenge of tranquil forces, property and wealth, industry and market, comes the time of apparently optimistic innovation and of real and pessimistic senescence. It is not decadence, which served civilization as a profound season of uneasy rethinking. It is just unwitting decay, civilizational drift, the virtual beginning of nothing, internal dissolution of the inner tissue of humanity, of the figure of the people, of the idea of the state, of class action. Portentous spirits intuited what was about to arrive: Tocqueville and Burckhardt for the 1800s; Weber and Schmitt for the 1900s. And few others. Marx is now for us the futuristic bridge linking these two epochs of thought. Without him, the two centuries would just be known as conservative *Kultur*. With him, they can even be understood as revolutionary *Kultur*. Within which one finds the self-critique of the revolution: not for the failed consequences but in its original framework. A world that must be understood.

But all of this is 'Europe'. In the closing episodes almost two centuries ago, modern antiquity came to an end: within the revolution, between the beginnings and the results.

---

19 Burckhardt, *Judgements on History and Historians*, p. 256.

20 Burckhardt, *Judgements on History and Historians*, p. 252.

21 Burckhardt, *Judgements on History and Historians*, pp. 256–57.

> Jena at the end of the eighteenth century. [. . .] Everywhere the earth resounds with battles, whole worlds are collapsing, but here, in a small German town, a few young people come together for the purpose of creating a new, harmonious, all-embracing culture out of the chaos. They rush at it with that inconceivable, reckless naivety that is given only to people whose degree of consciousness is morbidly high, and to these only for a single cause in their lives and then again only for a few moments. It was a dance on a glowing volcano, it was a radiantly improbable dream. [. . .] A spiritual tower of Babel was to be erected, with nothing but air for its infrastructure; it had to collapse, but when it did, its builders broke down too.[22]

In 1799, when the young Hegel was composing the 'enigma', *Freiheit und Schicksal*, Novalis (who was only ever young) wrote 'the lecture' or 'the sermon' *Die Christenheit*. There is a dual gaze on the immediate past in each of these texts: both, contradictorily, enthusiasm for the new forms that are being born, nostalgia for the old forms that are dying. They too are revolutionary conservatives. Novalis on the 'new European guild: the philanthropists and enlighteners;'[23] the 'priests and mystagogues'[24] of 'this new faith, which was stuck together out of pieces of mere knowledge', for which France is happy to form the womb. They mobilized all the erudition to 'ennoble [history] by making it into a domestic and civil portrait of family and morals'.[25] The programme: 'purging poetry from nature, the earth, the human soul and the sciences. Every trace of the sacred was to be destroyed, all memory of noble events

22 Georg Lukács, 'On the Romantic Philosophy of Life: Novalis' in *Soul and Form* (John T. Sanders and Katie Terezakis eds. Anne Bostock trans.) (New York: Columbia University Press, 2010), p. 42.

23 Novalis, 'Christianity or Europe', p. 71.

24 Novalis, 'Christianity or Europe', p. 70.

25 Novalis, 'Christianity or Europe', p. 71.

[. . .] spoiled by satire [. . .] the world stripped of colourful ornament'.[26] And yet we now 'stand high enough to smile back upon these former times and to recognize in those strange follies remarkable crystallizations of historical matter. Thankfully we should shake hands with those intellectuals and philosophers; for this delusion had to be exhausted for the sake of posterity and the scientific view of things had to be legitimated'.[27] And now, '[m]ore charming and colourful, poetry stands like an ornate India in contrast to the cold, dead pointed arches of an academic reason'.[28] Fabrizio Desideri is right to read here, here too:

> the romantic project of a fusion between the 'modern' world of enlightened rationality and traditional Catholic universalism as effective form of political unification (*complexio oppositorum*); what lies between individual freedom and the 'historical constitution' of Christianity [. . .]. A future, then, that lacks even the minimal traces of restoration, but the utopian-messianic one of a conjunction between the idealistic-subjective principle of revolution and the naturalistic-organic one of history.[29]

Once again, revolution and tradition, from another standpoint, from another vision of the world, of humanity, and of events. Innovation and history, the modern and the past, the ancient in culture and the new of the times: our—buried—problems, that must be disinterred at the end of the 1900s.

Then moments, passages, paths, returns: symbolic, allusive. By now, all true writing must be translated. We must read and must be read,

---

26 Novalis, 'Christianity or Europe', p. 70.

27 Novalis, 'Christianity or Europe', p. 74.

28 Novalis, 'Christianity or Europe', p. 74.

29 Desideri, in Novalis, *Opera filosofica*, VOL. 2 (Fabrizio Desideri ed.) (Turin: Einaudi, 1993), pp. 609–10; and for a more measured reading of the text, see his 'Nota introduttiva'.

adding to the text to be read. Like Scripture, the Holy one that—as Gregory said—grows *cum legente* [with the reader]. Novalis saw in 1793 the effect of a continuation of Protestantism as something permanent, which he declared to be 'something completely contradictory',[30] *eine Revolutions-Regierung*, a revolutionary government, or a government of the revolution. The beginning of Protestantism 'glowed from a passing fire from heaven; but shortly afterwards a withering of the holy sense is apparent. The worldly had now won the upper hand'.[31] '[*D*]*er Periode des praktischen Unglaubens*' [the period of practical unbelief approaches].

> With the Reformation Christianity was done for. From hence forth it existed no more. Catholics and Protestants or Reformers stood further apart for one another in their sectarian conflict than the Moslems and pagans. The remaining Catholic states continued to vegetate, not without vaguely feeling the corrupting influence of the neighbouring Protestant states. *Die neuere Politik erst entstand in diesem Zeitpunkt* [the new politics arose during this time]: individual powerful states sought to take possession of the vacant universal see, now transformed into a throne.[32]

In that moment, only then, in that point of epochal passage, was born 'modern politics': within the civil wars of religion, in the collapse of Christianity, in the process of the birth of the modern state, in a Europe emerging from 'practical irreligiosity'. The Reform was also a 'sign of the times'.[33] From Germany to Europe, the 'better minds of all nations had secretly grown mature'. And for its sake, against it, a political experiment took place that had never been seen in the entire course of universal

30 Novalis, 'Christianity or Europe', p. 66.

31 Novalis, 'Christianity or Europe', p. 67.

32 Novalis, 'Christianity or Europe', p. 67.

33 Novalis, 'Christianity or Europe', p. 69.

history, a society of men and women aiming squarely at a higher purpose, with self-sacrifice and for the good of a cause.

> The old Roman Senate did not conceive its plans of world domination with greater certainty of success. Never before was greater intellect used in the execution of a great idea. This society will be a model for all societies that have an organic longing for infinite expansion and eternal permanence. But it will be proof that the unguarded moment alone spoils the cleverest undertakings [. . .]. What was lost in Europe they attempted to regain in other parts of the world [. . .]. Everywhere they founded schools, infiltrated confessionals, mounted rostrums, busied the presses; they became poets and philosophers, ministers and martyrs, and remained in the most wonderful unanimity about doctrine and action throughout the vast expanse from America to Europe and to China [. . .]. If it were not for weak superiors, for the jealousy of princes and other ecclesiastical orders, and for court intrigues and other unusual circumstances, which interrupted their bold course [. . .] who knows how old the world would still seem? [34]

It's the Jesuits not the Bolsheviks, the *Societas Jesu* not the CP(b) [Bolshevik Communist Party]; we find ourselves in the 1500s, not the 1900s. But how modernity resembles itself in its epochs, its struggles, its attempts, and failures! Or better, how it resembled itself when there was still the fact and the sense of the historical event; and for it, and against it, the political will to think/act! Novalis could turn to the political spectacle of his time and discover the old world and the new fighting each other. We no longer can. Now, between the old and the new there is no war, there is a holy alliance. Postwar Europe is no longer Europe. Here the end of Christianity becomes the Christianity of the end. And in a

34 Novalis, 'Christianity or Europe', pp. 68–69.

convergent accord, the death of communism concludes the decline of the West.

Communismus der Geister [the communism of the spirits], 'Disposition', is a fragment, a rough draft by the young Hölderlin. Credit to Domenico Carosso for having brought it to our attention.[35] I shall summarize. 'Sundown. Chapel. Vast, rich land. River. Forests. The friends. The chapel alone still illuminated. The conversation comes to the middle ages. The monastic orders according to their ideal meaning.' *Die Orden gefallen*: 'the orders fallen'. Let us then 'start from the exact opposite principle': *von der Allgemeinheit des Unglaubens* (the same word Novalis used), from generalization, from universalization 'of unbelief'. '[L]amentation is fruitless, the task is to help.' *Christentum* and *Wissenschaft*: there must surely be a single truth. 'A beautiful evening draws to its end.' Light took leave. The murmuring of the Neckar welcomed the arrival of the night. 'Lothar! Does a secret ache not grip you too [. . .] this motionlessness induces anxiety and the remembrance of past beauty poisons; it has happened to me a hundred times as I had to turn back from the free ether of antiquity *in die Nacht der Gegenwart* [into the night of the present] [. . .] it is a tormenting feeling, the remembrance of splendors vanished, you stand like a criminal before history.' *Du kennst die Weltgeschichte; und wo ist es Alles*? '[Y]ou know world history; and where is it all?' The question does not concern the dead material

35 Domenico Carosso, *Il comunismo degli spiriti. Forma e Storia in un frammento di Hölderlin* (Roma: Donzelli, 1995). Friedrich Hôlderlin, 'The Communism of Spirits' (Hunter Brolin trans.) *Tripwire. Journal of Poetics*, 14 (2018): 258–60 (available online: https://bit.ly/3ym4xH4) (last accessed 18 May 2024). See also the very useful addendum to the translation by Bruno. C. Duarte, 'Apocryphal Politics: Hölderlin's Communism of Spirits', which discusses the complex history of the text and ongoing questions of attribution (pp. 261–72). The fragment has also translated in *The Germanic Review: Literature, Culture, Theory* 97(1) (2022), with an introduction and an interpretive essay by Joseph Albernaz. [Trans.]

which that era has handed down to us. It concerns 'the form in which it happened'. The form 'is the only thing that can present us with a point of comparison for our situation, since the material is always something given; form however is the element of the human spirit in which freedom acts as law and reason becomes contemporary; now compare that age with ours'.[36]

Vergleiche jene Zeit und unsere [compare that age with ours]: the theoretico-political cipher of our times. We must resist the temptation, though strong, given the 'ugly' times, to read these texts under the suggestive heading of 'beauty and truth'. Carosso finds a continuity between *Communismus der Geister* and that other unsettling text, dated 1797, attributed at one time or another to one or other of the three friends of the Stift in Tübingen, Hölderlin, Schelling, Hegel: *Das ältestes Systemprogramm des deutschen Idealismus*. It is here that is proclaimed the 'absolute freedom of all spirits, which carry the intellectual world in themselves, and which may not seek God or immortality *outside themselves*'.[37] The supreme act of reason is an aesthetic act because '*truth* and *beauty* are fraternally united only in *beauty*'. For this reason:

> Before we make ideas aesthetic, i.e. mythological, they will have no interest for the *people*. Conversely, before mythology is rational, the philosopher must be ashamed of it [. . .] mythology must become philosophical to make people rational, and philosophy must become mythological to make philosophers sensuous. Then eternal unity will reign among us.[38]

This was intended to be a 'political' programme. In the same way that *Freiheit und Schicksal* was a 'a youthful political fragment'—as Luporini

36 Hölderlin, 'Communism of Spirits', pp. 258–59.

37 'The Oldest Systematic Programme of German Idealism' in *The Early Political Writings of the German Romantics*, p. 4.

38 'Oldest Systematic Programme of German Idealism', p. 5.

called it when translating and commenting upon it, finding in it a discussion of the relationship between the intellectual and the masses (in 1947!). Another, later young-Hegel text seems to me closer: *Dass die Philosophie.*[39] 'A long time passes before an old ethical form can be surpassed by a new one'. And yet, 'once the new ethicality has grown to maturity in the spirit of the people and the opaque need for it has penetrated all souls, then the multitude no longer feels truly at ease but it remains unaware of what oppresses it, or of what else it wants to obtain.' There is thus need of a *nur eines leichten Druks*, 'just a little pressure' for the old bark to fall away and the new one to come to light. *Die grossen Menschen sind*, 'it is the great men that grasp nature in it; they understand the living form and truth of the ideal step that the ethical nature of man can ascend to; these more observant natures do nothing but say the word and the people follow'. But then, *die Macht ihres Geistes*, the force of their spirit (politics?) 'sets itself to work only on one side' (*an einem Ende*), at one extremity. Instead, nature (ethical nature, history?) wants 'the whole'. Hence it 'shakes them down (those men) from the heights at which they had been placed and puts others there'. But in the case when from that side it is possible to grasp the totality then, before the 'horrors' (*die Schrekken*) of the objective world', before 'all the constrains of ethical reality' (*alle Fesseln der sittlichen Wirklichkeit*), in the face of 'all the alien points of support for remaining in this world', one must bravely enter into the struggle with the old forms of the world spirit in the same way that Isaac fought God. Only the great man—that is, for us that great subjective collective force, the communism of spirits, the Europe that holds together tradition and revolution—can entwine, or better, entwine

39 Tronti refers the Italian reader to Bodei, *Scomposizioni*, pp. 253–55. Another Italian translation has since come out: G. W. F. Hegel, *Il bisogno della filosofia (1801–1804)* (C. Belli and J. M. H. Mascat eds and trans) (Milan: Mimesis, 2014). I am unaware of any English translation of this text and have translated directly from the Italian. [Trans.]

again 'individuality with destiny' so as to give it *eine neue Freiheit*, 'a new freedom'.

The difference between the end of the 1700s and the end of the 1900s: behind one, the revolutionary *Terreur*; behind the other, today, there is the Glorious Restoration.[40] And we anti-Enlightenment thinkers cannot give ourselves the aesthetic luxury of being romantic. Then the *Sehnsucht* [nostalgia] of the ancient past nourished itself with the hope of new life, of the new freedom. Today the *nostàlghia* of modern antiquity inevitably suffers from a 'historic desperation'. It is here that we must linger to understand. 'Perhaps this is the epoch: the "stellar" conflict between the shepherd-less herd of the last men and the declining ones [*tramontanti*], messengers of the Overman. The latter want to go towards the twilight [*tramonto*] of the history-destiny that has led to the last man (and therein lies their insuperable limit)'.[41] There is a stellar affinity between Eckhart's 'noble man' and Nietzsche's 'Overman'. It is true that we, *Untergehenden* [declining, setting], left without aim or *polis*, neither *civitas* nor *respublica*, much less *Gemeinschaft* [community], we are now 'intractable' characters practically and politically. But this we must acknowledge. So here the idea of a European Archipelago is convincing but not sufficient. Like all politics at the end of the twentieth century, it serves to increase the utility and limit the damage of history to life. It is a defensive apparatus, an action of containment, a *katechon* of a tremendous and compelling process: that of the new modernity that kills the ancient greatness of the modern. Let those able to engage in such a politics do so. But they should realize that they will only be permitted at best to carry out 'that' history, to accomplish that fate without freedom. 'The last man'—the *homo oeconomicus democraticus*—has won: for that is not only what the ordinary citizen, the common man and woman is,

40 In English in the original. [Trans.]

41 Massimo Cacciari, *L'arcipelago* (Milan: Adelphi, 1997), p. 153.

it is the very personality of the leader.[42] Not only the man of the people, also the figure of the prince. Who indeed is the last man? *Also sprach Zarathustra*, Prologue, Part 5: is it the one who will take root on a 'soil [that] will be poor and tame, where no tall tree will be able to grow from it anymore'?[43] is it the man who will not launch his arrow beyond himself, until the 'string of their bow will have forgotten how to whir'? The one who will live in the time 'when human beings will no longer give birth to a dancing star?' What '[n]o shepherd and one herd'[44] means is that the shepherd is now the first of the animals of the herd. This democracy is the self-government of the last men. The extinguishing of politics. Communism, which is to say, Europe realized and upended. See the beautiful note that closes, or opens, Cacciari's *Arcipelago*. Perhaps an icon of the *Übermensch* exists: 'the figure of the Risen one painted by Piero in Sansepolcro', with his gaze that pierces with 'implacable humility' from the remotest anticipation. But it should be set alongside a contrary image, the one Karl Kraus speaks of in *The Last Days of Mankind*:[45] the first world war, a hill, a cross, the strike of a howitzer, the cross destroyed, the body of Christ, arms outstretched, still hanging, as if in emptiness, over the void. The art of war. The 'sleepers' awaken. Now powerless the light of the Resurrected 'shows itself to the blind'. We will see, will see only within great history. If there is to be any.

---

42 'Leader' in English in the original. [Trans.]

43 Friedrich Nietzsche, *Thus Spoke Zarathustra* (Adrian Del Caro trans.) (Cambridge: Cambridge University Press, 2006), p. 9.

44 Nietzsche, *Thus Spoke Zarathustra*, p. 10.

45 Karl Kraus, *The Last Days of Mankind* (Fred Bridgham and Edward Timms trans) (New Haven, CT: Yale University Press, 2023).

A Final Motif

THESES ON BENJAMIN

I. It was not capitalism that defeated the workers' movement. The workers' movement was defeated by democracy. This is the problem that the century sets before us. It is the fact, *die Sache selbst* [the thing itself], that we must now think.

II. The workers' movement confronted capitalism as an equal. A confrontation, between the nineteenth and twentieth centuries, within great history. Alternating phases. Reciprocal outcomes of victories and defeats. But workers' labour-power, as internal part of capital, could not escape it. The murky depths of the failure of the revolution lies here. Attempts, reasonable and mad to change the world, all fell. The long reformist march has not had any more success than the storming of heaven. But the workers changed capital. They forced it to change. The workers' defeat took place not on the social terrain. It happened on the political terrain.

III. The twentieth century is not the century of social democracy. It is the century of democracy. Traversing the age of wars, it imposed its hegemony. It is democracy that triumphed over class struggle. Over the course of the century, authoritarian and totalitarian political solutions functioned as demonic instruments of a democratic providentialism. Democracy, like the monarchy of yore, is now absolute. It was not the practice of totalitarian democracies that advanced but the totalizing idea of democracy itself. Ironically, it did so at the same time as the dissolution of the concept of 'the people', foreseen by Kelsen's genius. Following the defeat of Nazi-Fascism and of socialism, twice over it became the value chosen. The workers' movement did not develop its own idea of democracy, let alone put it to the test—neither in the East nor in the West. It did not grasp it, did not traverse it as a field of struggle. The workers' movement of the twentieth century could only ever be democratic. But the century of democracy killed it. This trauma lies, and acts in obscurity in the collective unconscious of the European left—its militancy, leadership and culture.[1]

IV. Prophetically, Tocqueville glimpsed the anti-political future of modern democracy. The *demoralization politique* arrived promptly and—at the end of the century—the *athéisme politique* achieved completion. The great liberal saw the end of modern politics realized in American democracy, a powerful statement of the world's future. Umberto Coldagelli acutely grasped in Tocqueville's distinction between the science of politics and the art of government, the 'substantive dualism' of democracy and freedom. The direct consequence was that 'the safeguarding of freedom comes to depend exclusively upon the capacity of the art of government to oppose the spontaneous propensity of the "political state" to flatten itself onto the "social state".'[2] He then quotes the following version of the 1840 *Démocratie*: 'Sentiments and ideas are renewed, the heart grows larger and the human mind develops only by the reciprocal action of men on each other. I have demonstrated that this action is almost nil in democratic countries. So it must be created there artificially. And this is what associations alone are able to do.'[3]

1 'Leadership' in English in the original. [Trans.]

2 'Introduzione' to Alexis de Tocqueville, *Scritti, note e discorsi politici (1839–1852)* (Milan: Bollati Boringhieri, 1994), p. *xvi*.

V. The artifice of the political relation contrasts with the naturalness of the social relationship: this is not a Jacobin invention, nor a Bolshevik imposition, it is the condition of the political in the modern era. It is another way of saying: political civilization versus natural sociality. Today there is the opportunity to translate this choice into a decision between freedom and democracy. Contrary to what one might think, Tocqueville teaches that the natural-animal aspect is democracy, and the historico-political one is freedom. Now that the science of politics describes the necessity of democracy, the task of the art of government is to introduce freedom. Another political freedom, after the liberty of the moderns, without falling back into the liberty of the ancients. It is not so ironic that while the dictatorships have rekindled the passion for freedom, democracies have extinguished it. If *Le Philosophe lisant* depicted by Chardin was bent over the book by George Steiner rather than over his folio, I believe he would confirm Milton's verse: 'all passion spent'.[4] The century of democracy that triumphs over dictatorships in war does not provide freedom in peace. At the end of the twentieth century, the historic clash between dictatorship and freedom, which saw the defeat of both of totalitarianism as well as authoritarianism, leaves—passionless—on the field, as if it were an unexploded bomb, the political conflict between democracy and freedom. To decipher this passage. The challenge is for thought but practice finds itself equally interrogated. The winning ideological assemblage, the cumulative ideological consensus and so the *pouvoir social* that follows from it, are now all inflected by liberal democracy. To insert a wedge into this practico-conceptual whole 'liberal-democracy'. To force into opposed senses the two potentially contradictory terms. Great politics can only return on the front of this good war.

3 Alexis de Tocqueville, *Democracy in America: Historical-Critical Edition*, VOL. 3 (Indianapolis: Liberty Fund, 2010), p. 900.

4 George Steiner, *No Passion Spent* (London: Faber and Faber, 1996).

VI. A practice of freedom in contrast to the practice of *homo democraticus*. An idea of democracy in contrast to the practice of *homo oeconomicus*. Pressing these two buttons with the fingers of thought, we should try to start anew the investigation into new forms able to give meaning to political action. On the one hand, there are the *moeurs* and the *croyances*, on the other, the *goût di bien-être materiel* and the *mollesse du coeur*. Democracy guarantees and brings about the latter; freedom needs the former. Choose. Because they are alternatives. An unprecedented spirit of division is required. Dividing the neutral citizen into two differently gendered beings. For each man and woman, to convert the modern individual into a person. Reconnecting the past to the future, this can happen only if each is separated from the present. No longer can we consider, with Benjamin, 'now' (*Jetztzeit*) as the location for the Marxian revolutionary dialectical leap. Ever more with Heidegger, we are forced to consider 'now-time' (*Jetzt-zeit*) as *Weltzeit*, inauthentic worldly time. Here too, between time and the hour [*l'ora*], between the epoch and the now [*l'adesso*],[5] one must strike with the red wedge[6] of the living contradiction. The white circle is this world that by now is dead.

VII. Not liberty *to* or liberty *from*, positive freedom or negative freedom, 'liberty' or 'freedom',[7] liberty of the ancients and liberty of the moderns. Not even a political philosophy of liberty: this was provided by liberalism. But: philosophy of freedom, what Marxism was unable to provide. The object of the former was, at once external, juridical and social liberty, the constitutional freedoms of the market, the public guarantee for the

---

5 *L'ora* can mean 'now' as well as 'hour'. It should be understood here as in John 4:23: 'But the hour cometh, and now is'. *L'adesso* is how Tronti renders *Jetztzeit* in contrast to Benjamin's notion of 'now-time' or *Jetzt-zeit*. [Trans.]

6 The reference is to El Lissitzky's 1919 lithographic propaganda poster, 'Beat the Whites with the Red Wedge!' (*Klinom krasnym bey belykh*!). [Trans.]

7 The two terms are in English in the original. [Trans.]

private atom, rights which are precious and poor, precious in order to live together with others, poor if one is to exist setting out from oneself. The object of the latter, human freedom *itself*, that which Marx attributed to the 'eternal nobility of the human species', the beyond-human Christian freedom, Spinoza's *mentis libertas* [*seu*] *beatitude*,[8] the non-lonely solitude of the great spirit to put it in the terms of the Luporini of the philosopher-of-existence period.[9] The error of the Marxian perspective was not of having critiqued *libertas minor* but to have done so without contemporaneously taking on, theoretically and politically, *libertas major*. This was the political disaster. Only on the basis of true human freedom could one carry out a critique of false, bourgeois liberty. A destructive critique of their assumed human generality along with a positive adoption of their modern foundation as inheritance; only from here could one have moved beyond. In Kantian terms: the insufficiency of *Unabhängigkeit*, of the independence of individuals but at the same time its condition of possibility, its transcendentality to found freedom as the *Autonomie* of the human being, with the moral law within.

VIII. *Homo democraticus*, the isolated and massified individual, the more globalized the more 'particularized', guided from outside and from above until and while it cultivated its garden; the individual in the herd, the last man, described first by Nietzsche, by Goethe, as the subject that they saw arriving, 'the age of ease', a 'very anxious and doubtful' term Thomas Mann will say. The age of ease and vulgarity. Mann rediscovers Goethe's suggestion from 1830 once matters had reached fantastical and vertiginous heights in 1950. *Meine Zeit*, my time, 'the epoch of technology, of progress and of the masses': 'while I expressed it, I was largely

8 The phrase is from the Preface to Spinoza's *Ethics*, PART 5: 'Freedom of Mind, or blessedness'. See *Collected Works*, VOL. 1 (Princeton: Princeton University Press, 1986), p. 594. [Trans.]

9 Reference to Luporini, *Situazione e libertà nell'esistenza umana*. [Trans.]

hostile'. But, he warned: 'It is always risky to believe oneself privileged due to the particular abundance of one's epoch, because a more complicated time can come and it always does.'[10] It is easy to see the tragedy of socialism in the period between the middle and end of the twentieth century; it is more difficult to glimpse the exhaustion of democracy's drama. But it is here that democracy definitively surrenders to being a public function of *homo oeconomicus*. The democracy of interests: this is its final name. In the last 50 years, democracy has become corrupted or reached completion [*compiuto*][11]—depending on whether one sees the problem from the standpoint of a radical democrat or from that of the critic of democracy. I believe it has run its course [*compiuto*]. Is democracy incapable of reform in the same way as socialism was? I would like to say to Pietro Ingrao,[12] this is the doubt of the defeated. To solve it, or to attempt to, one must abandon intellectual facileness and confront the complexity that has intervened in politics.

IX. Ingeborg Bachmann wrote of Musil's character, 'he gives a mirror image to the world of his time': 'Ulrich understood in time that the epoch in which he lives, which is endowed with more knowledge than any earlier epoch, an immense knowledge, seems unable to intervene in the course of history.'[13] What was understood in time, was in time forgotten. To the point that no one notices that history is without epoch

---

10 Thomas Mann, *Romanzo di un romanzo* (Milan: Mondadori, 1964), p. 243. To my knowledge, no translation of *Meine Zeit* exists in English. I have therefore translated from the Italian. [Trans.]

11 The Italian *compiuto*, bears with it not only the sense of having 'been accomplished' or 'realized', but also the sense of having run its course, to have exhausted itself. [Trans.]

12 Pietro Ingrao was the leading figure of the PCI left from the 1960s till the self-dissolution of the party. [Trans.]

13 Ingeborg Bachmann, *Il dicibile e l'indicibile* (Milan: Adelphi, 1998), pp. 21–22.

any more. In fact, nothing happens. Events there are no more. There is only news. Look at the characters at the summit of empires. And reverse Spinoza's motto. There is nothing to understand. Tears only, or laughter. At the end of the millennium, Athens and Jerusalem watch with incredulity at the results of the ancient as of the modern. The end of communism and Christianity of the end, these two symbolic orders that still need interpreting; dark reservoirs in the folds of contemporary consciousness that themselves bring time to a close, but—and here's the novelty—without apocalyptic energies and with the silence of signs. The desperate cry of Father David Maria Turoldo: 'Lord, still send prophets / [. . .] to say to the poor to continue to hope / [. . .] to break the new chains / in this infinite Egypt of the world.'[14] The true God failed, the real defeat of God in the century is in the unkept promise of human freedom for every man and woman, for all men and women. This is what we mean: this freedom *in interiore homine*, need and negation must be grasped, unveiled in the tragic history of the twentieth century. From here we must set out again: not from new starting points but from paths interrupted.

X. Walter Benjamin to Stephan Lackner, 5 May 1940: 'We ask ourselves whether history might not by chance be forging an ingenious synthesis of two of Nietzsche's concepts, that of the good European and of the last man. As a result, there might issue forth that of the last European. All of us are struggling against becoming that last European.'[15] This is an

14 Father David Maria Turoldo (1916–1992), was a theologian, philosopher and poet. A member of the mendicant Servite Order, during the Nazi occupation of Milan he participated in the anti-fascist resistance. He later played an important role in the cultural and religious renewal of the Church. I have been unable to track down the bibliographical details for this fragment of a poem. [Trans.]

15 Walter Benjamin, *Gesammelte Briefe. Band VI. 1938–1940* (Frankfurt am Main: Suhrkamp, 2000), p. 442 (translated here from the Italian version in Tronti).

extremely timely reflection. This is what a prophetic political thought is. Before our disenchanted eyes, the incarnation of the last man in the good European is being realized, programmed according to the schedule of a democratically chosen economico-financial calendar. Here everything happens. The event becomes naked fact. Europe is born as the century dies: without passion due to the exhaustion of states and because of individual interests. History synthesizes what there is. What ought to be is not its concern. Politics had the task to overthrow the last man, not to represent him. But we have said: the end of modern politics. And *all* are happy with that. Everyone fights to become the last European. The competition takes place in the marketplace, where one hears 'the noise of the great drama' at the same time as 'the buzzing of poisonous flies'.[16] Stretching out before us, this history without epoch leaves us the choice between two anthropological perspectives. Bloch said: humanity is something that still needs to be discovered. Nietzsche said: humanity is something that needs to be overcome. The perspectives: the former, alternative; the latter, antagonistic. Up and till quite recently we would have said: one is politics, the other theory. No longer. Everything leads to a solution in thought. If the decline [*tramonto*] of the West is to be accomplished, as in Spengler, in the first centuries of the next millennium, the twilight [*tramonto*] of politics will be accomplished in the first decades of the next century.[17] To thought falls the task of pre-dicting, of speaking in the names of history's defeated.[18] Of humanity, meanwhile, there is nothing to discover. The Overman remains entirely to be thought.

---

16 Nietzsche, *Thus Spoke Zarathustra*, p. 36. Tronti misquotes—perhaps intentionally—the first of these phrases, writing *grande commedia*, which means 'great drama'. The standard Italian edition by Giorgio Colli and Mazzino Montinari (who also edited the standard German edition), is *grandi commedianti*, 'great actors'. See Friedrich Nietzsche, *Così parlò Zarathustra* (Milan: Adelphi, 1976), p. 55. [Trans.]

17 Written in 1998, Tronti is referring to our current period. [Trans.]

18 *Pre-dire*, normally written *predire*, 'to predict'. The hyphen emphasizes the idea that predicting here is fore-saying (*dire*, 'to say'). [Trans.]

XI. The ideal continuation to Marx's eleventh *Theses on Feuerbach*, that is, its twentieth-century reformulation, is Benjamin's twelfth thesis from *Über den Begriff der Geschichte*.[19] Let's observe: 'The subject of historical knowledge is the struggling, oppressed class itself [*die kämpfend, unterdrueckte Klasse*]. Marx presents it as the last enslaved class—the avenger class [*die rächende Klasse*] that completes the task of liberation in the name of generations of the defeated.'[20] This is a fact of consciousness that has always scandalized social democracy. It 'preferred to cast the working class in the role of a redeemer of *future* generations, in this way cutting the sinews of its greatest strength. Schooled in this way, the working class forgot both its hatred and its spirit of sacrifice, for both are nourished by the image of enslaved ancestors rather than by the ideal of liberated descendants.' It is rare to be able to subscribe to every word of a thought. This is one such case. This is the reversal of a standpoint, of one's side [*parte*]. 'Avenger class', the last enslaved one but also the first to possess sufficient strength. A motivation, political not ethical, for taking that side [*parte*]. To avenge an eternal past of oppression. This past is therefore the new subject of history, which alone can affect new political action. The rising sun was this passion, experienced and preserved in the body of one's past struggles. This passion was extinguished by the dogmatic presumption, typical of social democratic theory and practice, of an 'interminable' and 'unstoppable' progress of humanity, as if history proceeded 'through a homogeneous, empty time'.[21] Having forgotten hate, having forgotten the will to sacrifice, two virtues that are communist and Christian. Having cut the sinews of strength, which is

19 See Walter Benjamin, 'On the Concept of History' in *Selected Writings*, VOL. 4, p. 394. See also 'Lemmi: Futuro [*Zukunft*]' and 'Immagine [*Bild*]', in *Sul concetto di storia*, pp. 160ff.

20 I have partially modified the translation to conform more closely to the Italian. [Trans.]

21 Benjamin, 'On the Concept of History', p. 395.

what counts in struggle. Upsetting the meaning of action: that is *Bild*, not *Ideal*: the image of defeated comrades, not the ideal of redeemed brothers. For redemption concerns the 'oppressed past', not the radiant future. Only that historical movement, or that political subject is great, or is summoned to greatness, which can translate the contents of what has been into the forms that are about to come, always, always, always, against the present.

XII. 'In the idea of a classless society, Marx secularized the idea of messianic time. And that was a good thing. It was only when the Social Democrats elevated this idea to an "ideal" that the trouble began. This ideal was defined in Neo-Kantian doctrine as an "infinite task" [*der unendliche Aufgabe*]. And this doctrine was the school philosophy of the Social Democratic party.'[22] Homogenous and empty time became, here, the antechamber in which one had to await the revolutionary moment. 'In reality, there is not a moment that would not carry with it *its* revolutionary chance [*revolutionarën Chance*].'[23] What matters is a given political situation but 'it is equally grounded [. . .] in the power of the keys[24] which the historical moment enjoys vis-à-vis a quite distinct chamber of the past, one which up to that point has been closed and locked. The entrance to this chamber coincides in a strict sense with

22 Thesis XVIIa from 'Paralipomena to "On the Concept of History" ', *Selected Writings*, VOL. 4, pp. 401–2.

23 Benjamin, 'On the Concept of History', p. 402.

24 The English translation speaks of a 'right of entry', but I have retained the Italian, which is closer to the German *Schlüsselgewalt* and retains the Christian reference to Matthew 16:18–19: 'And I say unto thee, That thou art Peter, and upon this rock I will build my church; and the gates of hell shall not prevail against it. And I will give unto thee the keys of the kingdom of heaven: and whatsoever thou shalt bind on earth shall be bound in heaven: and whatsoever though shalt loose on earth shall be loosed in heaven'. [Trans.]

political action.'[25] What is essential is to recognize a sign of 'a revolutionary chance in the fight for the oppressed past'.[26] And here too it is right. But what of the times without signs? When history sleeps, must politics awaken it or should it slumber beside it, abdicating all vital acts? Even the Christian Giuseppe Dossetti[27] told us that politics was contingency, it is chance, occasion and not every so often but always, day in day out. And so one does not await the revolutionary *chance*,[28] one takes it; it does not arrive, it is already there in heterogenous and full time. Politics can regenerate itself, it can surpass its modern character only if it takes up 'the power of the keys' in a different sense, opposite to that which enabled it to operate as a future-oriented project, implicit in the present and issuing from it. It must decide to modify the past, to change everything that has been, open the closed room of history and produce the moment in which what always takes place does not cease. Not await the signs of the times but create them. For signs do not reveal the event, the signs are the event. To demonstrate in the contingency of daily action that everything that you are binding to the earth 'will be bound in heaven', and everything that you lose on earth 'shall be loosed in heaven' (Matthew 16:19). The end of the politics of the moderns is not the end of politics and it is not the return to the politics of the ancients. It is the

25 Benjamin, 'On the Concept of History', p. 402.

26 Benjamin, 'On the Concept of History', p. 396.

27 Dossetti (1913–1996) is a fascinating figure: jurist and politician and intensely anti-fascist, he joined the resistance but, as a deeply evangelical Christian, refused to carry arms. A Christian Democratic politician in the postwar governments, he often stood against the right of his party, was against NATO and was always engaged in social reforms. In 1956, he took his vows and was then made a priest. [Trans.]

28 In German (which is here identical to both French and English) in the original. I have italicized future instances where Tronti uses *chance* to allude to Benjamin's *revolutionarën Chance*. [Trans.]

occasion of that *discontinuum* in politics that the given situation does not offer but that the revolutionary *chance* can impose.

XIII. A revolution in the idea of politics: this is the first power of the keys bestowed upon us by the oppressed past and the generations of the defeated. Revolution as political praxis: this must be set before the eyes of critique. There is no longer a distinction between revolutionary act and revolutionary process. *Chance* is neither the one nor the other. We no longer need to ask whether the revolutionary subject is the class or the party. The halting of what occurs does not take place because of the will to power. Marx's '[dialectical] leap in the open air of history'[29] has come crashing down, its wings broken on the arid terrain of politics. The point of differentiation is no longer between reformist gradualism and revolutionary rupture. It is between continuity and discontinuity. And since within continuity no reformist practice is possible, so discontinuity is no longer identifiable with revolutionary action. The revolutionary *chance* is not revolutionary action. It is a standpoint, a way of political being, a form of political action, it is the now, always of political behaviour. In the face of, against the 'reified continuity of history', politics is practised in nature in 'intermittent bursts' of actuality, where 'all that is past [. . .] can achieve a higher level of actuality than at the moment of its existence'.[30] Among the preparatory materials for Benjamin's theses, one encounters piercing shards of thought: 'The history of the oppressed is a *discontinuum*', i.e. 'The *continuum* is of the oppressors.'[31] The concept of the 'tradition of the oppressed' must be seen 'as the *discontinuum* of the past in opposition to history as the *continuum* of events'.[32] But, should

29 Benjamin, 'On the Concept of History', p. 395.

30 See Benjamin, 'Lemmi: *continuum* Kontinuum' in *Sul concetto di storia*, p. 155.

31 Benjamin, 'Lemmi: *continuum* Kontinuum', p. 153.

32 Benjamin, 'Lemmi: *continuum* Kontinuum', p. 153.

the point of catastrophe be located in the continuity of history as the later Benjamin appears to think, or should it be cultivated in the discontinuity of politics as the end of the century appears to suggest? Here lies the in-decision of research, that looks to the extreme aspects of the horizon of problems, no longer with the hope of finding solutions but rather with the responsibility of escaping the sickness of time, which consists in being subordinate to a present future.

XIV. *Ex praeterito—Praesens prudenter agit—Ni futuru*[*m*?] *actione*[*m*?] *deturpet* (On the basis of the past—the present acts prudently—lest it spoil future action): this is the inscription, divided into three according to a triad of men and animal heads at the top of the 'Allegory of Prudence', or 'Allegory of Time governed by Prudence' that the aged Titian executed between 1560 and 1570. The wolf of the past, the lion of the present, and the dog of the future. Panofsky says that the painting glorifies Prudence as able to wisely utilize the three Forms of Time associated to the three Ages of Life. Titian did not depart from a well-established 'tradition—except that the magic of his brush imparted a semblance of palpable reality to the two frontal heads in the centre (that of the man in the prime of life and that of the lion) while dematerializing, so to speak, the two profile faces on either side (those of the old man and the wolf on the left, those of the youth and the dog on the right): Titian gave visible expression to the contrast between that which is and that which either has been or has not yet begun to be.'[33] 'Prudence', a great category of modern politics,[34] has marked twentieth-century success [*fortuna*] and failure [*sfortuna*], and produced the century's victories and tragedies. It is the 'dismal science' of the doctrine of state at the time of the absent

33 Erwin Panosfky, *Problems in Titian: Mostly Iconographic* (New York: New York Press, 1969), p. 103; see also Panofsky's *Meaning in the Visual Arts* (Garden City: Doubleday Anchor Books, 1955), pp. 146ff.

34 See the journal *Filosofia politica* 1(2) (1987).

sovereign.[35] The present must know from the past above all what should not happen in future. This is the gap that current events [*l'attualità*] impose upon us: to defend ourselves from the form of the future that all the contents of the present are constructing. Current events: Father Time without Great Epoch, the 'lion' without the 'fox', strength without prudence, politics without politics, which is to say, history left to itself, minor history, cyclical, the eternal return of the always the same, accelerated, modernized, via inner conservative revolutions. The old wolf's face is the tiger leap into the past of which Benjamin speaks. The mature face of the lion is the great twentieth century that has been extinguished in the current reified continuity of history. This brings about a virtual, abstract, domesticated form of future. One must act now lest what follows ruins this action. But does the criterion of the political still have a *chance*, whether revolutionary or otherwise, in the current contingency of historical events?

XV. *Kultur* and *Zivilization*: taking up again the broken thread of a debate, picking it up at the end of the century from the place of its beginnings. With our words, fitted to today, the distinction is the following: *Zivilization* is modernity; *Kultur* is civilization. One could speak of bourgeois modernity and human civilization. But this would be too emphatic and no longer acceptable. One cannot inflect the bourgeois and the human according to nineteenth-century rules. Today's bourgeois is the 'last man'. And the man of today has nothing to do with that of yesteryear. As the *Bürger* in Thomas Mann, 'our' Mann, the one from before 1918, is the opposite of the *bourgeois*, in the same way that the *Arbeiter* [worker], not Jünger's but Marx's, is the opposite of the *citoyen*. Our dream: the rugged pagan race containing great bourgeois culture,

35 See Giacomo Marramao, 'Il sovrano assente: la dottrina dello Stato come "triste scienza" ' in *Dopo il Leviatano* (Turin: Bollati Borringhieri, 2000), pp. 23–47.

'that great, severe, tormented bourgeoiseness of the soul' that Claudio Magris has written about.[36] However, between the two, modernity/civilization, there has been an eternal, historic conflict, as well as a provisional political consensus. In the various passages of the twentieth century, consensus and conflict expressed themselves in various forms. The age of war radicalized the contradiction between *Kultur* and *Zivilization* but the time of peace that ensued did not even ask itself the question. We must understand whether one can take up again the civilizing function that the workers' movement had before war pushed it into the trenches. The wars and peace of the twentieth century leave this legacy. But for it to be gathered up one would need heirs: a movement of ideas and forces able to insert into the body of the modern, the soul and forms of a *Kultur*, of a Civilization; it does not matter that it is new, it can even be ancient, what matters is that it exhibits the signs of a contrast when compared to the current barbarization of human social relations. To civilize modernization: this is the task within which everything else must situate itself—struggles, organization, government, projects, tactics. Insert *Kultur* in the unstoppable organizational projects of globalization, digitalization, virtualization. The greater the danger of modern barbarism, the more what saves can intervene to withhold, messianically arresting what occurs. After the end of modern politics, I see more *katechon* than *eschaton* in the response to *what is to be done*?

XVI. '*Aber Freund*! *Wir kommen zu spat*.'[37] Freely translated: 'But friend, we have come too late.'[38] This is the *Stimmung* that binds the figures and the motifs, the passages and the pauses, the prestos and the adagios of

---

36 See Claudio Magris, 'I saggi di Thomas Mann, una custodia per i *Buddenbrooks*' in Thomas Mann, *Nobilità dello spirito e altri saggi* (Milan: Mondadori, 1997), p. *x*.

37 Hölderlin, 'Brot und Wein' (1801).

38 Friedrich Hölderlin, 'Bread and Wine' in *Selected Poetry* (David Constatine trans.) (Hexham: Bloodaxe Books, 2018), p. 97.

reflection. The century of great opportunities was transformed, in the course of its history, into the century of small occasions. Possibility, in politics, is always tragic. The comedy of probability leaves everything as it is. It was possible to not do what was done. But it was also possible to carry out what was not. Research has a long way to go along these tracks. No longer in the dark. Although: this is a strange light that the twilight of politics throws on recent history. '*Aber das Irrsal hilft*',[39] helping to roam, to *err*, error (?)

---

39 Constantine's translation has 'But wanderings help', although *Irrsal* can also mean 'erring'. Tronti makes this explicit in the continuation of the sentence: where *errare*, 'to err', also means to wander. [Trans.]

Afterword

After the Twilight of Politics—the Night of History

1998: the date of the birth of *The Twilight of Politics*. The century officially died. In fact, it was already dead. Hobsbawm had already named it the 'short century', 1917–1989. It never really convinced me. Of course, it worked symbolically. I think the traumatic start-date of the Twentieth Century is 1914. Without the great war, no great revolution. And even the extraordinary first ten years of the century are fully within the Twentieth Century. More than that, they are foundational. The dissolution of all the forms that explode in figurative arts, in literature, in music, in science anticipate the thunderclap that launched the age of the European and world civil wars. At the other end, the epochal date that marks the end is not 1989 but 1991, the collapse of the Soviet Union.

The essence of the twentieth century is not contained in the brevity of its existence but is to be found in the tragic matter of its history, where the tragic belongs to the political, which needs to be noted and underlined. That's what the 'twilight of politics' meant. There was a Spenglerian suggestion of a decline of the West. An intellectual stand against the then-invasive 'mainstream'[1]: a thinking of the end when the ideology of the 'new beginning' raged. What was being offered was a work of mourning that one of the parties to the dispute, the bad heirs to the great events of the workers' movement, refused to confront.

1 In English in the original. [Trans.]

In truth, the end of the century should be situated within the 1980s, because the Twentieth Century did not die a premature, natural death. It was killed from above through an operation that was explicitly intended to cure the patient but that ultimately aimed to suppress him. The Trilateral Commission is the starting point of the offensive, the order of the day dictated by the dominant classes that were in trouble after the cycle of struggles in the years straddling the 1960s and 70s. Excess demand from the base of the social was denounced as an undermining of the public good. Order had to return to the chaotic capitalist cosmos. Stewardship followed, with Reaganite and Thatcherite policies. The *trente glorieuses*, 1945–75, was declared closed due to bankruptcy. A powerful ideological apparatus presented this as if it were the 'new that advances'. The winning keyword was: innovation. Progressive democrats were fascinated by it. Blind kittens, they failed to see the conservative manoeuvre taking giant leaps. A veritable age of Restoration opened. The fierce anti-twentieth-century reaction was nothing else but this. The laws of the market were set back on their throne, considered legitimate after the European and world civil wars had ended in victory for the armies that usurped politics, parties and the State.

So, politics: parties, the State. That is to say, modern politics. Not Politics in general, which one derives from the *polis*, the Athenian myth of the citizen's participation in the *res publica*. The latter, not coincidentally returns in current demagogic and populist tendencies, precisely in contrast to the modern idea of politics, the one which runs from Machiavelli to Weber, from Hobbes to Schmitt, which from the Sixteenth-to-Seventeenth centuries arrives in the Twentieth century where it achieved its highest form of expression. The politics that governs processes, such as the organization of forces, such as the relationship between masses and elites. That is, the political action of the great classes in struggle in modern capitalism. There is no capital without this form of politics, from an original accumulation that concentrates power in absolute monarchies, to the cycles of development and crisis, crisis and development, which will demand and will obtain liberalism for the freedom of the market and democracy for the dictatorship of production. They will write the liberal democratic Constitutions to keep in order inevitable and indispensable social conflict. It is not the case, as in vulgar historical materialism, of structure and superstructure; here the coupling of economy and politics is equivalent. *The Twilight of Politics* of the 1990s is the daughter, now grownup, of the *Autonomy of the Political* of the 1970s. And both would not have been possible without the experience of operaismo of the 1960s, which opened the books for me on the inadequacy of Marxist economism. I do not wish to vindicate intellectual coherence. I wouldn't know what to do with it. What matters and should be taken care of is the coherence of one's form of life. Passages of research and discovery are also leaps. And each of us retains their own endowment of tough decisions.

Thought is struggle. Struggle against one's time. Because that is one's enemy. Close combat with present history requires a defensive and offensive conceptual armoury that must be consolidated and renewed each day.

One of the scandalous theses produced by the adoption of this political criterion is that of the historic encounter between the workers' movement and modern politics. The encounter comes when the young Marx leaves the League of the Just and founds the Communist League. The passage of socialism from utopia to science does not explain it all but it tells us something essential. It does not say it all because at that time it was marked by a certain determinism that would forcefully condition so-called historical materialism. But it gives us the essential in refusing recipes for the cuisine of the future, the prefiguring of an abstract society of the free and equal, and rejects 'what wells up from each person's heart'[2] in the form of a future universal justice. In the same way that the bourgeoisie needed modern politics to realize capitalism, so the proletariat would need modern politics to realize socialism. And so the long history of subaltern classes comes to a close. But in ending it is not extinguished. That history must, in Hegel's terms, be 'sublated', conserving its subversive will while inflecting it with other means for other ends.

Modern politics, as encountered and practised by the workers' movement is not entirely and solely political realism. It is the realistic conduct of political action aimed at overcoming the present historical conditions. The ruthless, demonic analysis of Machiavelli's *The Prince* concludes, in Chapter 26, with the *Exortatio* for the arrival of a 'redeemer'. Because 'the barbarian dominion stinks in everyone's nostrils'.[3] And by citing Petrarch: 'Virtue will seize arms / Against frenzy'. It is essential then to have armies of one's own and not mercenary ones, and with these to have no 'other object nor any other thought, nor must he adopt anything as his art but war'.[4] With Marx, the workers' movement achieves a lucid scientific analysis of capital, with the aim of exiting capitalism and overcoming the present course of history. For this to occur it is essential to have one's own autonomous organization that cultivates no other thought or engages in any art other than class struggle. Class struggle is not civil war, it is war civilized, which is to say, conflict given form, struggle collectively and consciously organized. The proletariat is strong enough to avoid violence. Strikes, work stoppages, the refusal of labour within the process of the production of the wealth of nations are a political threat

2 Tronti uses the expression *pappa del cuore* or baby food of the heart, a vague *Senhsucht*, sentimental nostalgia. This is a reference to Hegel's critique of romantic sentimentalism in the Preface to his *Elements of the Philosophy of Right* (Allen W. Wood ed., H. B. Nesbit trans.) (Cambridge: Cambridge University Press, 1991), p. 15. [Trans.]

3 Machiavelli, *Prince*, p. 90.

4 Machiavelli, *Prince*, p. 90.

that jeopardizes the system's logic as a whole. It is subversive in itself and for itself. For this reason, it is at ease within the process of modern *Zivilization*. It aims, however, to overcome it inasmuch as it bears a higher idea of *Kultur*.

The protean power of capitalism lies in its extraordinary capacity of continuous self-transformation. It has seized human history and never again abandoned it. Still today, today still more so, as possessor of immense technological revolutions. To call oneself progressive to combat capitalist society is a paradoxical political nonsense. While there is capitalist domination, that form of progress does not stop. It cannot be stopped. The proletariat, having become organ of the factory, has learnt not to destroy the machines. They can be used for their own partisan interests in the struggle in production and one organizes oneself to make them into collective property, expropriating the expropriators. The means are ready-to-hand, and an end that only with difficulty can posit itself at the order of the day. Thus, 'politics against history' is not a bon mot to be embroidered with beautiful phrases; it is a strategic choice, the practical indication of a new frontier of general conflict. The course of history is now in the hands of those in command and it consists in programming the future as the eternal repetition of the present. The innovations of the postmodern exist but they have the following function: not of changing but of conserving. The globalization of the production of markets and consumption, the financialization of the economy, the technological virtualization of life, the dictatorship of communication, the geopolitics of power between nations-continents, the secularization of the sacred, and the consequent anthropological drift of the masses: this is the history that the winners are writing. Can politics seize these processes once again? Before rethinking 'what is to be done?' for the revolution, one must decide 'what is to be done?' with politics.

One can say of modern politics what must be said of the proletarian revolution: that the one and the other can still take place is confirmed by the fact that they have already happened. It is, then, a case of the modality of action, that it is not a case of inventing but of reprising. And it is not superfluous to add that the one and the other must be updated, both in their forms and contents, measured and practised in the contingency of the historical present, in a form more advanced and transformed. What does politics mean today in the age of anti-politics? What does revolution mean today in the age of revolt? How can one redefine the word party? How can one define anew the word class? Many questions, equally many problems. Perhaps if one were to focus on these themes several interrupted paths might reopen.

In the meantime, everyone must inflect in their own way, in accordance with the needs of their own research, the Weberian 'in spite of everything [let us continue]'.[5] The powerful process of rationalization, borne by capitalism, that has occupied the whole of the modern era, Weber saw as corrected and in a certain sense held in check not only by the resources of disenchantment but also by the 'experience of the irrationality of the world'[6] and, consequently, of the natural imperfectness of the human plant.[7] It is this historic contradiction that remains forever open and one

5 Max Weber, 'Politics as a Vocation' in *Political Writings* (Peter Lassman and Ronald. P. Speirs eds) (Cambridge: Cambridge University Press, 1994), p. 369. The phrase in square brackets appears in the Italian translation but not the English, although the meaning is implicit. [Trans.]

6 Weber, 'Politics as a Vocation', p. 362.

7 The expression *pianta uomo* comes from the famous Italian literary critic, Francesco De Sanctis (1817–1883) in his reading a of the writer and poet, Vittorio Alfieri (1749–1803). In his *Storia della letteratura Italiana* (Milan: Garzanti, 1964), De Sanctis writes: 'It is the new man who challenges his contemporaries. [. . .] And albeit in those days Italy was corrupt, it maintained a firm faith in a future Italy that yearned in thought for one like the ancient. At the foundation of this new Italy was the recreation of the plant man.' [Trans.]

must continue to see as open the 'small gateway'[8] through which the messianic message might continue to pass, as Benjamin suggested.

In *The Twilight of Politics*, prophecy was taken up *versus* utopia. I recently wrote a piece called 'Desperate Hopes' setting out from Bloch's concrete utopia.[9] If this is a new age of Restoration, where politics and subversion are spoken of with difficulty and with still greater difficulty do they meet, it is good to make hope a quotidian public practice and visual horizon for the future. Philosophy of praxis, understood in the Marxist and, more still in the Gramscian sense, is no longer given imminently. You must then secure your gaze on the beyond within a condition of enforced closure of everything outside. It is important to not abandon the 'already' and the 'not yet'. But both must be revisited. With Benjamin it is important to save the subversive charge of the past, with Bloch to reprise the cultivation of the 'dream of a thing'.

The framework that made the political history of the twentieth century lies behind us. We must put our path back within its frame. I do not know if today I would repeat the distinction I made between the great and the small Twentieth Century. The ideology of postmodernity has dissolved it. This squalid passing of the century has told us that what immediately preceded the current world disorder has been a single long state of exception that, in its own way, gave an order to the world and thereby a sense to human events. The one and the other are now lost, order and sense. But the rate of intensity of that lived history was so lofty and profound that it was unable to last the traditional one hundred years, it was forced to close much earlier. I now see the twentieth century like a romantic youthfulness spent and consumed in mad individual and collective undertakings. Everything from 1910 to the 1960s.

---

8 Benjamin, 'On the Concept of History', p. 397.

9 Mario Tronti, '*Disperate speranze*' (available online: https://bit.ly/4alF0Lr; also available in English: https://bit.ly/44PkpxC) (last accessed 18 May 2024).

After which, nothing. History does not end there. What begins again is the history as it has always been. One must contest the writing of that history by the victors. It is possible to do so only with an insurgent resurrection of modern politics, which is public action from above and from below, tactical manoeuvres and strategic eruption together, not separate, even less in opposition, destituent power and constituent power.

That world broken in two, always—in civil wars and in the Cold War, in the workers' revolution and in the totalitarian reaction—described, reflected, celebrated the dichotomous division of the capitalist socioeconomic formation. It was a real world. With the tragic features characteristic of real history. There one had to take sides, take up a position for one solution or other, to be a part, to feel, experience, to live the belonging to a point of view cost whatever it may in self-sacrifice; and to do so alongside others, beyond one's own egotistic singularity. And so, ethics of conviction and ethics of responsibility reunited, fused within the same person. Let's ask ourselves: why were such lofty, such towering literatures, such profound poetry and breaks and leaps in figurative arts and music, why such scientific discoveries that at once overthrew the traditional images of inside and out, of the human psyche and the world universes, why were they all concentrated in the Twentieth Century? Why did politics become, have to become political theology? And why did the history of the historians grasp at once the *longue durée* and the eruption of the event? But there is more and for me it is more significant. The class struggle that becomes daily life. Simple men and women reached a level of self-awareness and common destiny that had never been achieved previously and even less afterwards.

All of this has been interrupted, intentionally interrupted, and turned into its opposite. *The Twilight of Politics* at the end of the Twentieth Century, not only narrated a state of mind, a nostalgic one, but also an intellectual decision for battle. It registered in *interiore homine*. Because it was a history and politics lived dramatically. I hold very dear that *Stimmung* recalled in the final words of the book, illustrated by the warm words of my beloved poet, Hölderlin: '*Aber Freund*! *Wir kommen zu spät*' ['My friend, we have come too late']. Yes, I arrived in the world too late. I should have been born earlier, to have been able to participate in the history of the century rather than to witness the news reports of its conclusion. Then one would have been able to not do what was done and do what was not done. Now, at least for now, nothing more can be done, all has to be given up to the stupid 'spirit of the times'. But the last word is never spoken. It is always possible to wander through, that erring and that error . . . of those who command the course of history.

Mario Tronti
September 2020

Translator's Acknowledgments

Many thanks to Sunandini Banerjee and Diven Nagpal for their attentive, meticulous and patient editorial work and to Alberto Toscano for his efforts to iron out infelicitous expressions and for his invaluable contribution to several notes.

Bibliography

ACCORNERO, Aris. *Era il secolo del lavoro*. Bologna: Il Mulino, 1997.

ARENDT, Hannah. *The Promise of Politics*. New York: Schocken Books, 2005.

——. *Was ist Politik? Fragmente aus dem Nachlass* (Ursula Ludz ed.). Munich: Piper, 1993.

ASOR ROSA, Alberto. *Genus italicum. Saggi sulla identità letteraria italiana nel corso del tempo*. Turin: Einaudi, 1997.

——. *The Writer and the People* (Matteo Mandarini trans.). London: Seagull Books, 2021.

AUGUSTINE. *The City of God* (Henry Bettenson trans.). Harmondsworth: Pelican, 1972.

BACHMANN, Ingeborg. *Il dicibile e l'indicibile*. Milan: Adelphi, 1998.

BENJAMIN, Walter. *Gesammelte Briefe, Band VI: 1938–1940*. Frankfurt am Main: Suhrkamp, 2000.

——. *Selected Writings, Volume 4: 1938–1940* (Howard Eiland and Howard W. Jennings eds). Cambridge, MA: Belknap Press, 2003.

BILLINGTON, James H. *Fire in the Minds of Men: Origins of the Revolutionary Faith*. New York: Basic Books, 1980.

BLOCH, Ernst. *The Spirit of Utopia* (Anthony A. Nassar trans.). Stanford, CA: Stanford University Press, 2000.

——. *Traces* (Anthony A. Nassar trans.). Stanford, CA: Stanford University Press, 2006.

BODEI, Remo. *Scomposizioni. Forme dell'individuo moderno*. Turin: Einaudi, 1987.

BOLOGNA, Sergio, and Andrea Fumagalli, eds. *Il lavoro autonomo di seconda generazione. Scenari del postfordismo in Italia*. Milan: Feltrinelli, 1997.

——. *The Rise of the European Self-Employed Workforce*. Milan: Mimesis, 2018.

BOTERO, Giovanni. *The Reason of State*. Cambridge: Cambridge University Press, 2017.

BRECHT, Bertolt. *Collected Plays: Three*. London: Methuen, 1997.

BURCKHARDT, Jakob. *Considerazioni sulla storia universale*. Milan: SE, 1990.

——. *Judgements on History and Historians* (Harry Zohn trans.). London and New York: Routledge, 2007.

BURKE, Edmund. *Reflections on the Revolution in France and Other Writings*. New York: Everyman's Library, 2015.

CACCIARI, Massimo. *L'arcipelago*. Milan: Adelphi, 1997.

——. *The Withholding Power: An Essay on Political Theology* (Edi Pucci trans., Howard Caygill introd.). London: Bloomsbury, 2018.

CANETTI, Elias. *Crowds and Power* (Carol Stewart trans.). New York: Continuum, 1978.

CAROSSO, Domenico. *Il comunismo degli spiriti. Forma e Storia in un frammento di Hölderlin*. Rome: Donzelli, 1995.

CASSIN, Barbara, ed. *Dictionary of Untranslatables: A Philosophical Lexicon*. Princeton, NJ: Princeton University Press, 2014.

CHATEAUBRIAND, François-René de. *Memoirs from Beyond the Grave* (Alex Andresse trans.). New York: New York Review of Books, 2018.

CIGARINI, Lia. *La politica del desiderio* (Ida Dominijanni introd.). Parma: Nuova Pratiche Editrice, 1995.

CONSTANT, Benjamin. 'The Liberty of the Ancients Compared with that of the Moderns' in *Political Writings* (Biancamaria Fontana trans. and ed.). Cambridge: Cambridge University Press, 1988, pp. 308–28.

CRAINZ, Guido. *Il paese mancato*. Rome: Donzelli, 2003.

DAVIS, William. 'Hölderlin, Heidegger, and Hyperobjects' in *Wild Romanticism* (M. Poetzsch and C. Falke eds). London: Routledge, 2021.

DE SANCTIS, Francesco. *Storia della letteratura Italiana*. Milan: Garzanti, 1964.

DE TOCQUEVILLE, Alexis. *Democracy in America* (Harvey C. Mansfield and Delba Winthrop eds and trans). Chicago: University of Chicago Press, 2000.

——. *Democracy in America: Historical-Critical Edition*, VOL. 3. Indianapolis: Liberty Fund, 2010.

De Tocqueville, Alexis. *Scritti note e discorsi politici (1839–1852)*. Milan: Bollati Boringhieri, 1994.

Descartes, René. 'Discourse on the Method' in *The Philosophical Writings of Descartes*, vol. 1 (John Cottingham, Robert Stoothoff, and Dugald Murdoch trans). Cambridge: Cambridge University Press, 1985.

Dubois, Claude-Gilbert. *La conception de l'histoire en France au XVIe siècle (1560–1610)*. Paris: Nizet, 1977.

Eagleton, Oliver. 'Therborn's World Casting'. *New Left Review* 144 (November–December 2023).

Eckart, Meister. *Meister Eckart: An Introduction to the Study of His Works with an Anthology of His Sermons* (James M. Clark ed. and trans.). Edinburgh: Thomas Nelson and Sons, 1957.

Fanon, Frantz. *The Wretched of the Earth* (Constance Farrington trans.). London: Penguin, 2001.

Filippini, Michele, ed. *Leaping Forward: Mario Tronti and the History of Political Workerism*. Maastricht: Jan van Eyck Academie, 2012.

Furet, François. *The Passing of an Illusion: The Idea of Communism in the Twentieth Century* (Deborah Furet trans.). Chicago: University of Chicago Press, 1999.

Galli, Carlo. *Genealogia della politica. Carl Schmitt e la crisi del pensiero politico moderno*. Bologna: Il Mulino, 1996.

Gilbert, Felix. 'Bernardo Rucellai and the Orti Oricellari: A Study on the Origin of Modern Political Thought'. *Journal of the Warburg and Courtauld Institutes* 12 (1949): 101–31.

Ginsborg, Paul. *A History of Contemporary Italy*. Harmondsworth: Penguin, 1990.

Gramsci, Antonio. 'La rivoluzione contro Il Capitale'. *Avanti*, 24 November 1917.

——. 'Soviets in Italy (1920)'. *New Left Review* 1(51) (1968): 28–58.

——. *Pre-Prison Writings* (Richard Bellamy ed., Virginia Cox trans.). Cambridge: Cambridge University Press, 1994.

——. *The Prison Notebooks*, vol. 1. New York: Columbia University Press, 1992.

Grossmann, Henryk. *The Law of Accumulation and Breakdown of the Capitalist System* in *Henryk Grossman Works*, vol. 3 (Jairus Banaji and Rick Kuhn eds and trans). Leiden: Brill, 2022.

Hegel. *Early Theological Writings* (Richard Kroner ed., T. M. Knox trans.). Philadelphia: University of Pennsylvania Press, 1975.

——. *Elements of the Philosophy of Right* (Allen W. Wood ed., H. B. Nesbit trans.). Cambridge: Cambridge University Press, 1991.

——. *Il bisogno della filosofia (1801–1804)* (C. Belli and J. M. H. Mascat eds and trans). Milan: Mimesis, 2014.

——. *The Letters* (Clark Butler and Christiane Seiler trans). Bloomington, IN: Indiana University Press, 1984.

Heidegger, Martin. *The Question Concerning Technology and Other Essays* (William Lovitt trans.). New York: Harper Torchbooks, 1977.

Hexter, J. H. *More's Utopia: The Biography of an Idea*. New York: Harper Torchbooks, 1952.

Hobbes, Thomas. *Leviathan*. Cambridge: Cambridge University Press, 1996.

Hobsbawm, Eric. *The Age of Extremes: The Short Twentieth Century 1914–1991*. London: Abacus, 1994.

Hölderlin, Friedrich. 'Bread and Wine' in *Selected Poetry* (David Constantine trans.). Hexham: Bloodaxe Books, 2018.

Hölderlin, Friedrich. 'The Communism of Spirits' (Hunter Brolin trans.). *Tripwire: Journal of Poetics* 14 (2018): 258–60. Available online: https://bit.ly/3ym4xH4 (last accessed 18 May 2024).

——. *Selected Verse* (Michael Hamburger ed. and trans.). London: Anvil Editions, 1986.

Huizinga, Johan. *Erasmus and the Age of Reformation*. Princeton, NJ: Princeton University Press, 1984.

Inglese, Giorgio. *Introduzione a 'Il Principe'*. Turin: Einaudi, 1995.

Jonsson, Stefan. *Subject Without Nation: Robert Musil and the History of Modern Identity*. Durham, NC: Duke University Press, 2000.

Kosselleck, Reinhart. *Futures Past: On the Semantics of Historical Time*. New York: Columbia University Press, 2004.

KRAUS, Karl. *The Last Days of Mankind* (Fred Bridgham and Edward Timms trans). New Haven, CT: Yale University Press, 2023.

LENIN, Vladimir I. 'Notes of a Publicist' in *Collected Works*, VOL. 33. Moscow: Progress Publishers, 1980.

——. *Collected Works*, VOL. 26. London: Lawrence & Wishart, 1964.

LEOPARDI, Giacomo. 'Bread and Wine' in *Selected Poetry* (David Constantine trans.). Hexham: Bloodaxe Books, 2018.

——. *Canti* (Jonathan Galassi trans.). New York: Farrar Strauss and Giroux, 2010.

LESSING, Gotthold Ephraim. *Philosophical and Theological Writings* (H. B. Nisbet ed.). Cambridge: Cambridge University Press, 2012.

LÖWITH, Karl. 'Correspondence concerning modernity'. *The Independent Journal of Philosophy* 4 (1983): 107.

——. 'The Occasional Decisionism of Carl Schmitt' in *Martin Heidegger and European Nihilism* (Richard Wolin ed.). New York: Columbia University Press, 1995.

LUFT, David S. *Robert Musil and the Crisis of European Culture 1880–1942*. Berkeley, CA: University of California Press, 1980.

LUPORINI, Cesare. *Situazione e libertà nell'esistenza umana*. Rome: Editori riuniti, 1994[1945].

MACHIAVELLI, Niccolò. *The Prince* (Peter Bondanella trans.). Oxford: Oxford University Press, 2005.

MAGRIS, Claudio. 'I saggi di Thomas Mann una custodia per i Buddenbrooks' in Thomas Mann, *Nobilità dello spirito e altri saggi*. Milan: Mondadori, 1997.

MALRAUX, André. *Man's Fate* (Haakon M. Chevalier trans.). New York: Modern Library, 1934.

MANDARINI, Matteo. Review of *Workers and Capital* by Mario Tronti (David Broder trans.). *International Review of Social History* 65(3) (2020): 547–50.

MANN, Peter Gordon. 'The Good European in the Great War: Thomas Mann's Reflections of an Unpolitical Man and the Politics of the Self, Nation and Europe'. *Journal of European Studies* 47(1) (2017): 39–40.

MARRAMAO, Giacomo. 'Il sovrano assente: la dottrina dello Stato come "triste scienza" ' in *Dopo il Leviatano*. Turin: Bollati Borringhieri, 2000.

MARX, Karl. *Capital: Volume I* (Ben Fowkes trans., Ernest Mandel introd.). Harmondsworth: Penguin, 1990.

MARX, Karl, and Friedrich Engels. *Collected Works*, VOL. 3. London: Lawrence & Wishart, 1975.

——. *Collected Works*, VOL. 5. London: Lawrence & Wishart, 1976.

——. *Collected Works*, VOL. 6. London: Lawrence & Wishart, 1976.

MILANESI, Franco. *Nel Novecento: Storia teoria politica nel pensiero di Mario Tronti*. Milan: Mimesis, 2014.

MORE, Thomas. *Utopia*. Cambridge: Cambridge University Press, 2002.

MÜNTZER, Thomas. *Sermon to the Princes* (Wu Ming introd., Alberto Toscano pref. and annot., Michael G. Baylor trans.). London: Verso, 2010.

NEGRI, Antonio. 'Proletarians and the State' in *Books for Burning* (Timothy S. Murphy ed.). London: Verso, 2005, pp. 118–79.

——. *Political Descartes: Reason, Ideology and the Bourgeois Project* (Matteo Mandarini and Alberto Toscano trans and intros). London: Verso, 2007.

NIETZSCHE, Friedrich. *Beyond Good and Evil: Prelude to a Philosophy of the Future* (Rolf Peter-Horstmann and Judith Norman eds, Judith Norman trans.). Cambridge: Cambridge University Press, 2002.

——. *Così parlò Zarathustra*. Milan: Adelphi, 1976.

——. *Thus Spoke Zarathustra* (Adrian Del Caro trans.). Cambridge: Cambridge University Press, 2006.

NOVALIS. 'Christianity or Europe: a Fragment' in Frederick C. Beiser (ed.), *The Early Political Writings of the German Romantics*. Cambridge: Cambridge University Press, 1996.

——. 'Miscellaneous Observations' in *Philosophical Writings* (Margaret Mahony Stoljar ed. and trans.). Albany: SUNY Press, 1997.

——. *Opera filosofica*, VOL. 2 (Fabrizio Desideri ed.). Turin: Einaudi, 1993.

PANOSFKY, Erwin. *Meaning in the Visual Arts*. Garden City: Doubleday Anchor Books, 1955.

——. *Problems in Titian: Mostly Iconographic*. New York: New York Press, 1969.

POLANYI, Karl. *The Great Transformation: The Political and Economic Origins of Our Time*. Boston: Beacon Press, 1957[1944].

PONS, Silvio. 'L'unione sovietica nella politica estera di Togliatti'. *Studi storici* 33(2–3) (1992): 444.

QUINZIO, Sergio. *La croce e il nulla*. Milan: Adelphi, 2006[1984].

——. *La sconfitta di Dio*. Milan: Adelphi, 1992.

——. *Mysterium iniquitatis*. Milan: Adelphi, 1995.

——. *Un commento alla Bibbia*. Milan: Adelphi, 1979.

ROBINSON, Joanne Maguire. *Nobility and Annihilation in Marguerite Porete's 'Mirror of Simple Souls'*. Albany, NY: State University of New York, 2001.

SCHMITT, Carl. 'Donoso Cortés in Berlin (1849)'. *Telos* 125 (2002): 97.

——. 'The Age of Neutralizations and Depoliticizations'. *Telos* 96 (1993): 130–42.

——. *Ex Captivitate Salus: Experiences 1945–1947* (Matthew Hannah trans.). Cambridge: Polity Press, 2017.

——. *Le categorie del politico* (Giovanni Miglio and Pierangelo Schiera eds and trans). Bologna: Il Mulino, 1972.

——. *Political Romanticism* (Guy Oakes trans.). Cambridge: MIT Press, 1986.

——. *Political Theology* (G. Schwab trans.). Chicago: University of Chicago Press, 2005.

——. *Roman Catholicism and Political Form* (G. L. Ulmen trans.). Westport: Greenwood Press, 1996.

——. *The Nomos of the Earth: In the International Law of the Jus Publicum Europaeum* (G. L. Ulmen trans.). New York: Telos Press, 2006.

SCHUMPETER, Joseph. *Capitalism, Socialism and Democracy*. London: Unwin University Books, 1974.

SPINOZA, Benedict. *A Theologico-Political Treatise* (R. H. M. Elwes trans.). New York: Dover, 1951.

STRAUSS, Leo, and Karl Löwith. 'Correspondence concerning modernity'. *The Independent Journal of Philosophy* 4 (1983): 107.

TAUBES, Jacob. *Occidental Eschatology* (David Ratmoko trans.). Stanford, CA: Stanford University Press, 2009.

——. *The Political Theology of St. Paul* (Dana Hollander trans.). Stanford, CA: Stanford University Press, 2003.

——. *To Carl Schmitt: Letters and Reflections* (Keith Tribe trans.). New York: Columbia University Press, 2013.

TRENTIN, Bruno. *La città del lavoro. Sinistra e crisi del fordismo*. Milan: Feltrinelli, 1997.

TRONTI, Mario. 'Ancora su utopia proseguendo una discussione'. *Infiniti mondi* (2020). Available online: https://bityl.co/OXPf (last accessed 18 May 2024).

——. 'Autonomy of the Political' (1972) (Andrew Anastasi, Sara Farris, and Peter Thomas trans). *Viewpoint Magazine*, 26 February 2020. Available online: https://bit.ly/4bGk6aF (last accessed 18 May 2024).

——. 'Desperate Hopes'. *Autonomies* (2020). Available online: https://bityl.co/OXPj (last accessed 18 May 2024).

——. 'Disperate speranze'. Available online: https://bit.ly/4alF0Lr. Also available in English: https://bit.ly/44PkpxC (last accessed 18 May 2024).

——. *Il destino dei partiti* (Enrico Melchionda ed.). Rome: Ediesse, 1996.

——. *La sinistra nel labirinto* (Massimo Illardi ed.). Genoa: Costa and Nolan, 1994.

——. *The Weapon of Organization: Mario Tronti's Political Revolution in Marxism* (Andrew Anastasi ed. and trans.). Brooklyn, NY: Common Notions, 2020.

——. *Workers and Capital* (David Broder trans.). London: Verso, 2019.

WEBER, Max. 'Politics as a Vocation' in *Political Writings* (Peter Lassman and Ronald Speirs eds, Ronald Speirs trans.). Cambridge: Cambridge University Press, 1994.

——. *Economy and Society*. Berkeley: University of California Press, 1978.

ZEDONG, Mao. 'On the Correct Handling of Contradictions Among the People' (27 February 1957) in *Selected Works of Mao Tse-tung*, VOL. 5. Beijing: Foreign Languages Press, 1977. Available online: https://bit.ly/3yDSTXS (last accessed 21 May 2024).

ZWEIG, Stefan. *The World of Yesterday* (Anthea Bell trans.). Lincoln, NE: University of Nebraska Press, 2013.